INDIANA UNIVERSITY

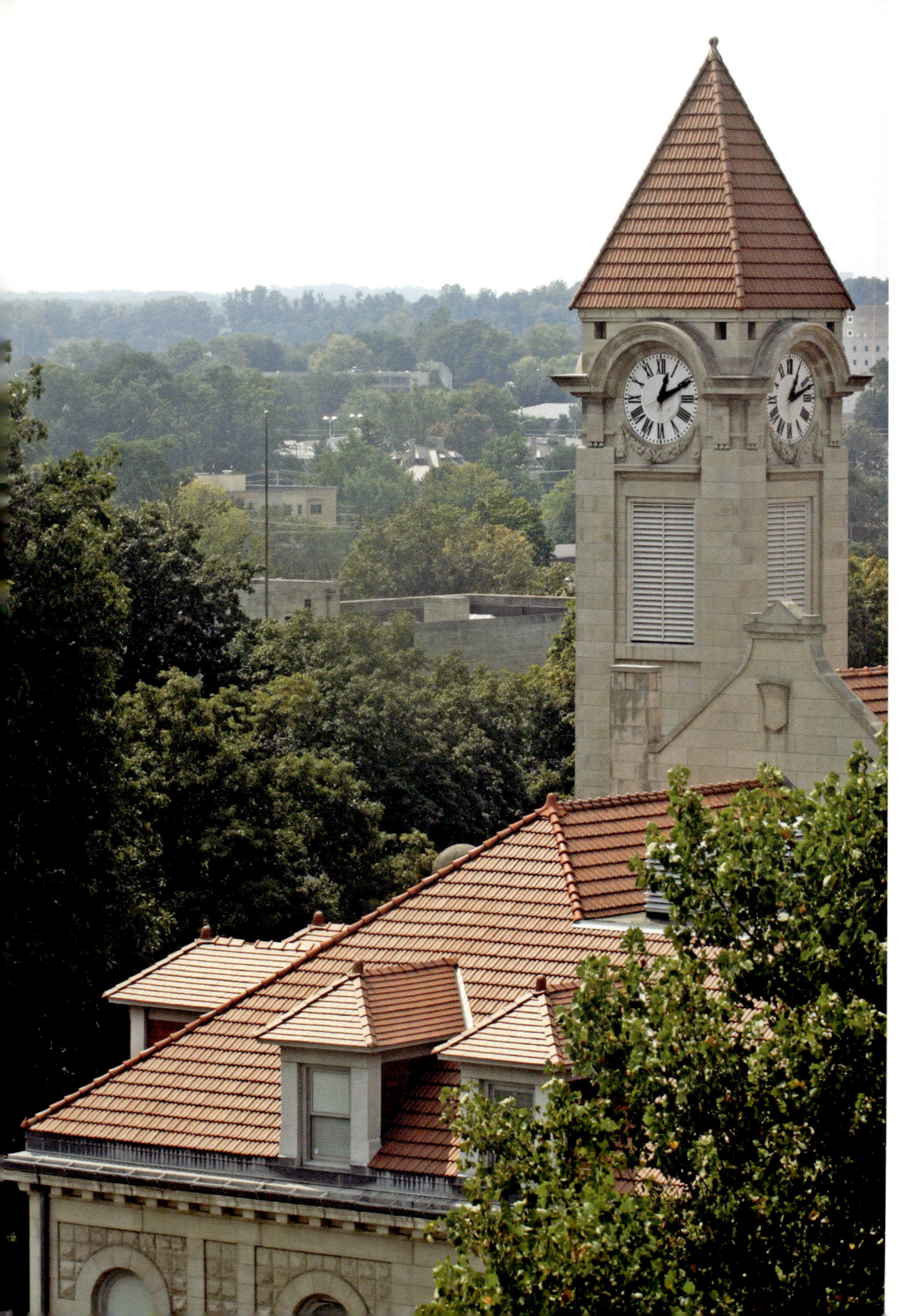

Overleaf
Limestone carving on the IU Auditorium exterior. *Rob Guillen*

Aerial view of the Student Building.

The campus should be a place of beauty
that students can walk around
and think grand thoughts.

HERMAN B WELLS
Indiana University President
1938–1962

INDIANA UNIVERSITY PRESS
Bloomington & Indianapolis

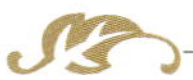

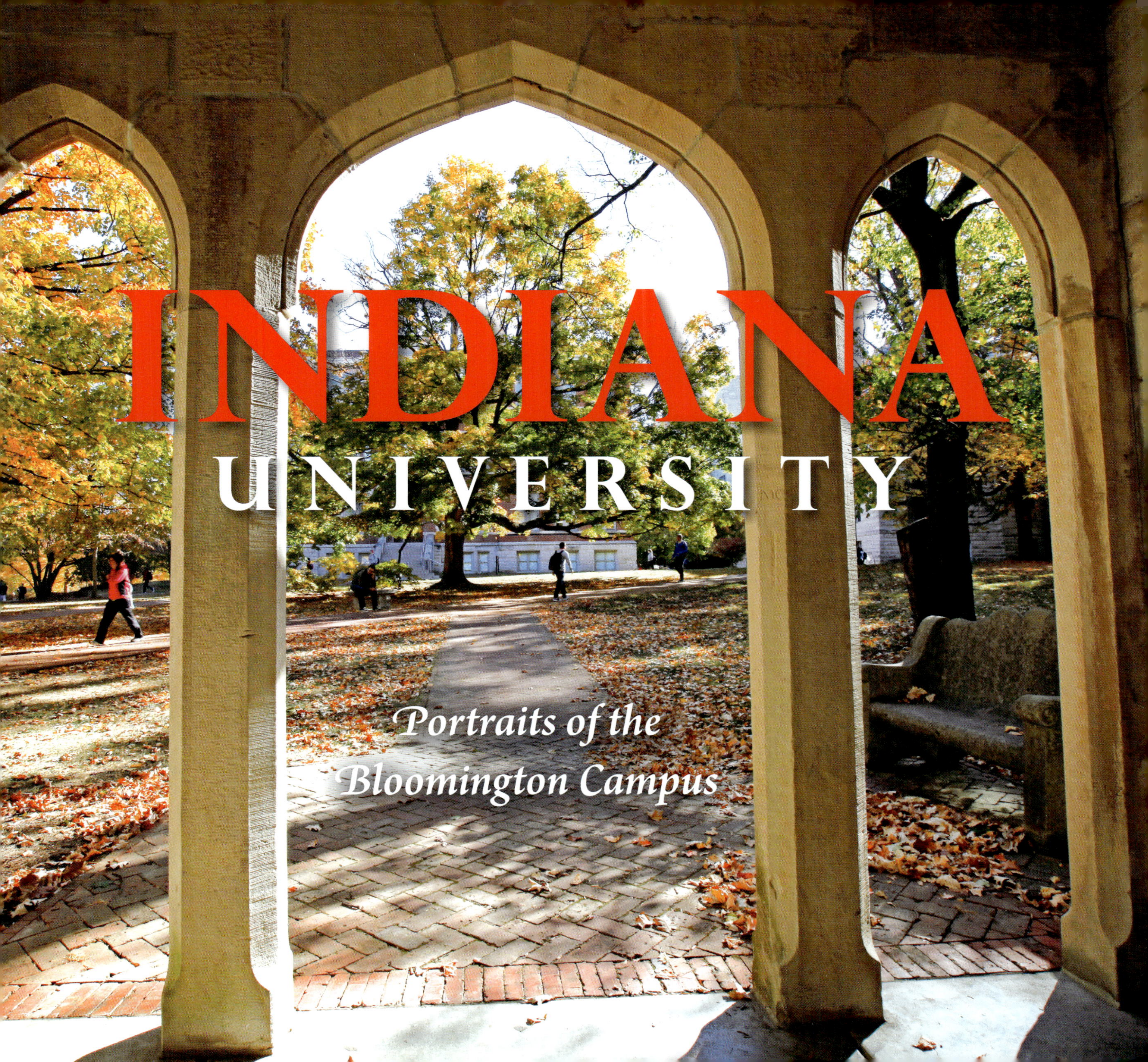
INDIANA
UNIVERSITY
Portraits of the
Bloomington Campus

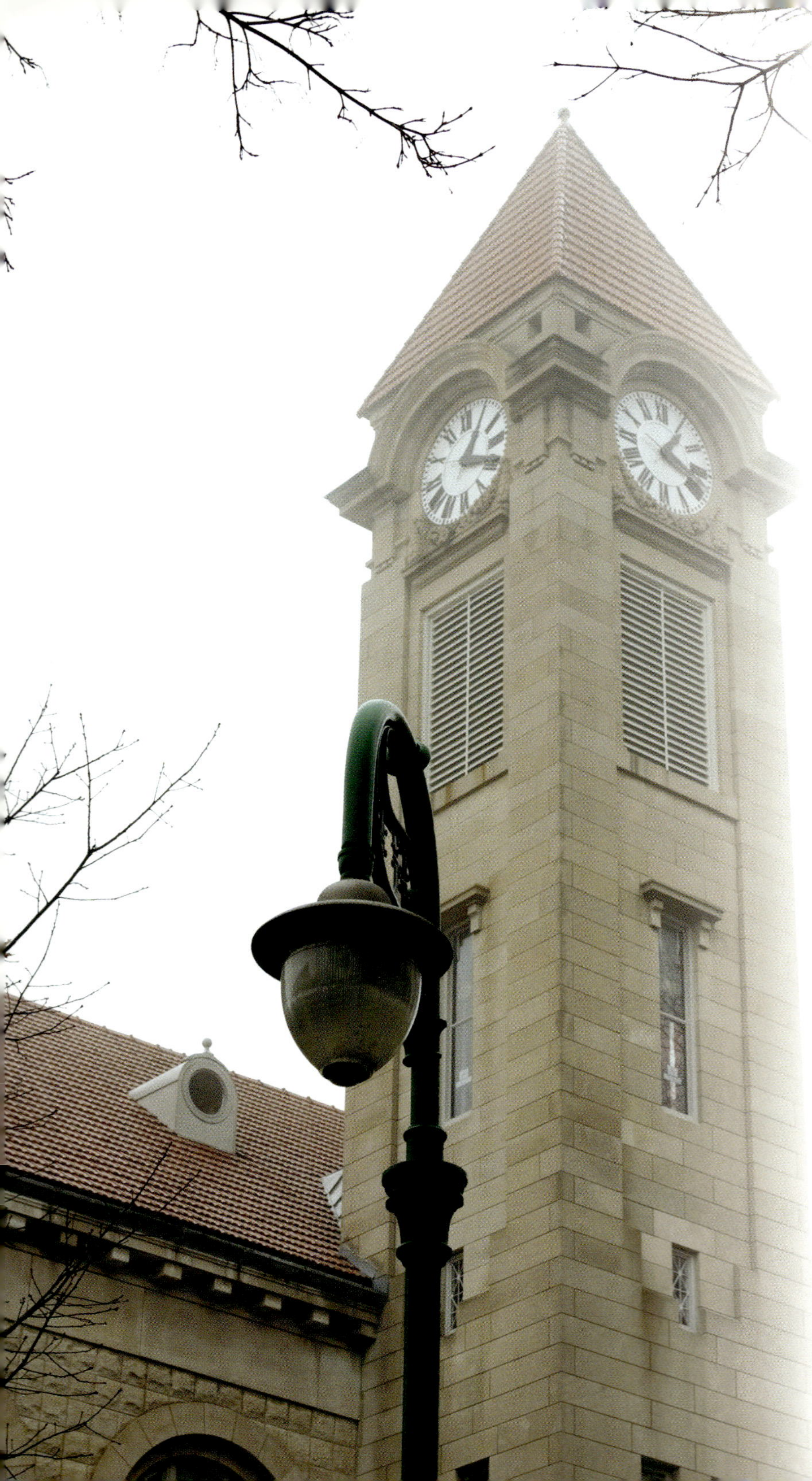

This book is a publication of

Indiana University Press
Office of Scholarly Publishing
Herman B Wells Library 350
1320 East 10th Street
Bloomington, Indiana 47405 USA

iupress.indiana.edu

Telephone 800-842-6796
Fax 812-855-7931

This book is printed on acid-free paper.
Manufactured in Korea

Cataloging information is available from the Library of Congress.

ISBN 978-0-253-01404-7 (pbk)

1 2 3 4 5 19 18 17 16 15 14

Overleaf, Rose Well House.
Clock Tower, Student Building. *Chris Robb*

Contents

Preface xi

Old Crescent Buildings

Franklin Hall 2
Student Building 3
Maxwell Hall 7
Owen Hall 8
Wylie Hall 8
Lindley Hall 9
Kirkwood Hall 10
Swain Hall East 11
Swain Hall West 18
Rawles Hall 19

Campus Landmarks

Sample Gates 1
Clock Tower 3
Herman B Wells Sculpture 14
Dunn's Woods 20
Rose Well House 26
Indiana Memorial Union 34
Beck Chapel 40
Jordan Hall Greenhouse 47
Showalter Fountain 64
Arboretum 80
Arboretum Gazebo 82
Metz Carillon 91

Athletic Venues 95
About the Photographers 111

Hail to Old IU

WORDS BY J.T. GILES

Come and join in song together,
Shout with might and main;
Our beloved Alma Mater,
Sound her praise again.
Gloriana Frangipana, E'er to her be true.
She's the pride of Indiana,
Hail to Old IU!

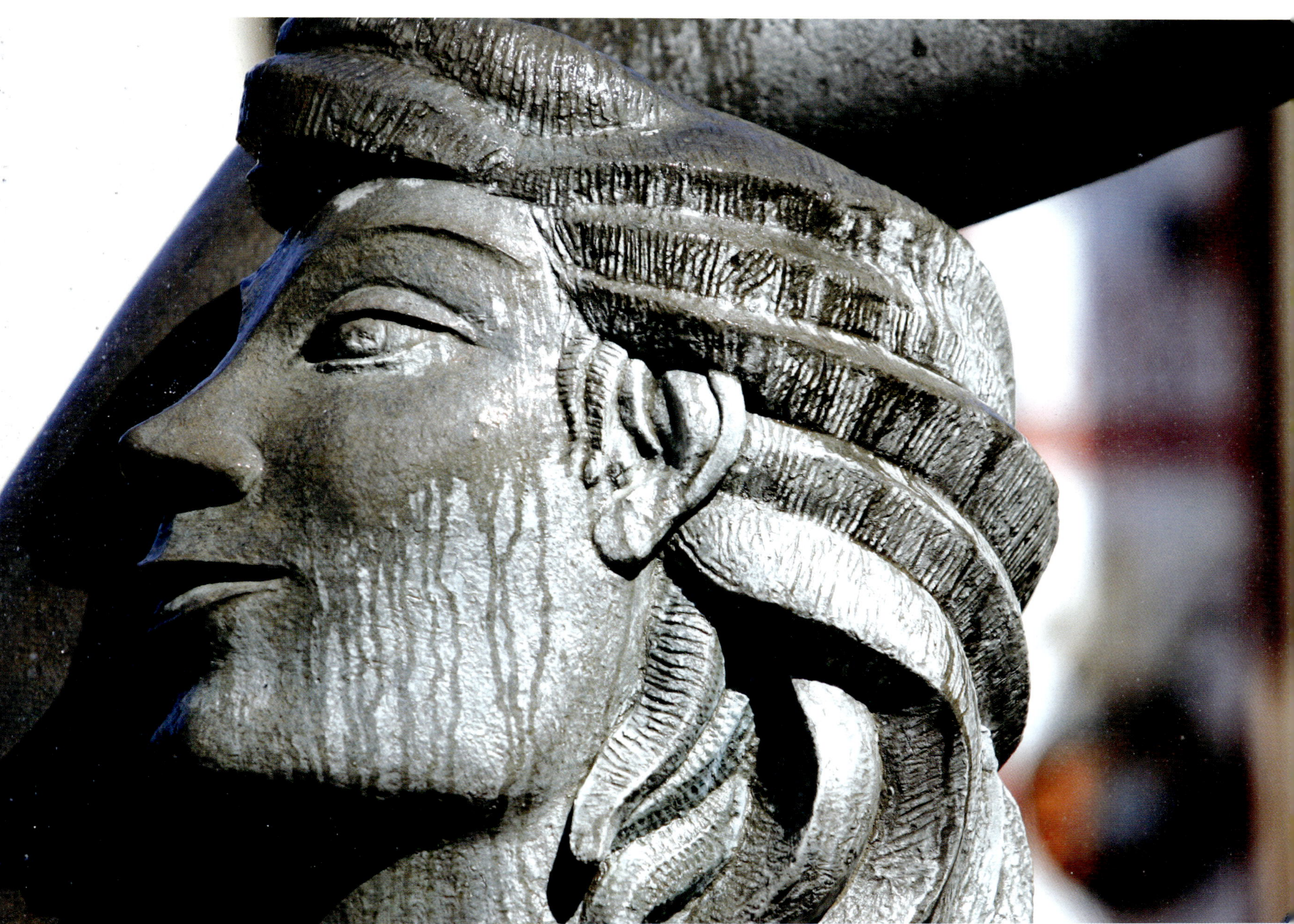

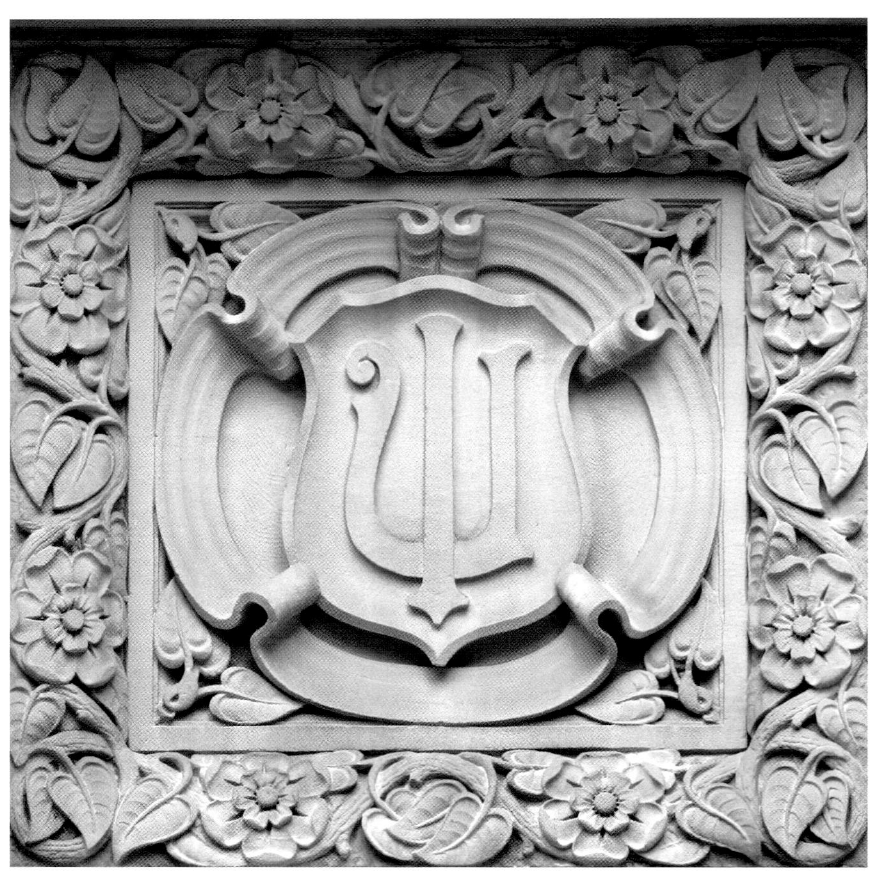

Overleaf

Showalter Fountain statue.

Above

Limestone carving.

Preface

In 1820, the State Seminary of Indiana was founded in the small town of Bloomington. Within a few years, the first building was completed and classes began with an initial enrollment of ten men. From these humble beginnings, the school and its location would change to develop into the flagship campus of Indiana University.

Today the campus has expanded to nearly 2,000 acres and serves more than 40,000 students. Recognized as a leading university in research, the arts, and international studies, the school attracts students from all over the world.

Over the years, the campus has grown into one of the most beautiful in the United States. It has witnessed students grow into adults, go on to make contributions to their fields of study, and become leaders in industry, outstanding citizens in their communities, and loyal and supportive alumni of Indiana University.

As you thumb through the pages of this book, we hope you will experience the spirit of Indiana University as if you were taking one of the walking tours of the Bloomington campus. Starting from the Sample Gates, wandering through the Old Crescent and Dunn's Woods, and continuing along the many well-worn paths of campus, you will see the grandeur and the fine details of limestone buildings, exquisite landscaping and quiet corners for contemplation, and students in pursuit of their studies and their recreations.

We would like to take this opportunity to thank all of the IU alumni and donors who allowed us to share their stories and memories of their time on campus. We would also like to recognize the staff members who devote their energies and creativity to making the university grounds and buildings a beautiful place for all to enjoy.

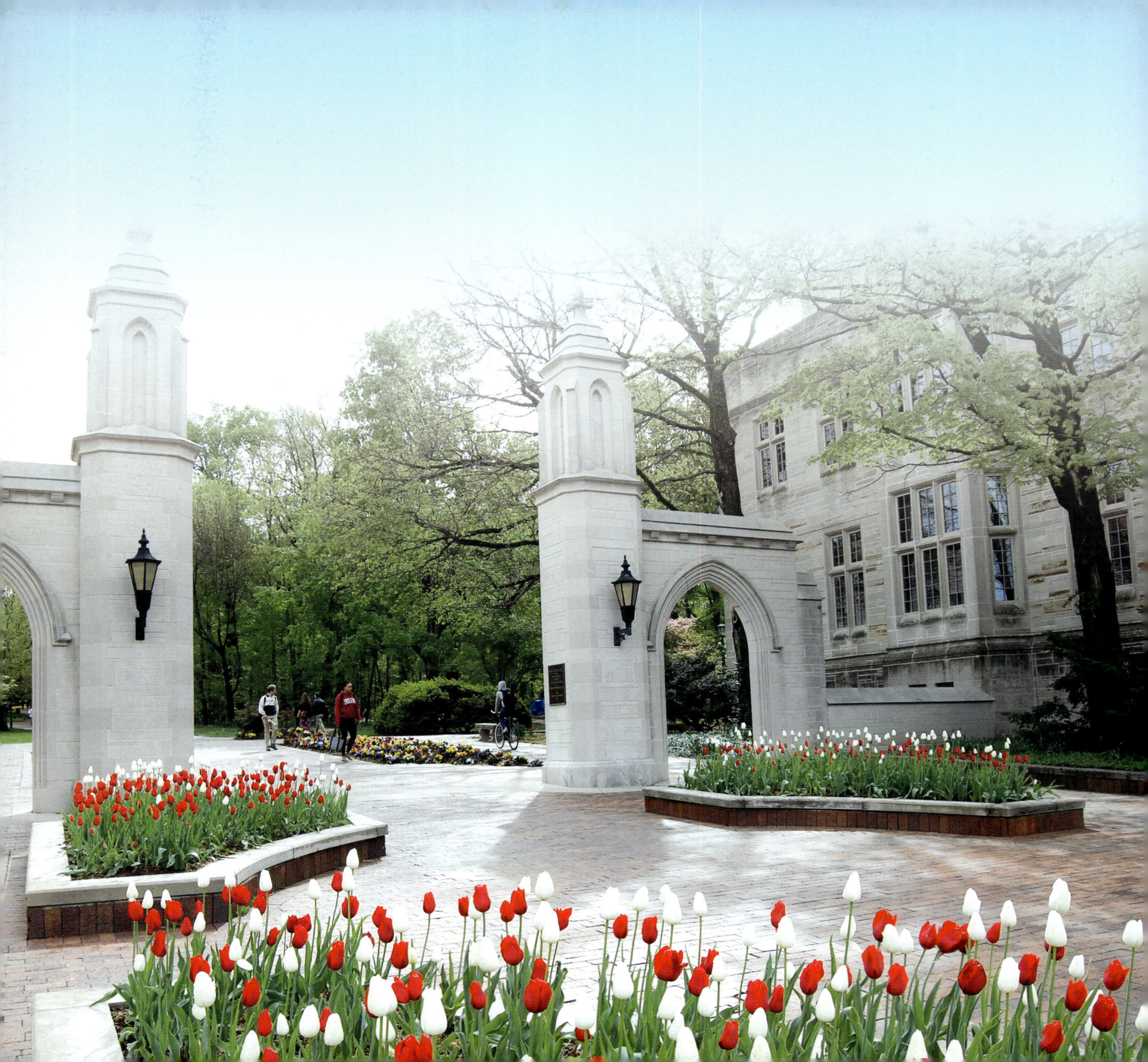

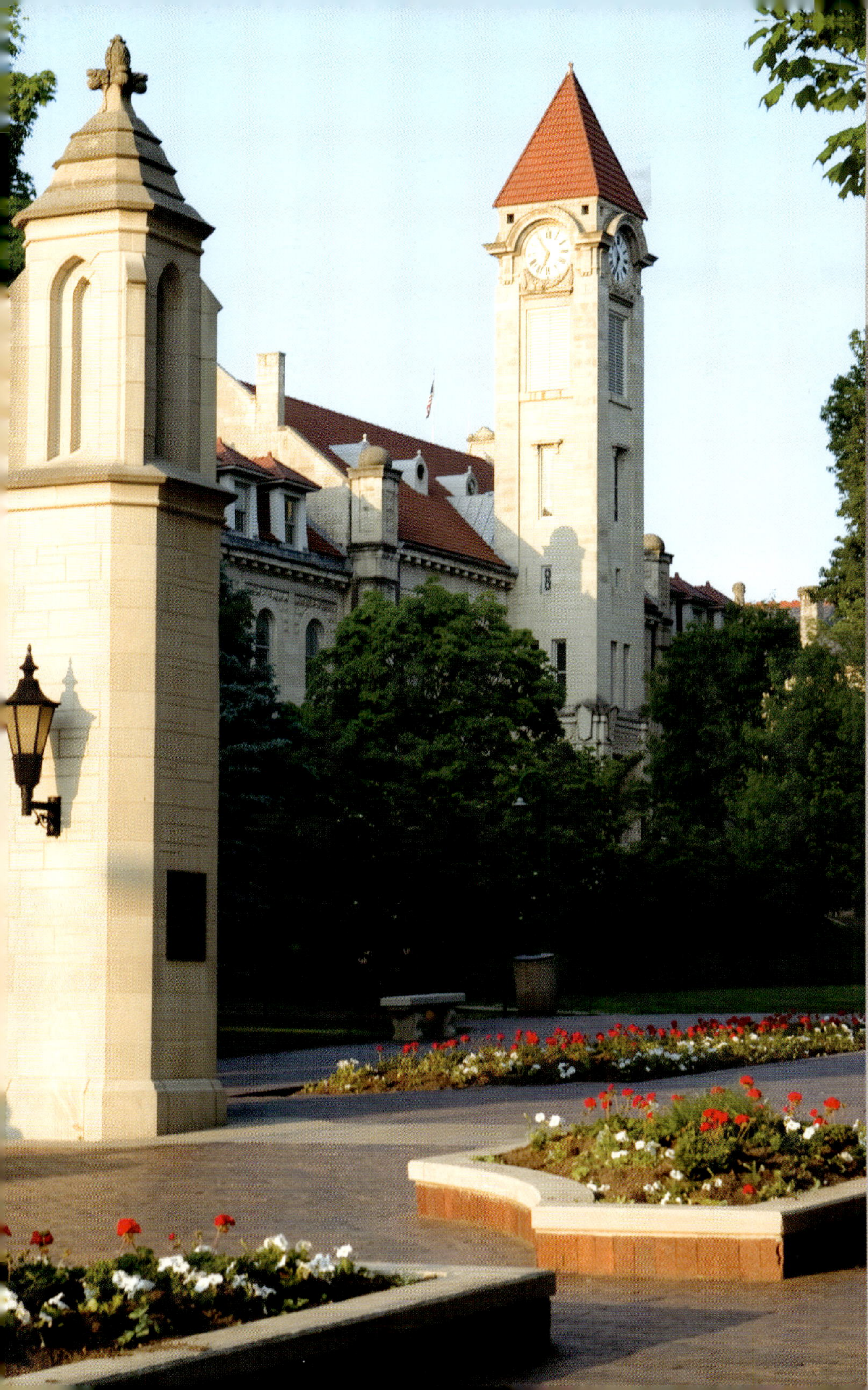

sample gates

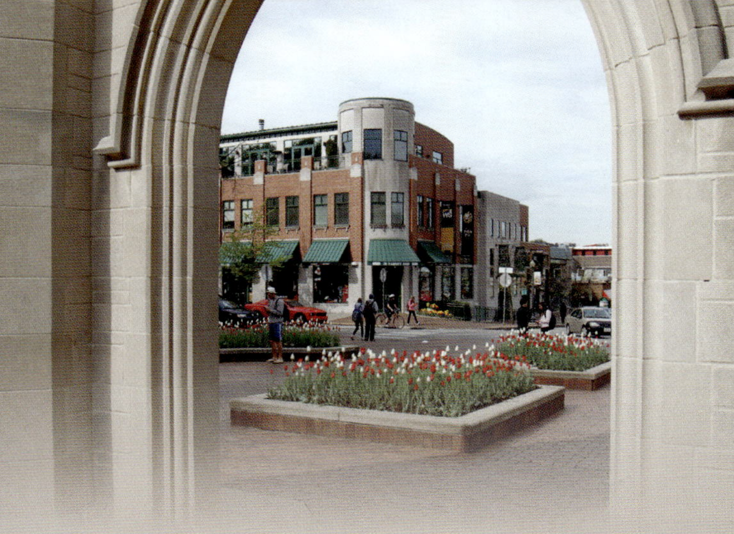

Sample Gates, left. *Chris Robb*

Sample Gates in the spring, above and facing.

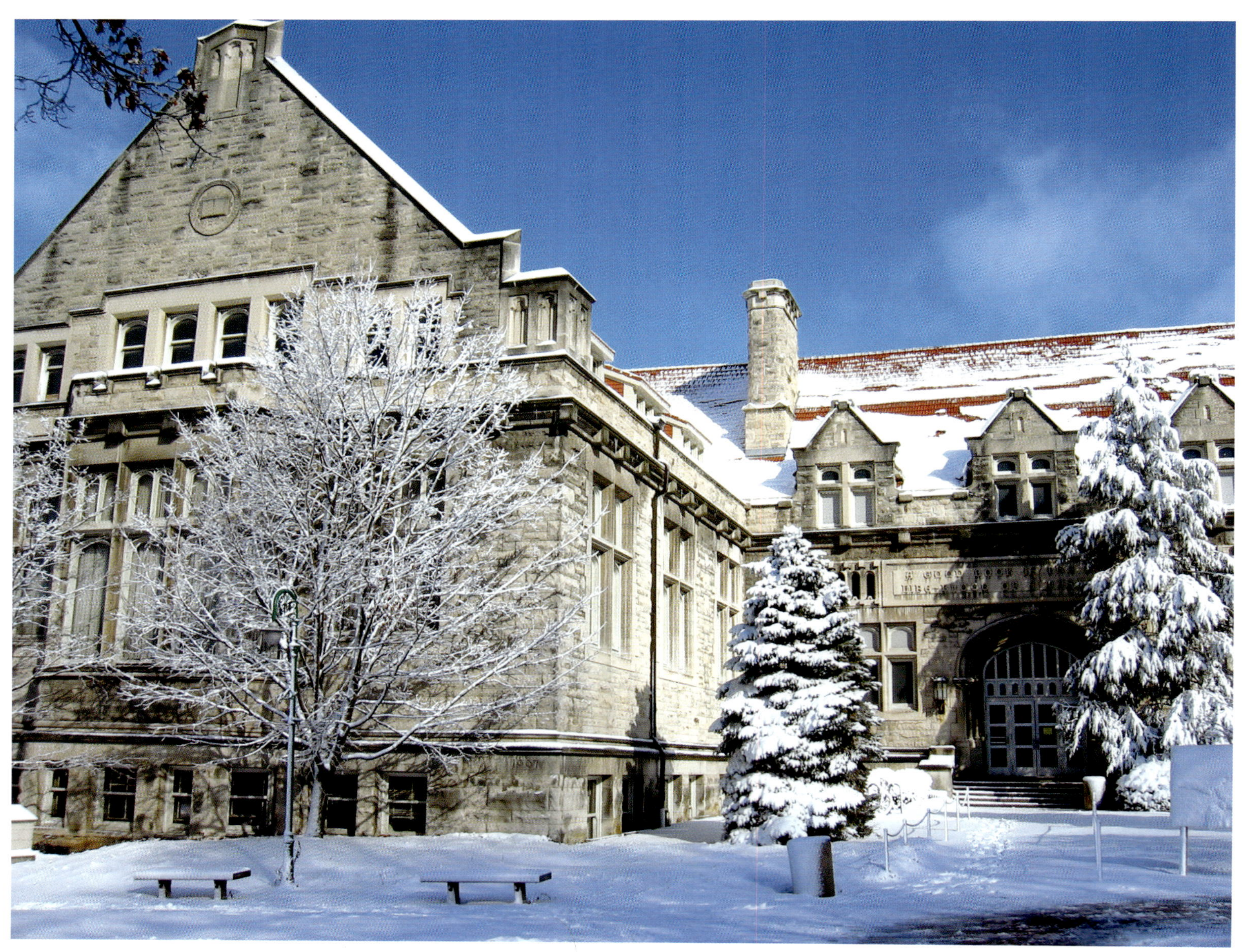

Franklin Hall, which houses Presidents Hall, dedicated in 2013. *Chris Robb*

clock tower

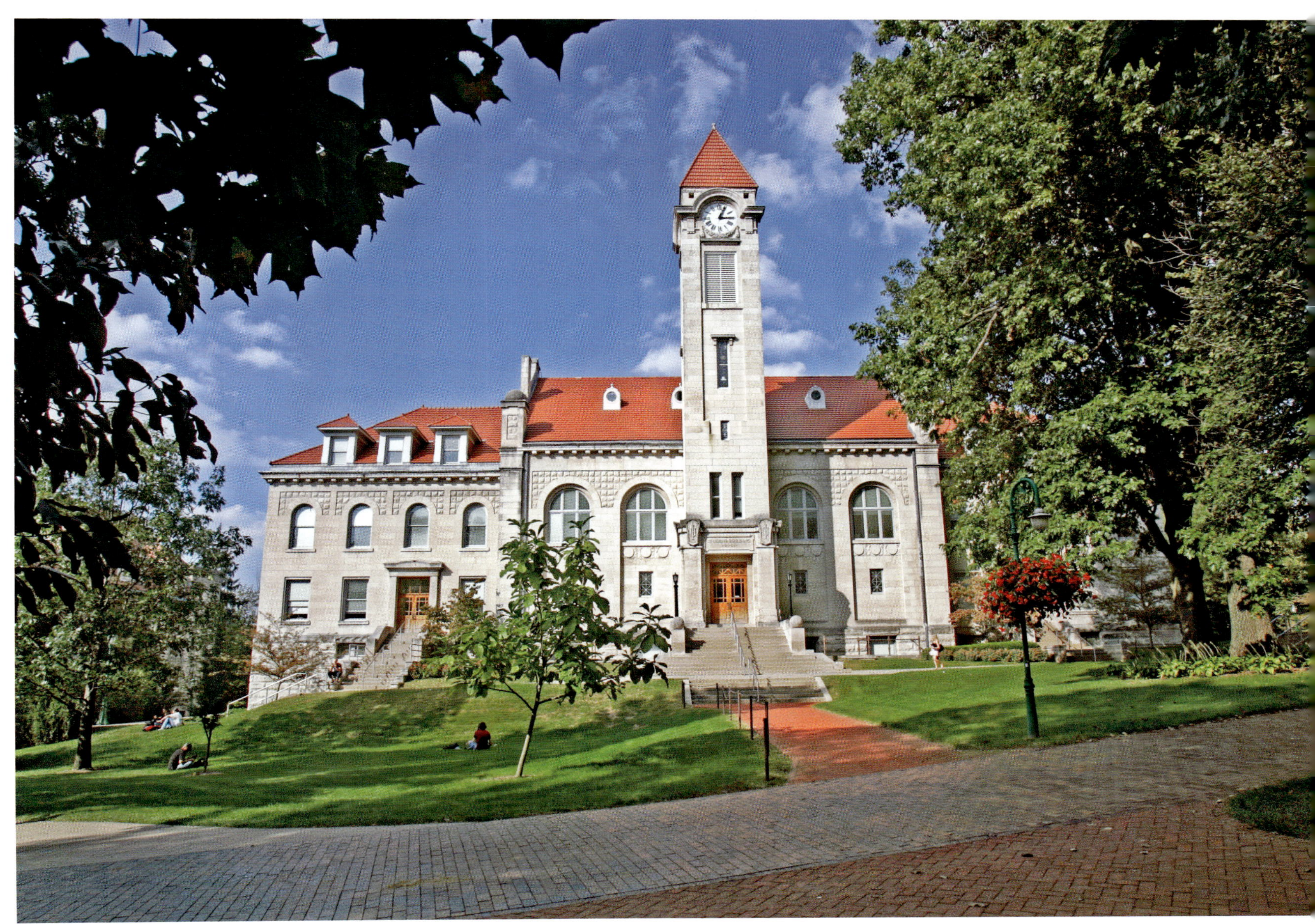

The Clock Tower on the Student Building.

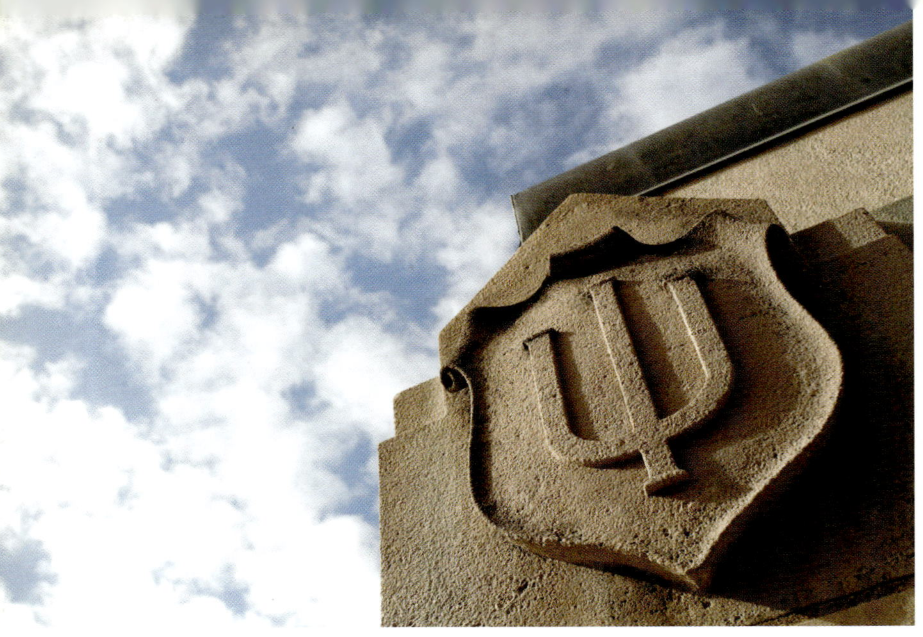

I met my husband, Frank, in front of the beautiful doors of the old library. There were these fresh guys that were trying to get my phone number. I tried to ignore them, then suddenly, Frank came along and told them to shove off. Sixty years later, we now have four children and two grandchildren, all of whom graduated from IU; it's sort of a family tradition. Frank's and my home was near campus. I used to walk daily past the beautiful library with my children in strollers and tell them they would all go to IU when they grew up. I was certainly right.

—*Becky Hrisomalos*, B.A. ENGLISH AND SPEECH, 1952; M.S.W. SOCIAL WORK, 1985

Frank Hrisomalos, B.S. PHARMACY, 1950; M.D., 1956

Limestone IU carving.

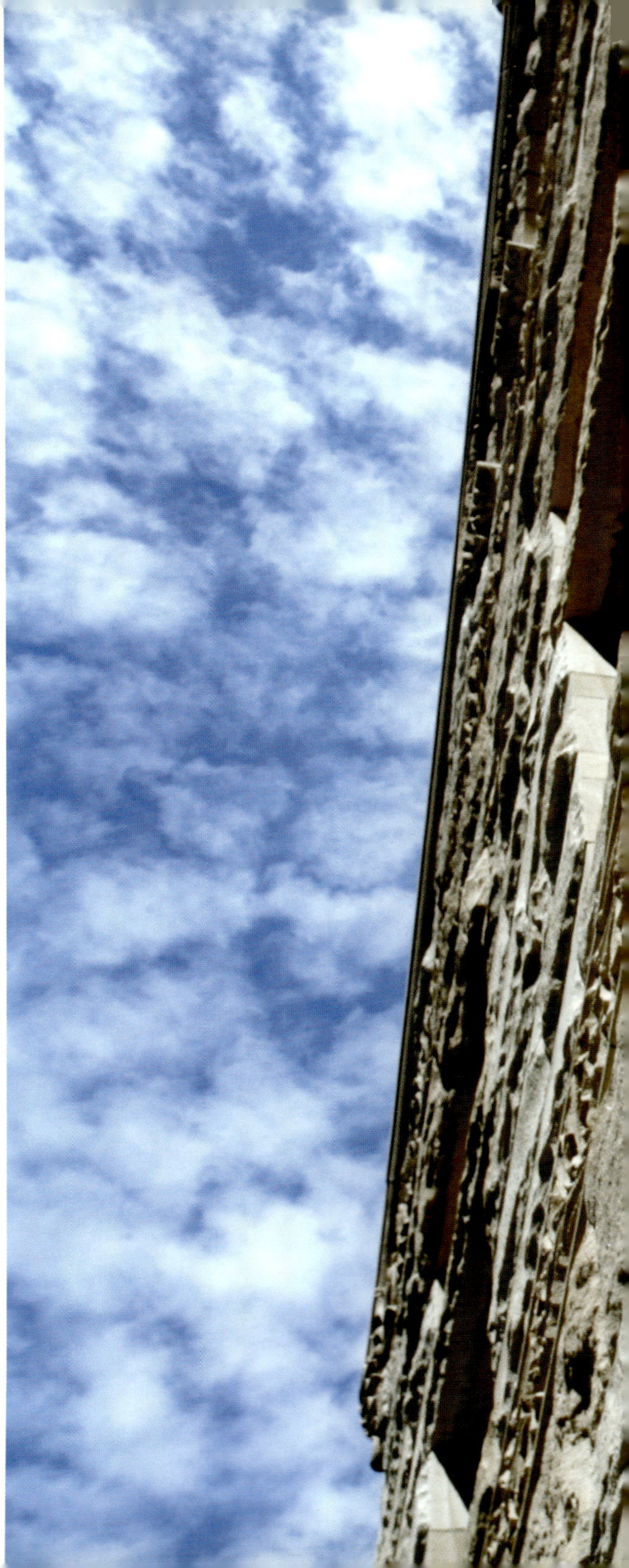

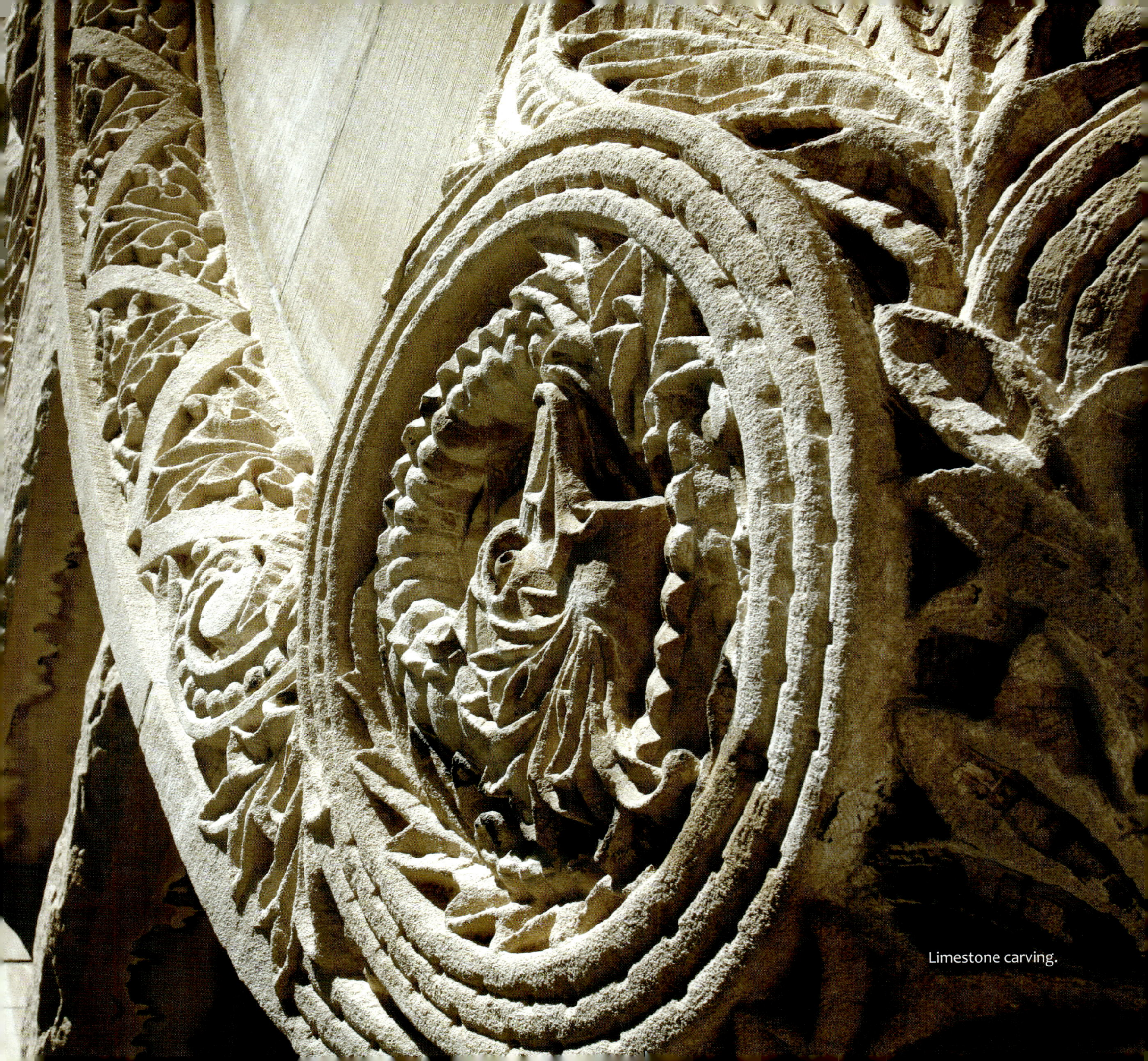

Limestone carving.

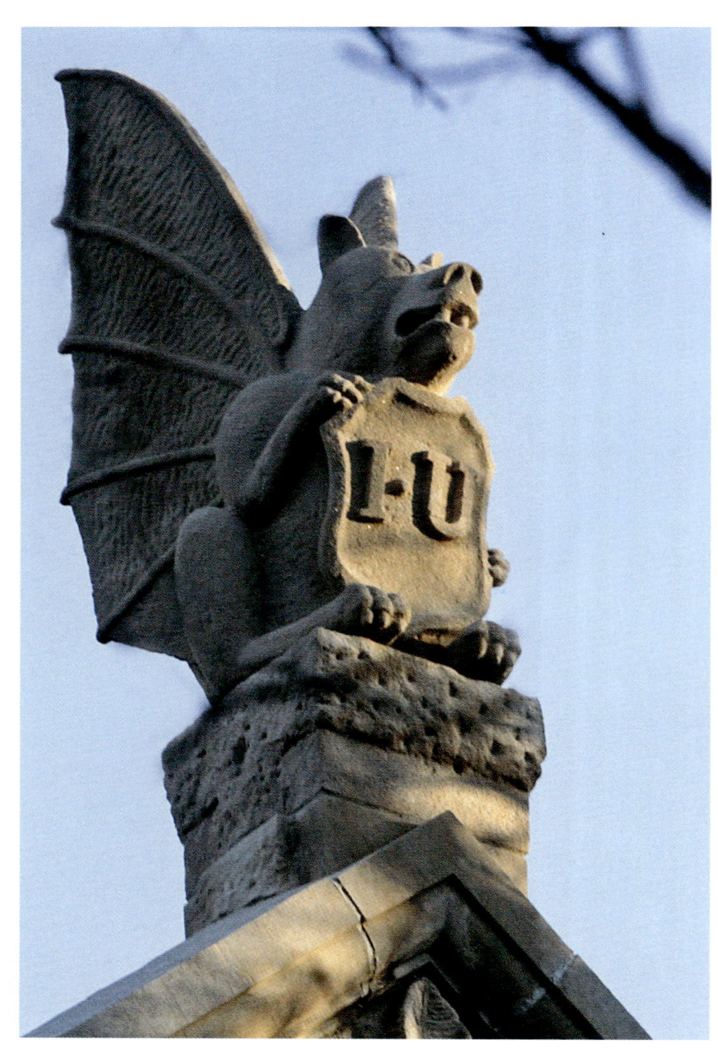

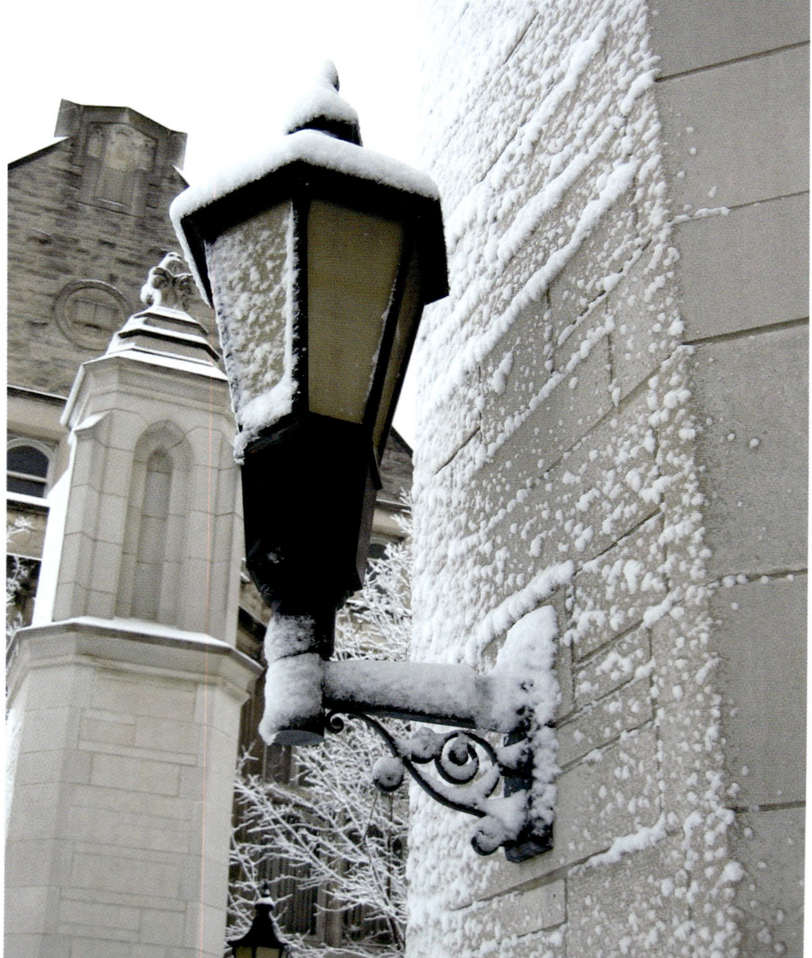

The gargoyle at the top of Maxwell Hall.

Winter's mark.

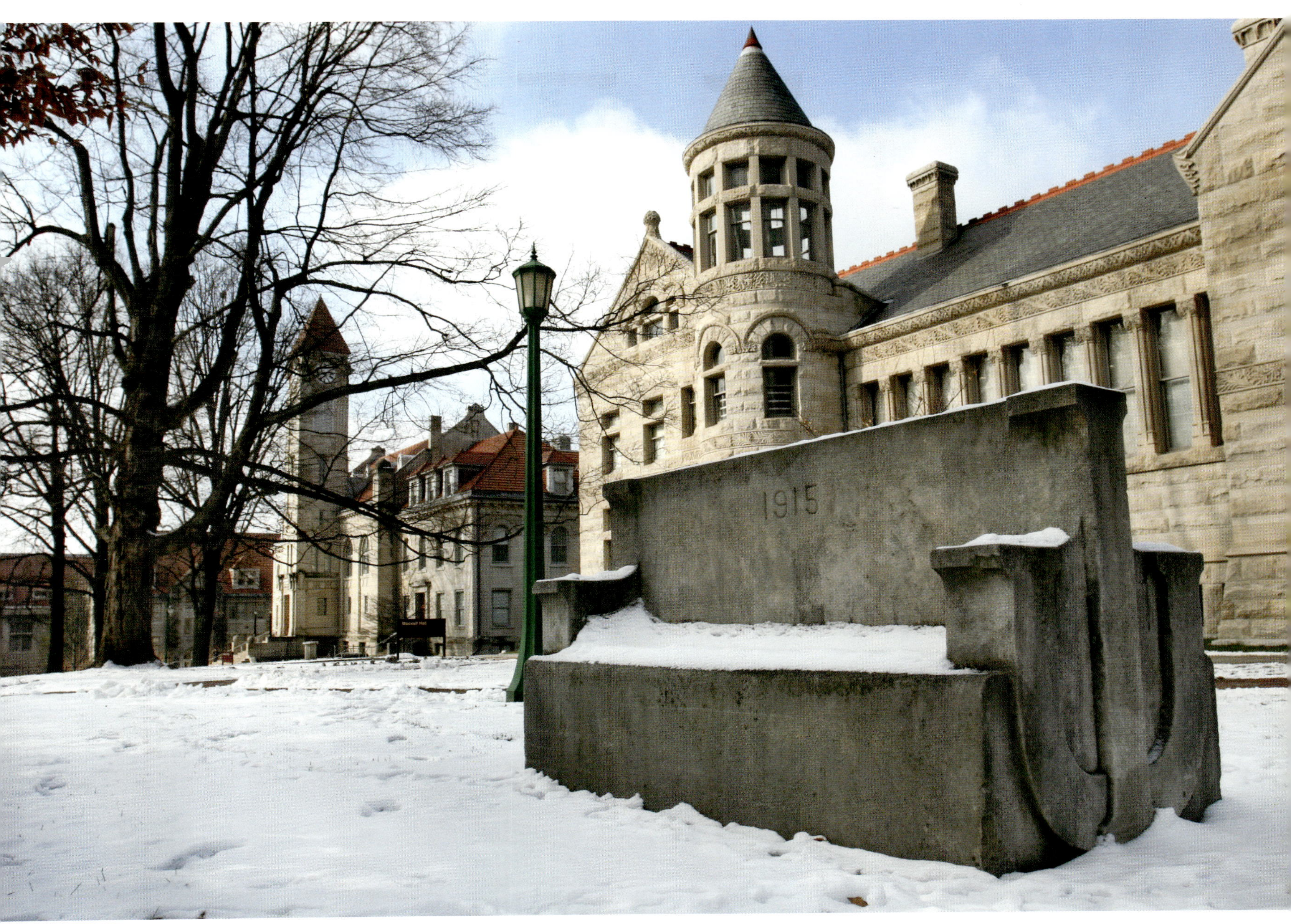

IU stone bench near Maxwell Hall.

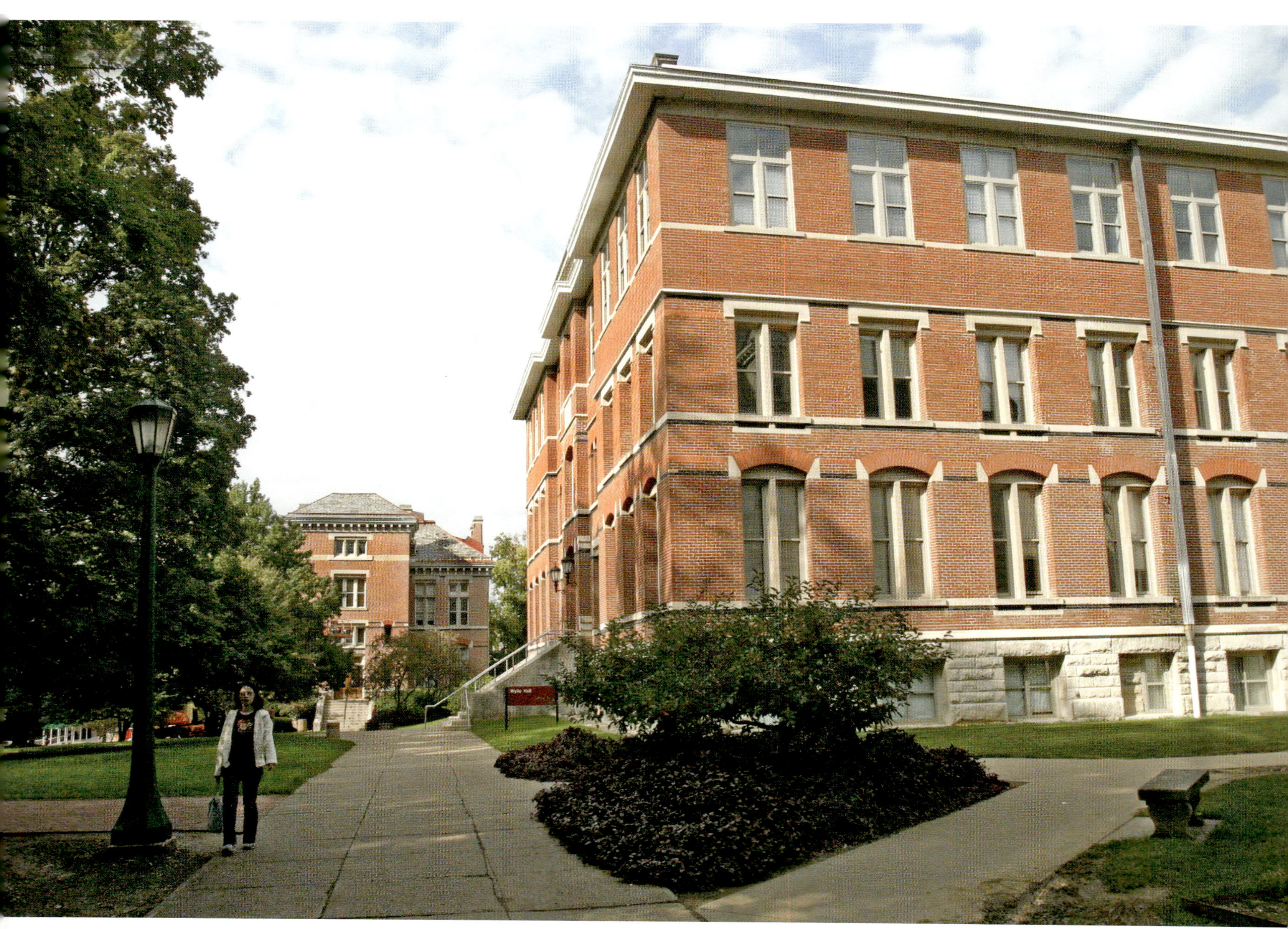

Owen Hall and Wylie Hall border Dunn's Woods.

The Old Crescent and Dunn's Woods have always held special meaning for me. To see the names of the buildings and the years they were built provides a sense of continuity. Generations of IU students have used these buildings and they are being restored so that future generations will use them. They all face Dunn's Woods, a peaceful and beautiful place in the midst of all the activity of the campus. Just walking through it gives me a feeling of calmness.

—Dr. Harold D. "Pete" Goldsmith

DEAN OF STUDENTS,
IU BLOOMINGTON 2009–

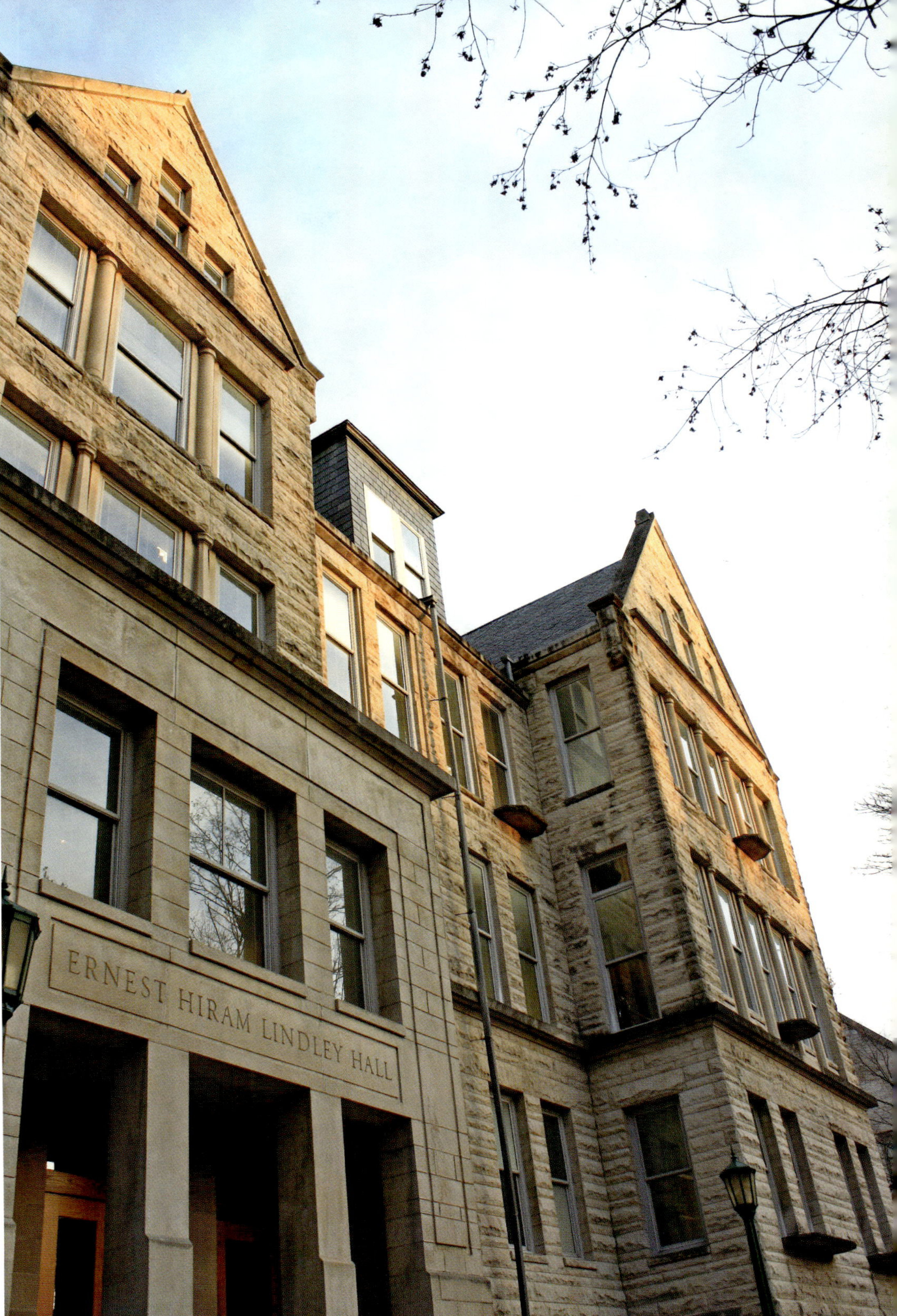

Lindley Hall catches the autumn afternoon sun.
Mandy Hussey

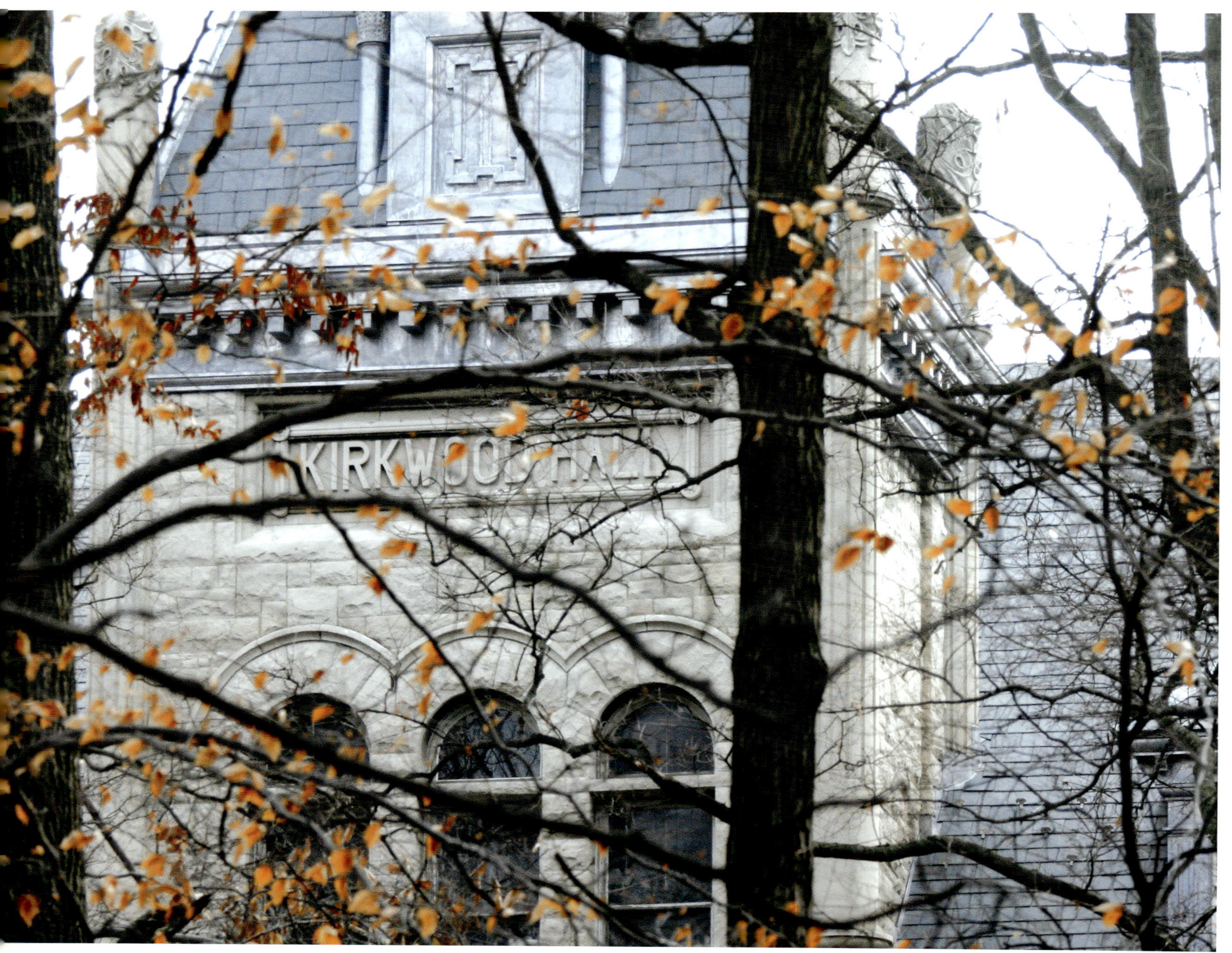

Kirkwood Hall.

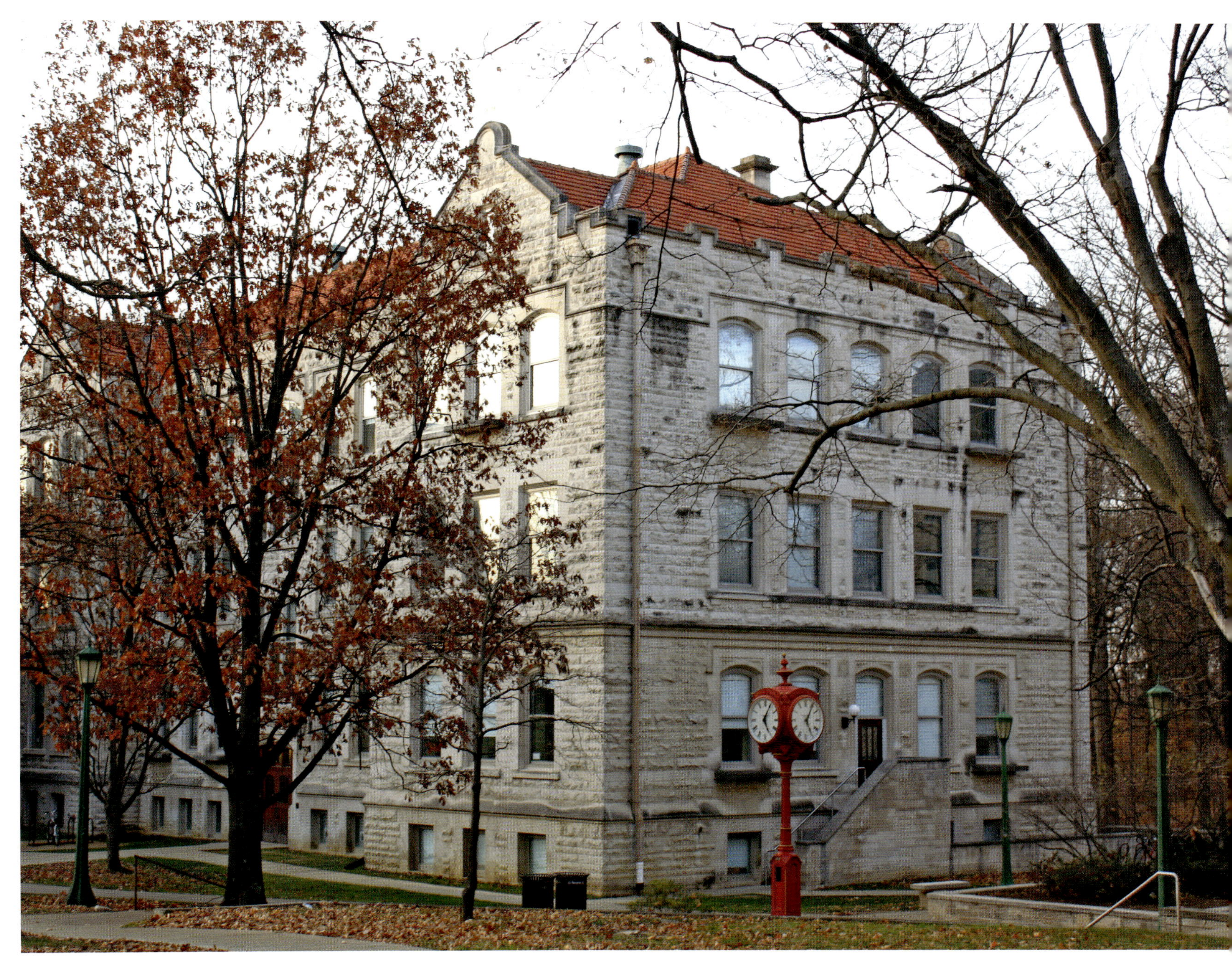

Swain Hall East. *Mandy Hussey*

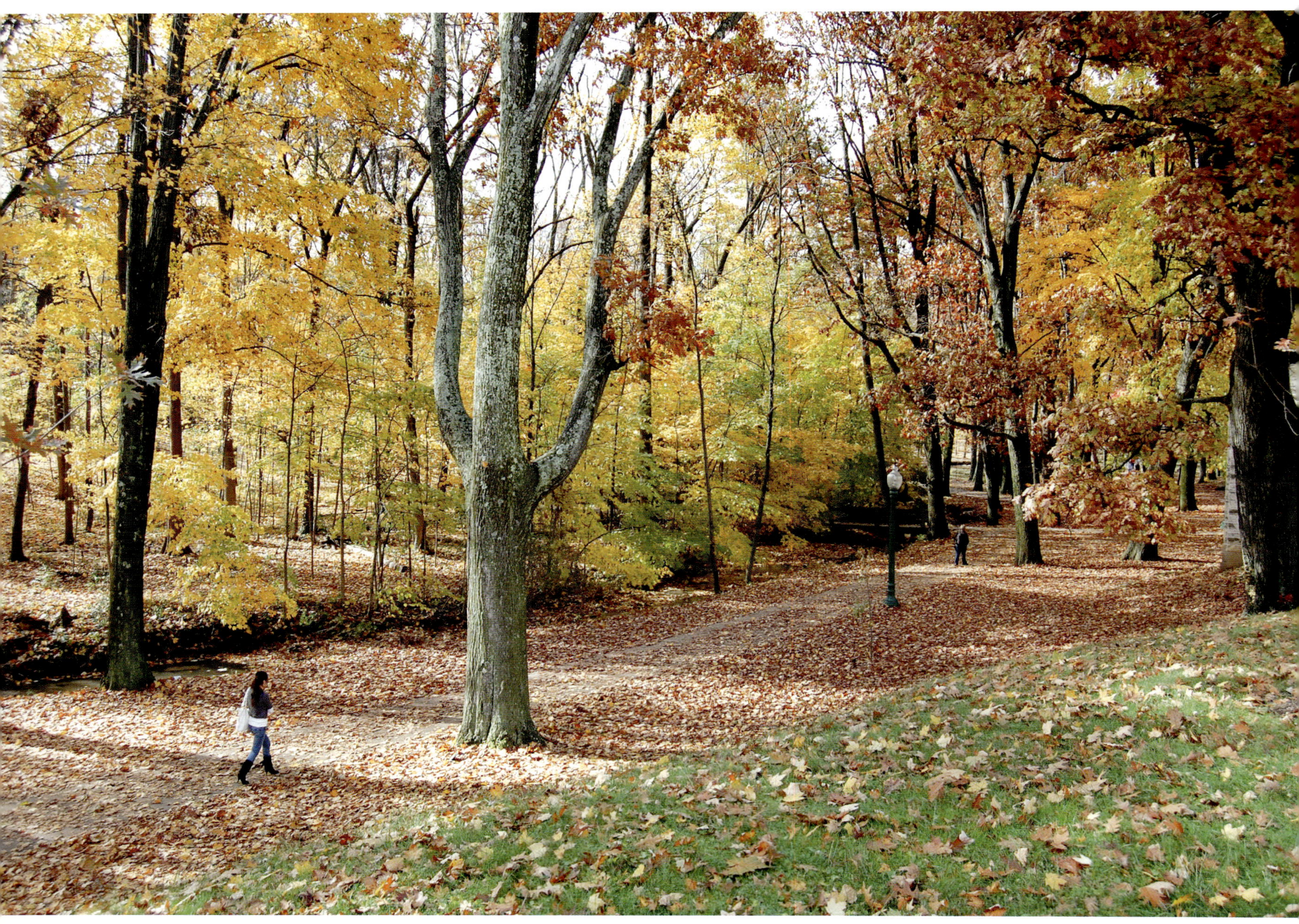

Walkways among the colorful trees.

A carpet of leaves.

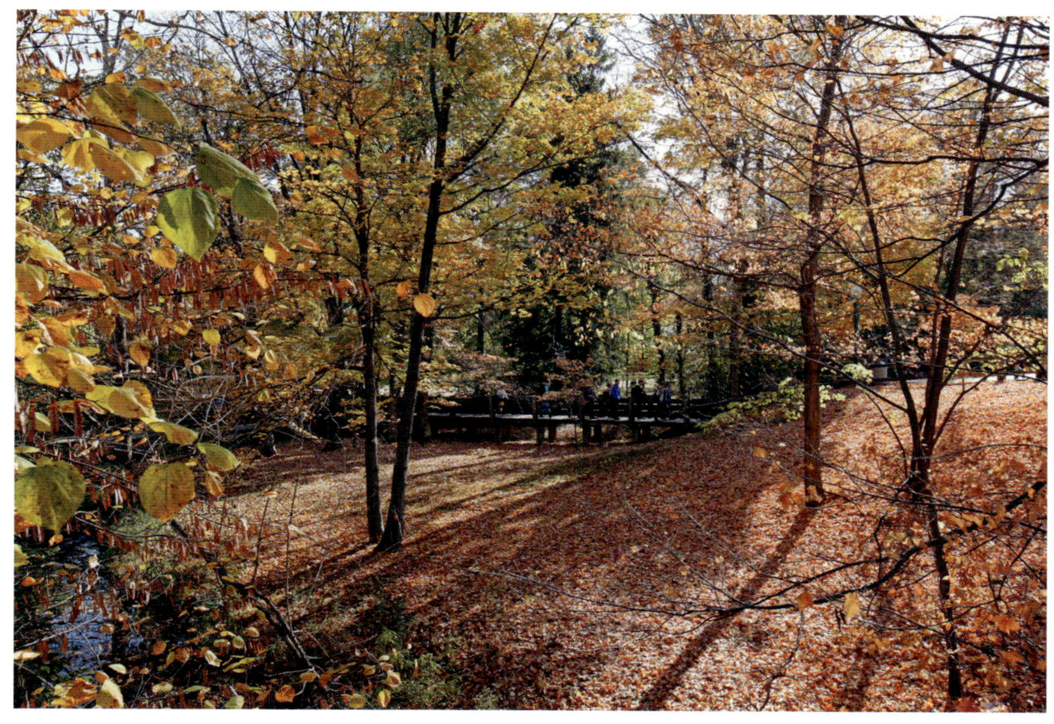

My husband and I loved our time at Indiana University during the late '60s and early '70s. It was an exciting period in America's history and for the students at IU. We spent many hours walking through the campus to the Student Foundation and to class. Since we enjoyed the beauty of the campus while attending IU, we have donated funds to support the continued beautification. By purchasing a grove of trees, we hope that others will take our lead and provide similar donations. We have nothing but fond memories of our time in Bloomington.

— *Sally Springer,* B.S. BUSINESS, 1968
Steve Springer, B.S. BUSINESS, 1968; M.B.A., 1970

herman b wells sculpture

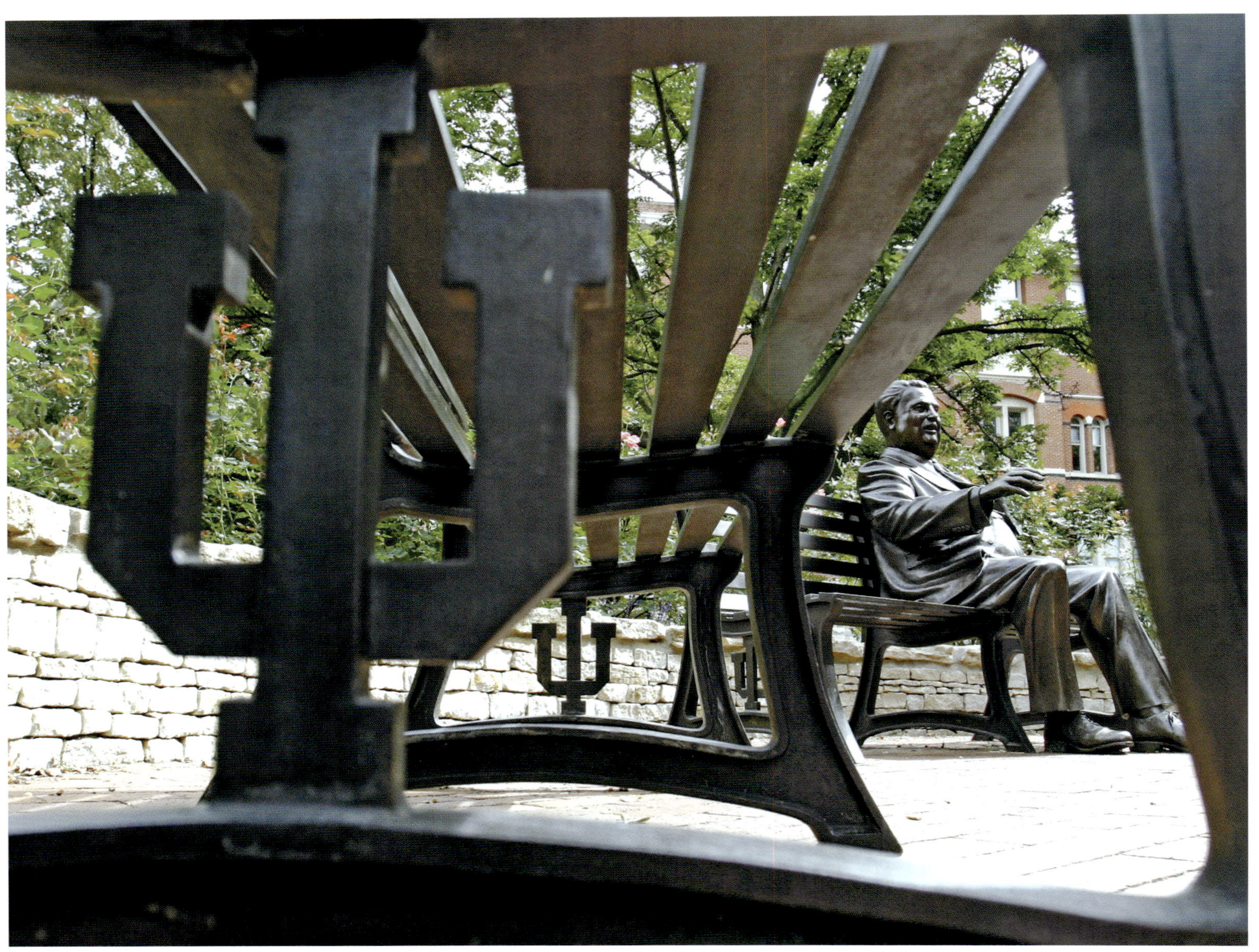

Herman B Wells sculpture near Maxwell Hall.

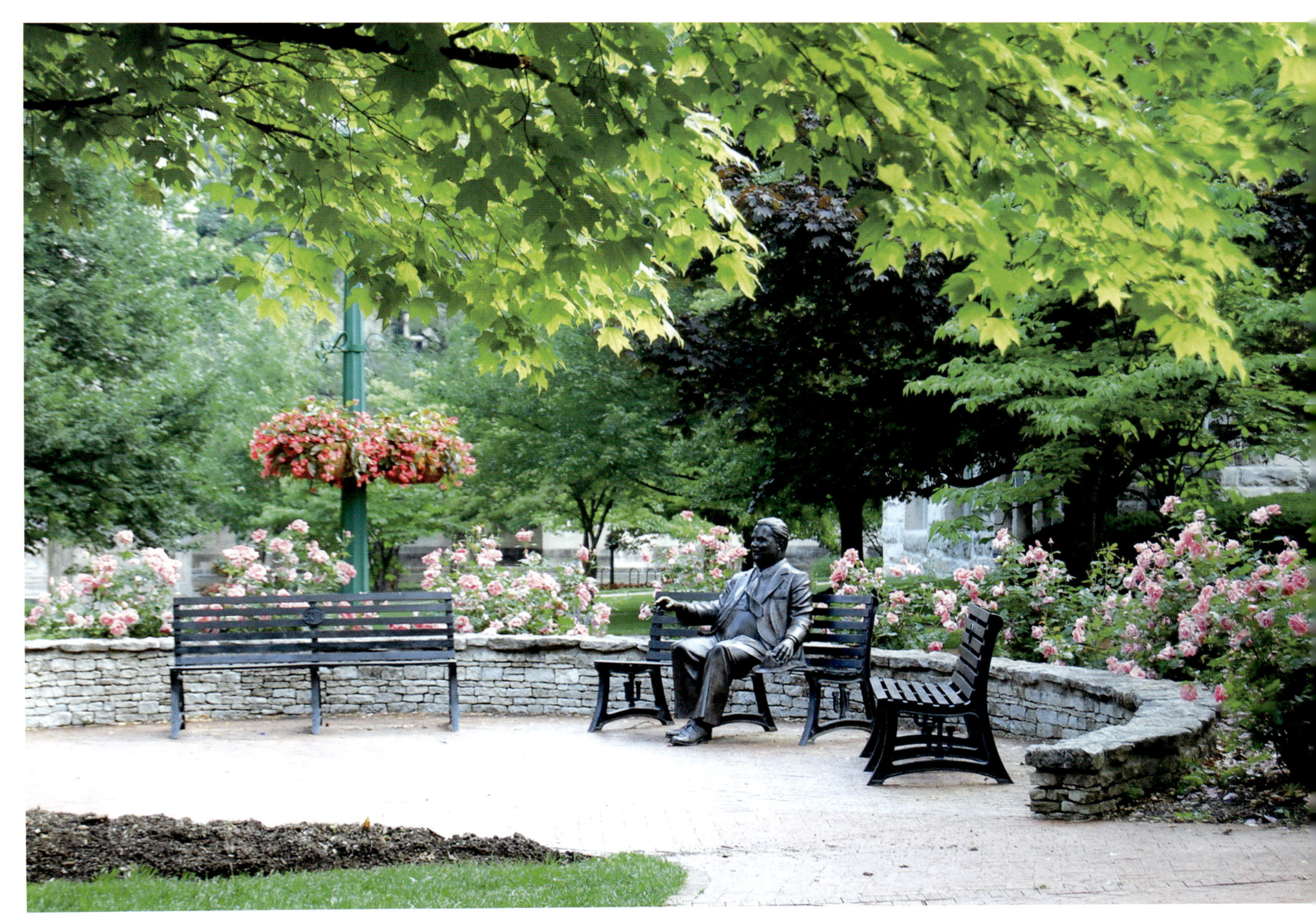

Surrounded by summer's beauty.

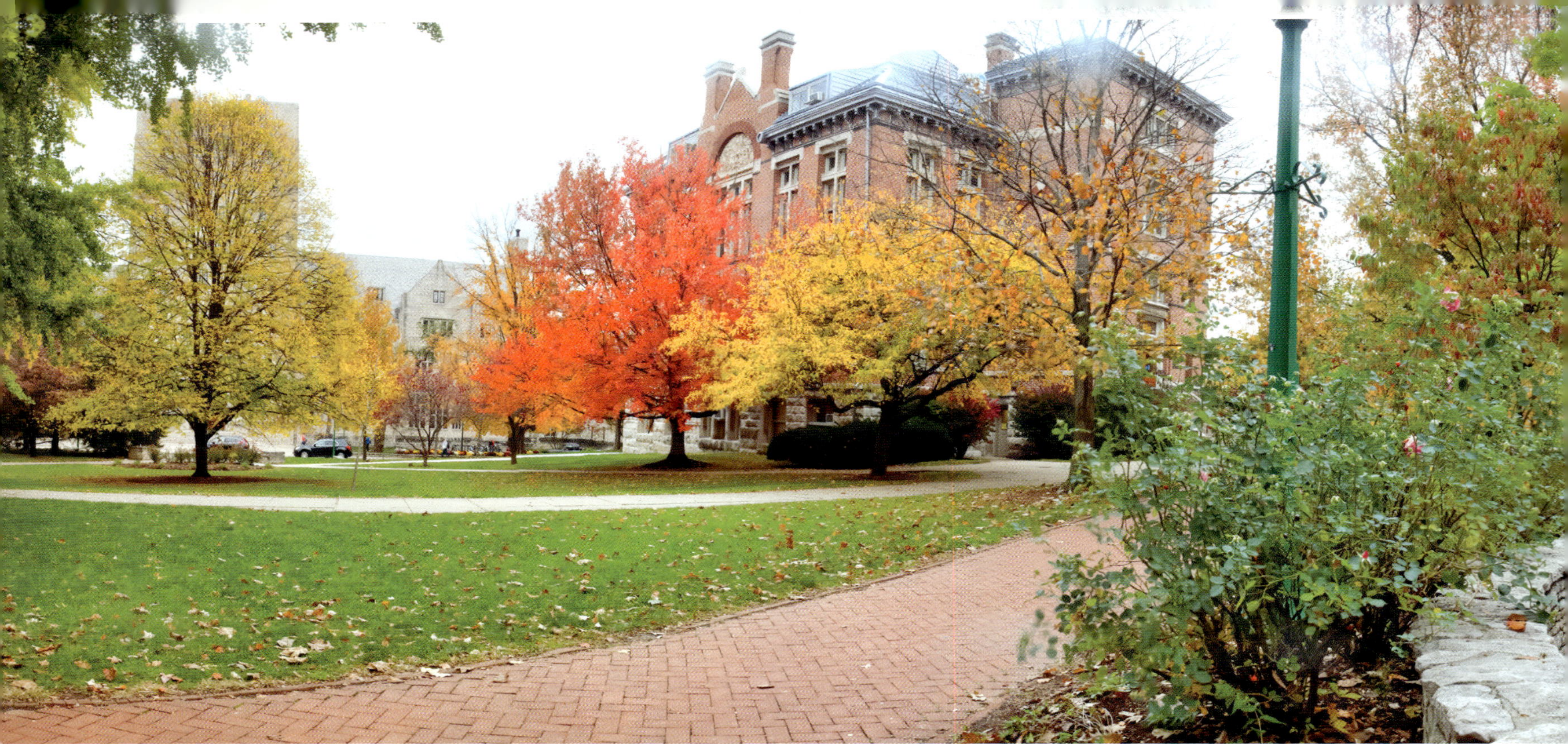

Our frequent, early-Sunday-morning strolls through the heart of the beautiful IU campus are calming yet invigorating, both physically and spiritually. We feel a sense of gratitude when we pass the beautifully preserved area where the old football stadium stood, because it was a scholarship to play there that led to my optometry degree and then the privilege of giving back as an IU optometry professor. In the original quadrangle, we are able to thank Herman B Wells, seated on his bench, for the forethought and insistence that the natural beauty of the campus be preserved. There we feel the strong connection of those before us and future students, all permanently and positively imprinted by this beauty.

—*Vic Malinovsky,* B.S. OPTOMETRY, 1971; DOC. OPTOMETRY, 1973
Janice Malinovsky, B.S. EDUCATION, 1971; M.S. EDUCATION, 1992

Panoramic view of Herman B Wells Plaza.

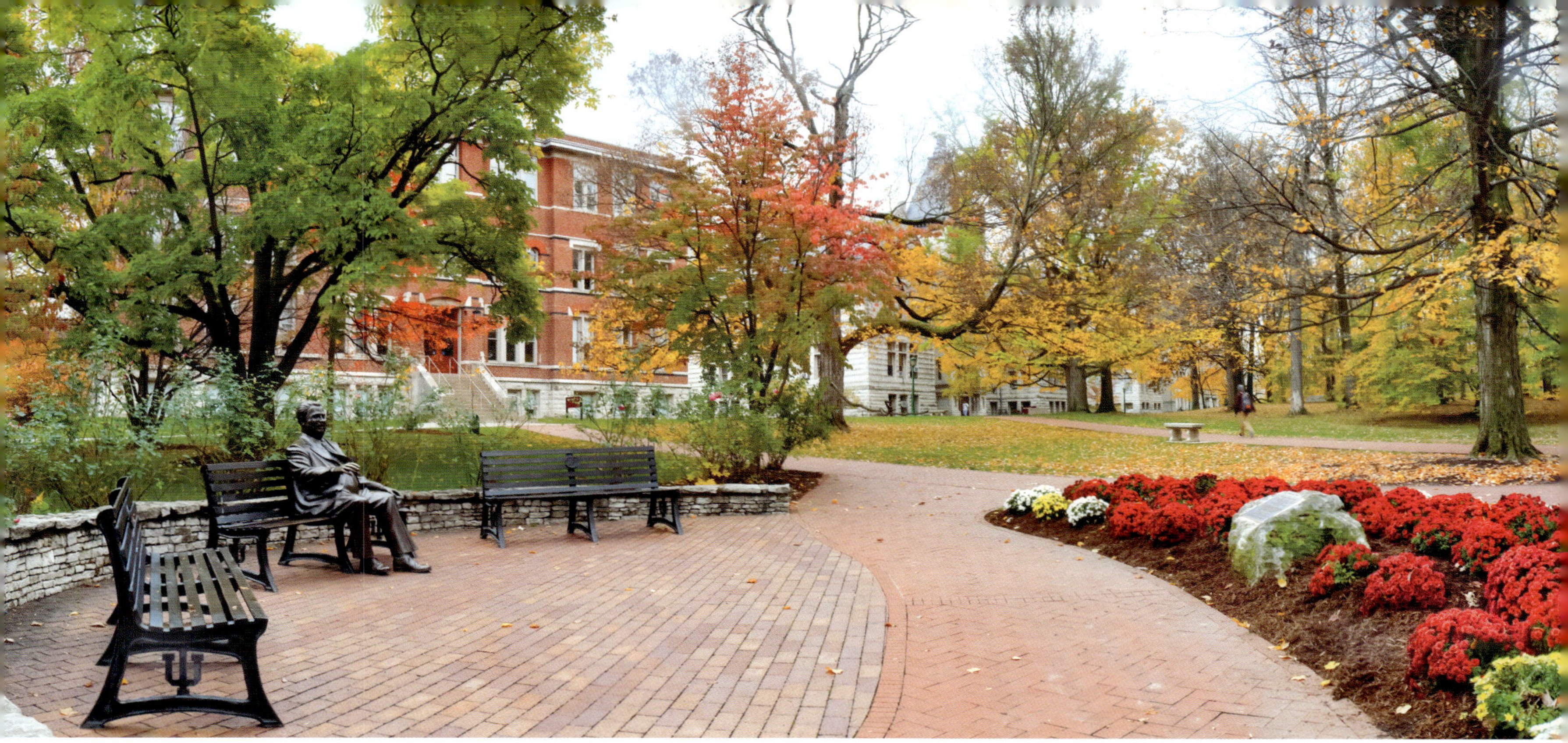

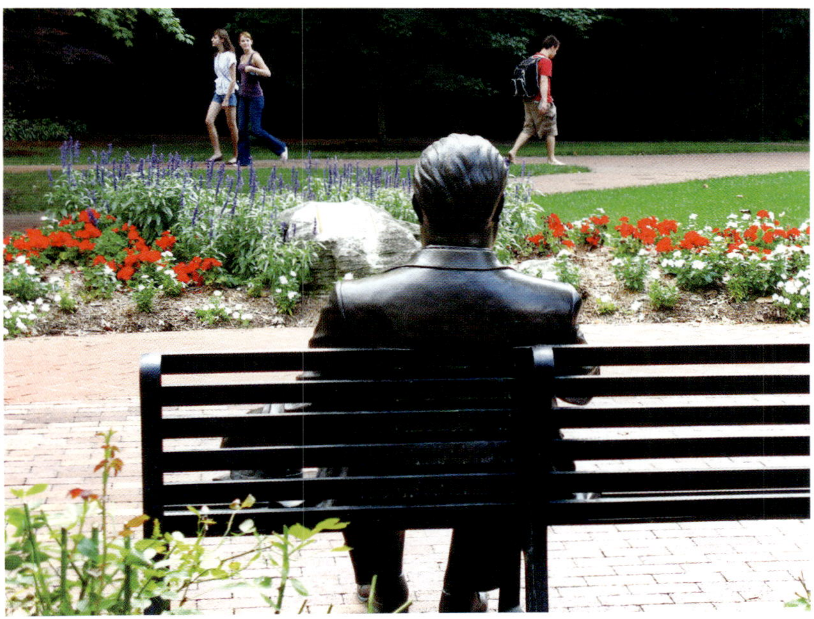

Traditionally, IU has focused on developing the entire person, not just his or her intellect. Under President Wells's leadership particularly, this effort included not only a campus characterized by green space, beautiful buildings, and art objects but also one filled with attractive living units, residence halls and Greek houses alike. The student's entire surroundings were designed to be stimulating and educational, thereby creating the campus IU has today.

—*Robert H. Shaffer, Professor Emeritus*

DEAN OF STUDENTS, IU BLOOMINGTON 1955–1969

Looking out over the plaza.

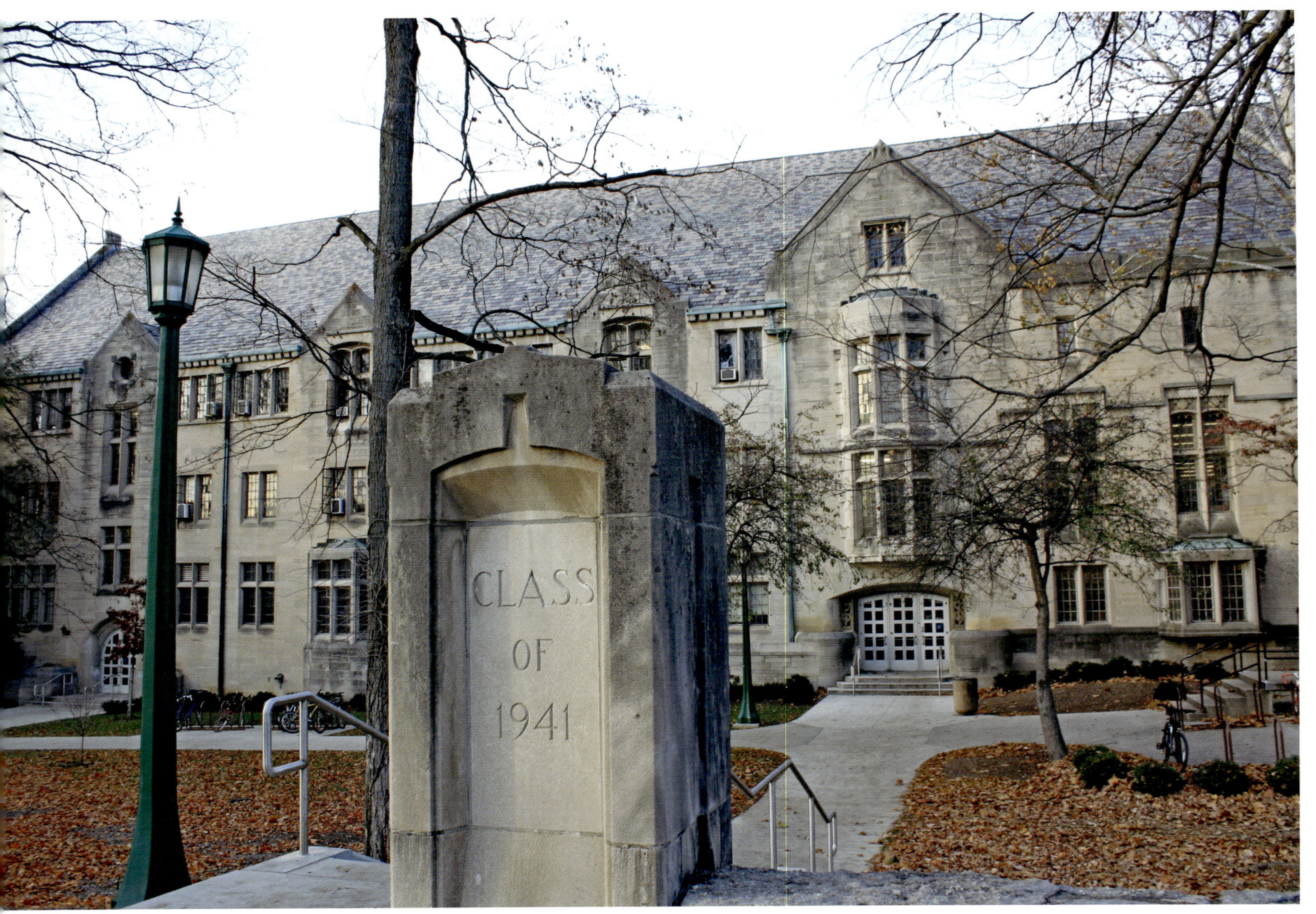

Swain Hall West. *Mandy Hussey*

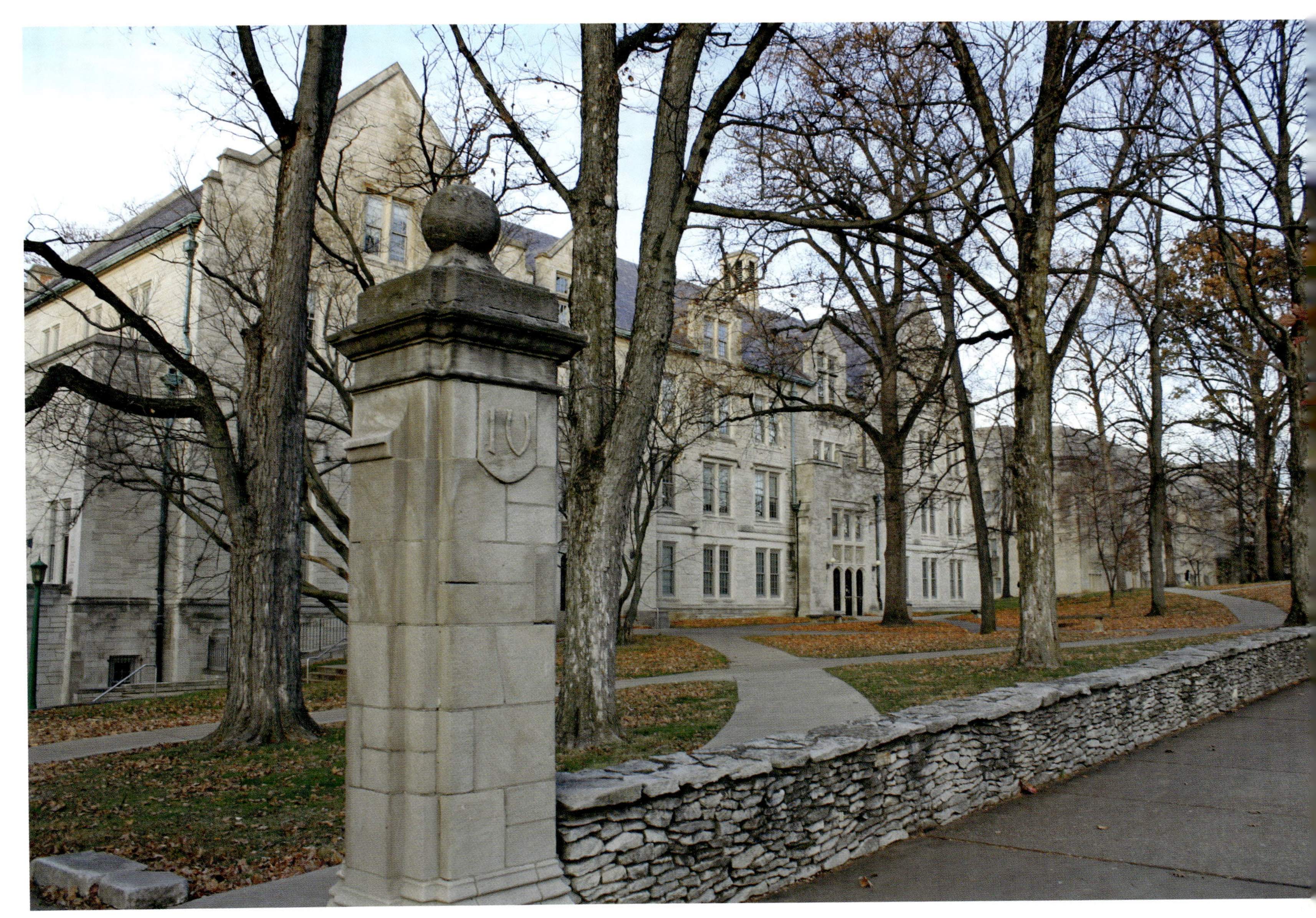

Rawles Hall. *Mandy Hussey*

dunn's woods

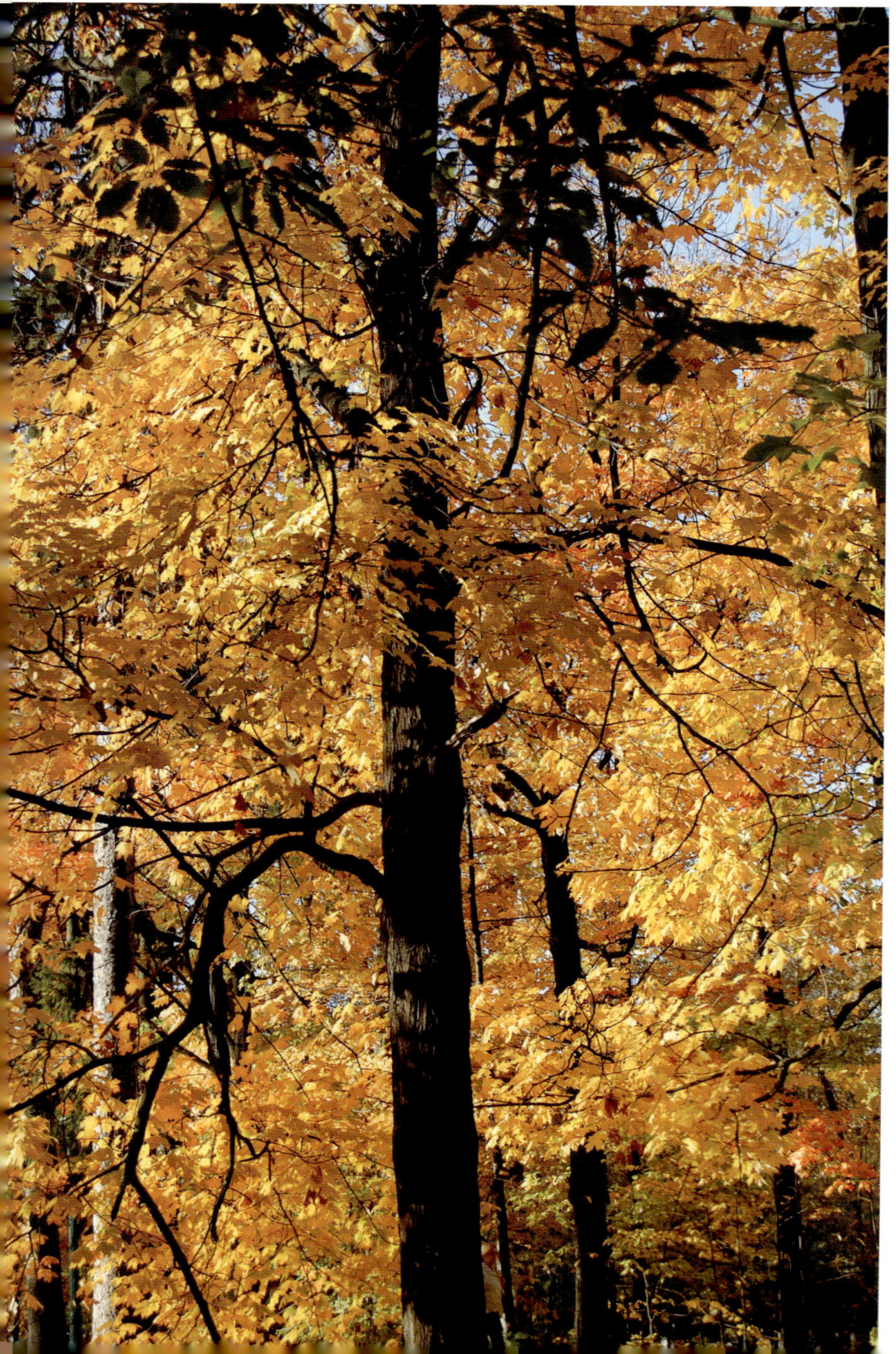

When I was an art student, I spent a lot of time in the cluster of temporary-frame–WWII buildings that constituted the Fine Arts Center near the Old Crescent area. Each day, I would step out into Dunn's Woods and be amazed by its magnificence. Among my fond memories are the times that our art classes went outdoors to paint and sketch amidst the trees, inspired by the color, light, and beauty of the surrounding campus.

—*Gayle Cook,* B.A. FINE ARTS, 1956

Brilliant golden trees in Dunn's Woods.

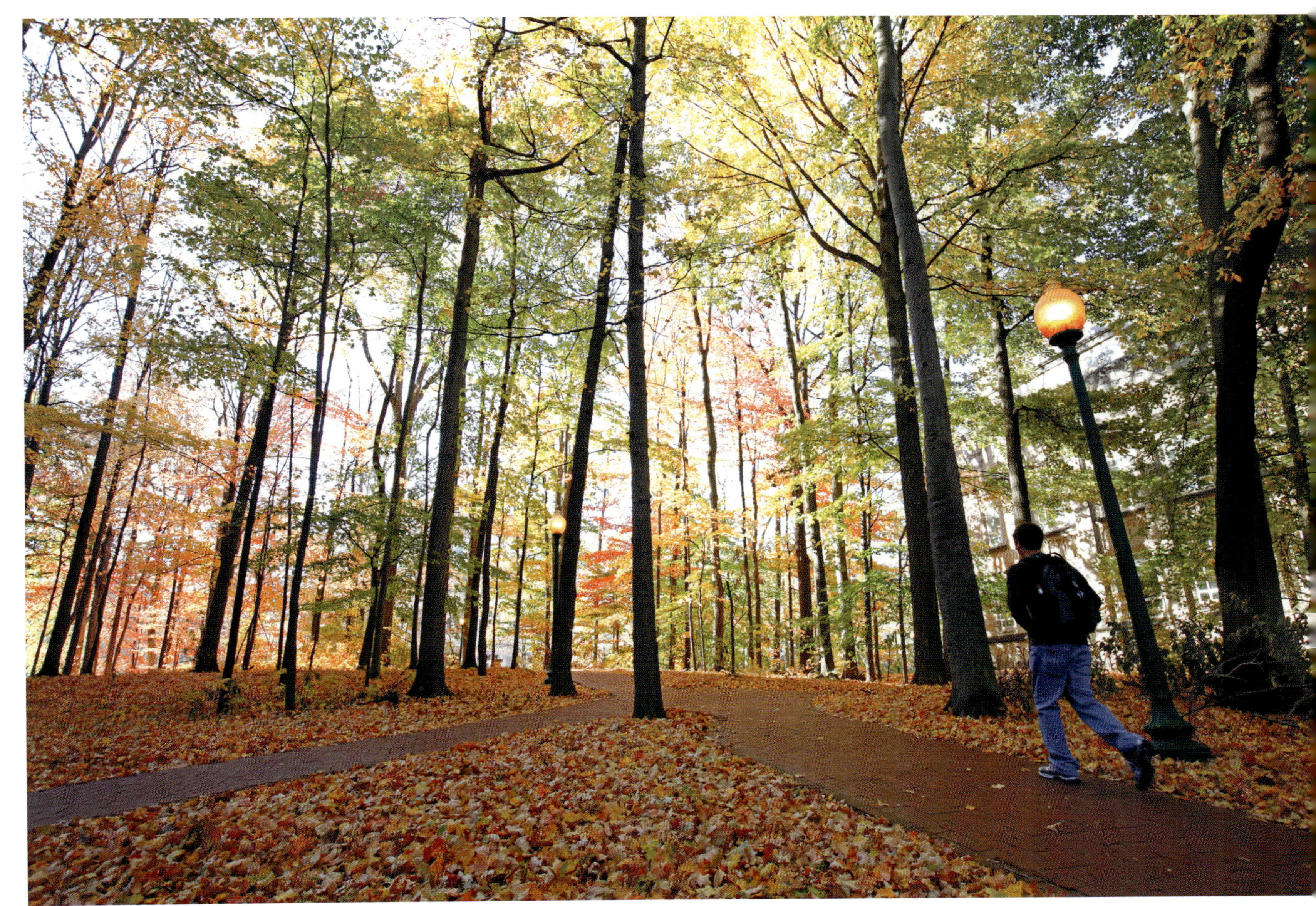

The path to class.

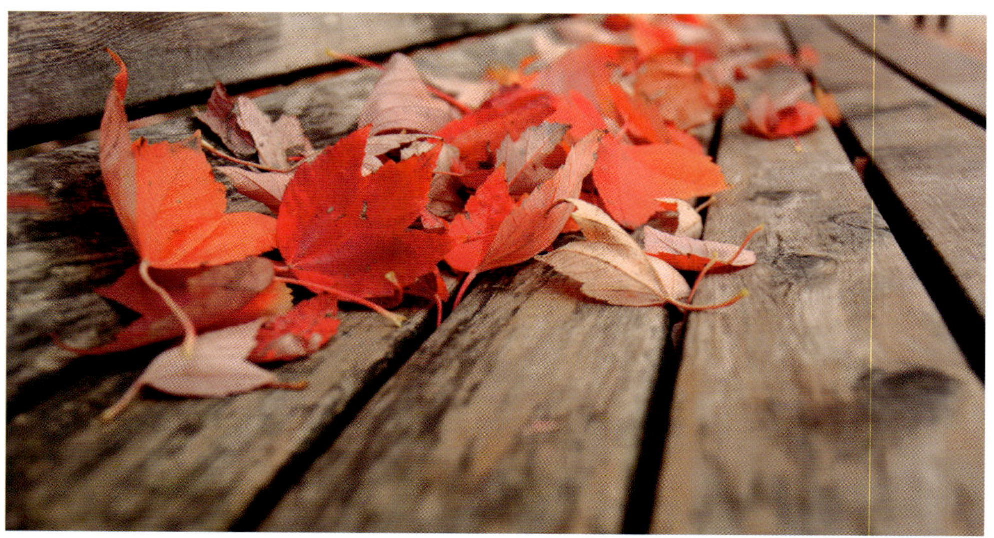

I met my wife, Nancy, the first day of our freshman year at IU. We spent our second date talking for hours on a wooden bench halfway through the woods in the center of campus. That was when I realized I had met the woman I was going to marry. Forty-five years later, that wood slat bench is still there . . . and so's the marriage.

—Michael Uslan

B.A. HISTORY, 1973; M.S. EDUCATION, 1975;
DOC. JURISPRUDENCE, 1976

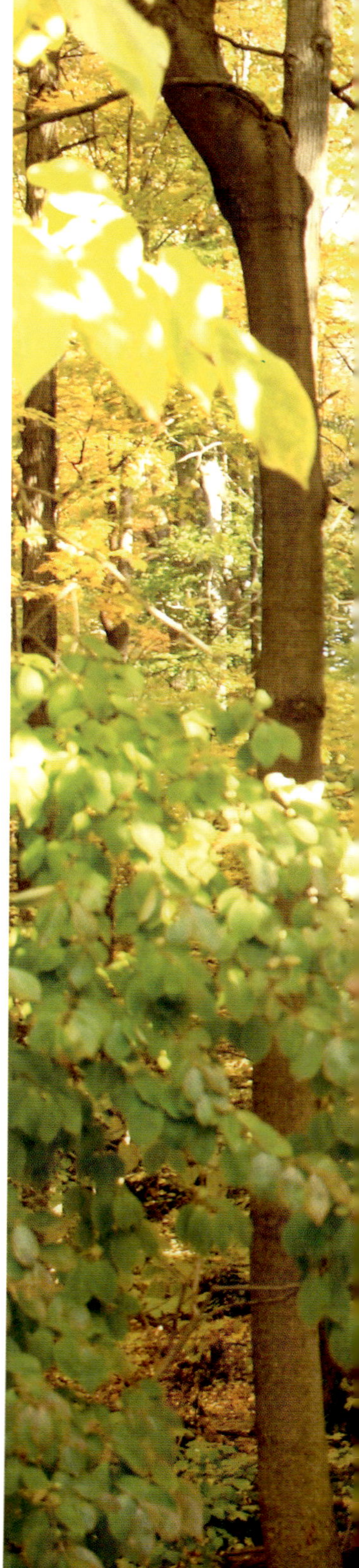

Lampposts line the paths in Dunn's Woods.

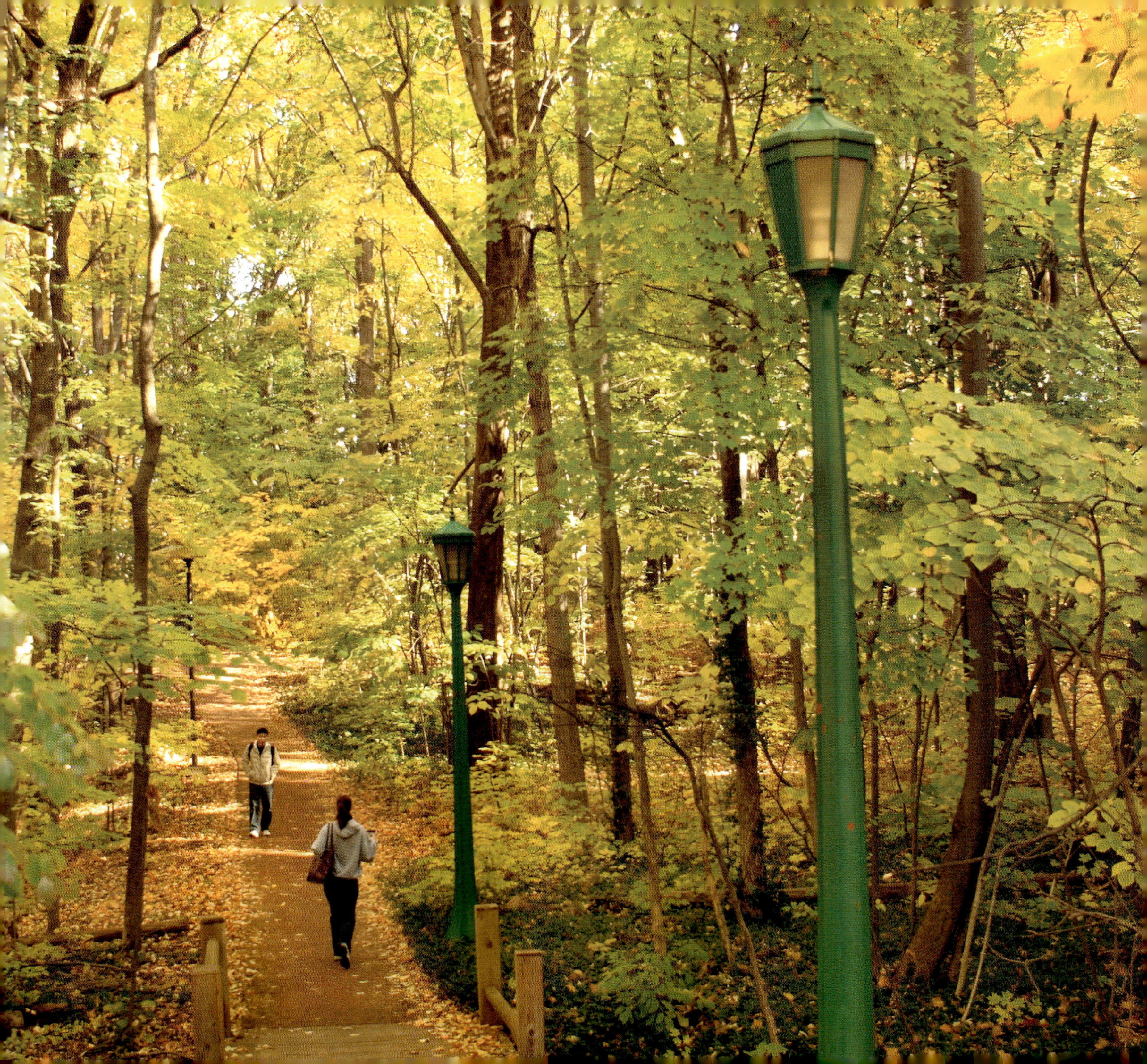

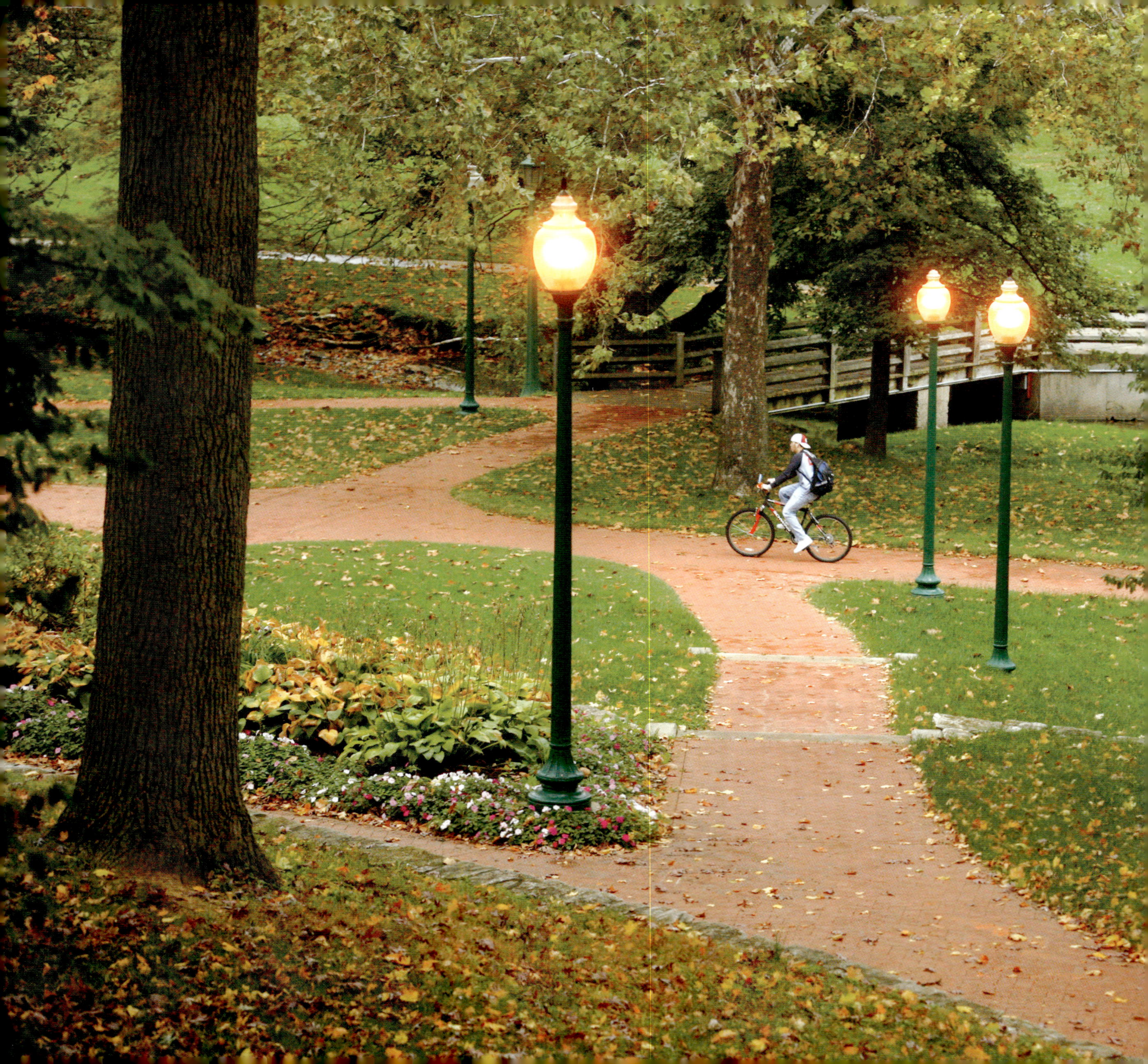

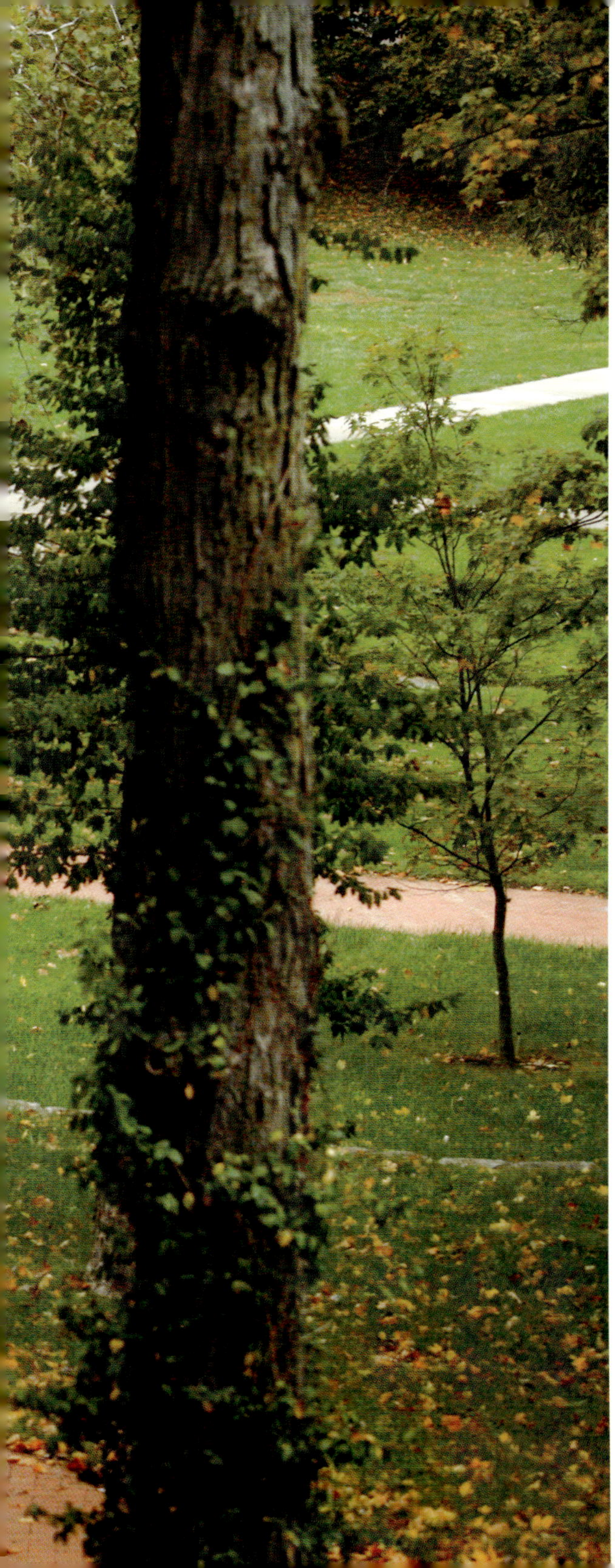

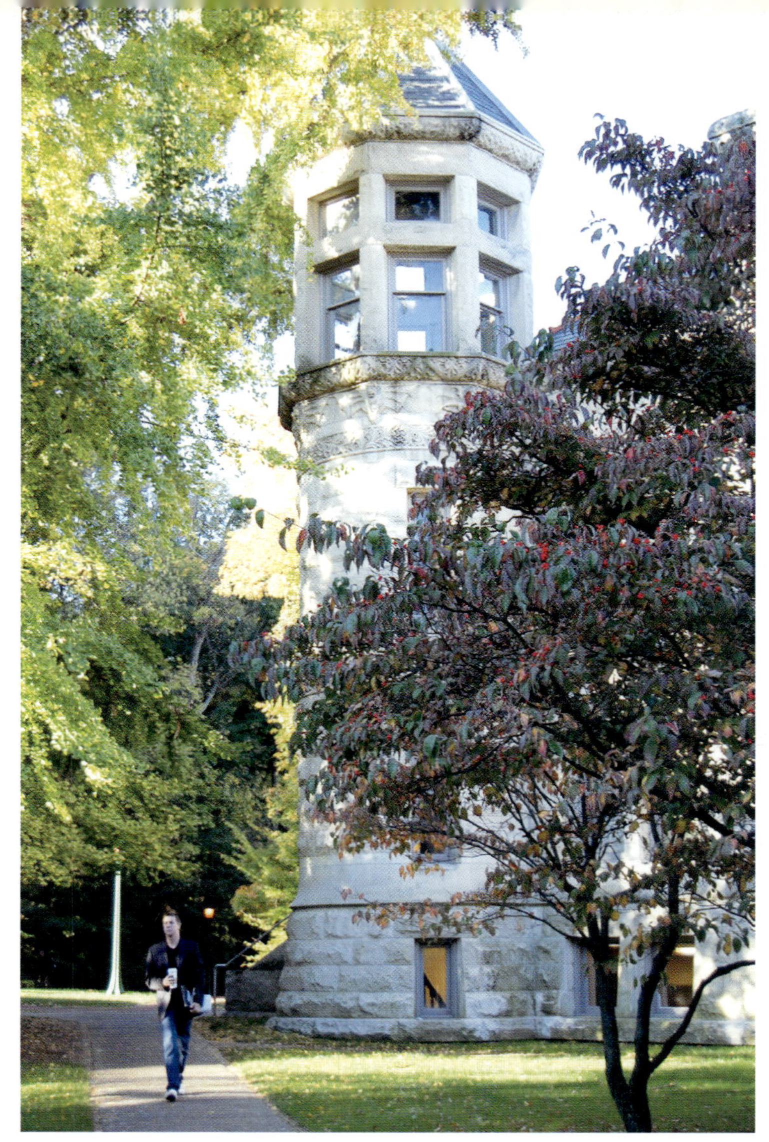

Paths.

Ginkgos near Maxwell Hall.

rose well house

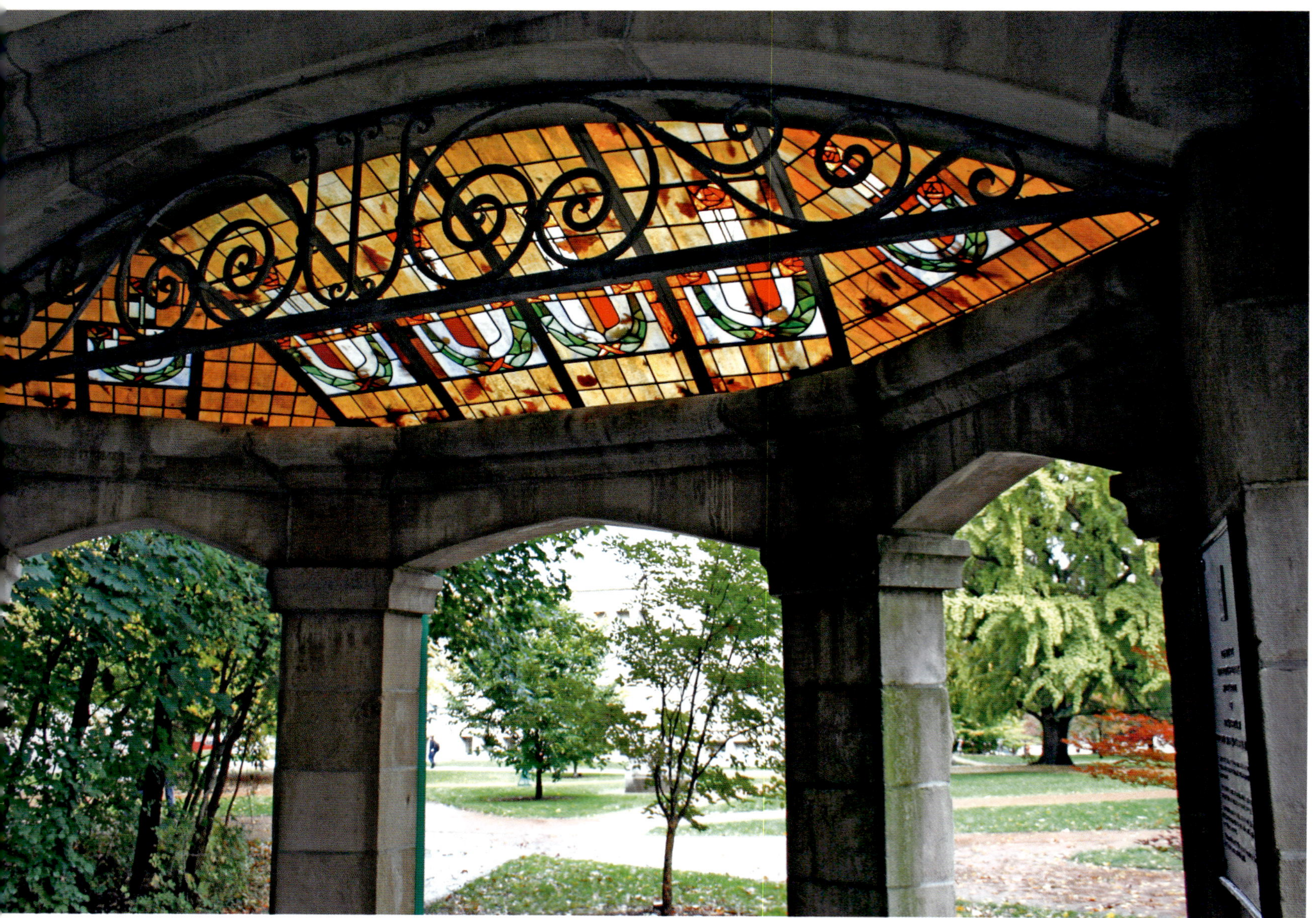

Rose Well House stained glass. *Milton Hamburger*

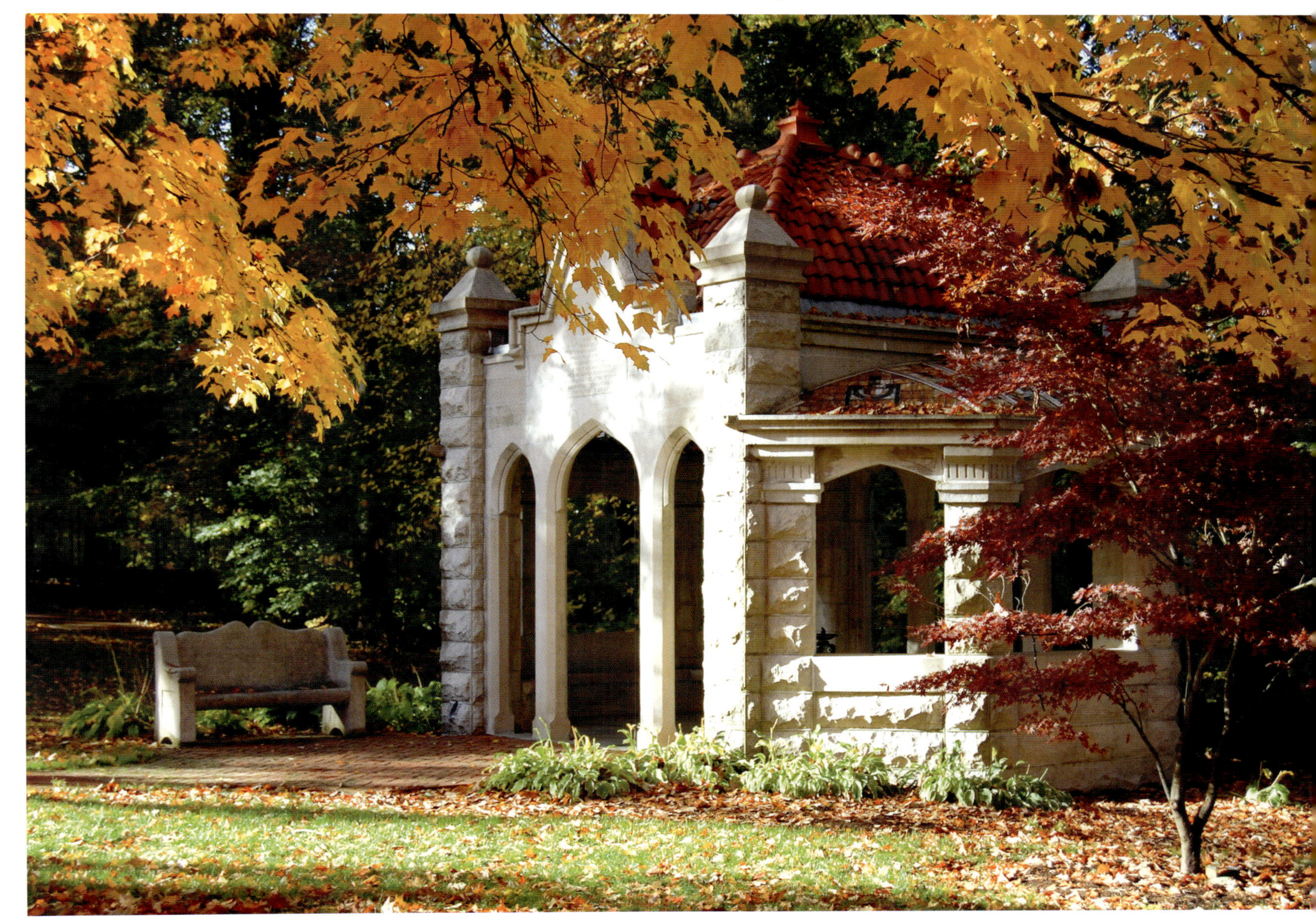

Rose Well House.

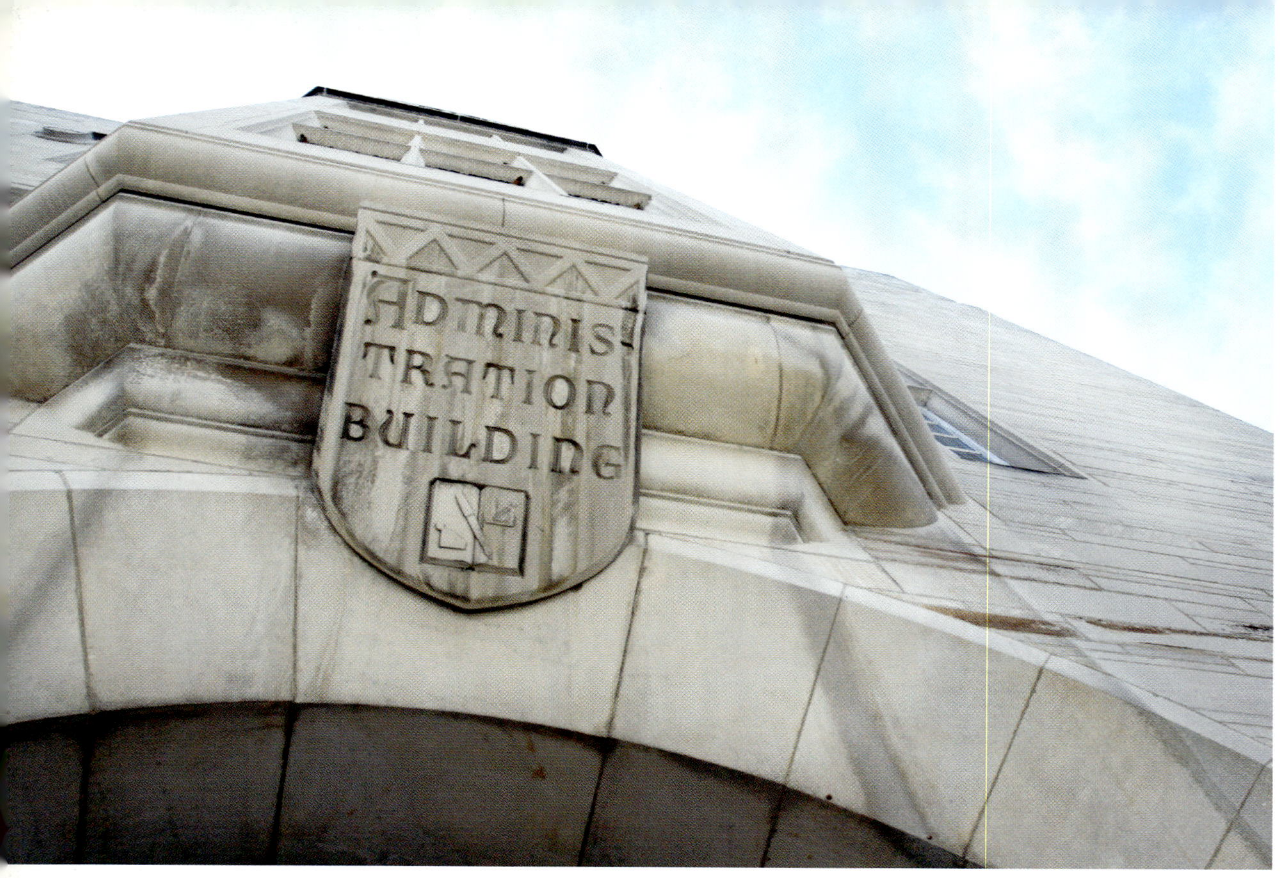

The Bloomington campus was alive with an air of excitement and expectancy for the 1945 school year in September. The end of World War II, just a month before, had turned loose a torrent of expectations, as well as thousands of returning veterans. Our student population would boom over the course of the school year, from 6,000 to more than 12,000, and continue going up. As new freshmen, Billie, my future wife, and I enjoyed the excitement and the heightened activity. Introduced by a mutual friend at the Delta Zeta house on Seventh Street, I was struck by her brown-eyed beauty. Later, I called her for a Coke date and we enjoyed that momentous event next afternoon at the small pharmacy across from the Administration Building on Indiana Avenue. Our little five-cent glasses of fountain Coke became our touchstone for campus life, leading to library dates and strolls all over campus. One such evening stroll near the campus wishing well was the site of a bright harvest moon shining down on our first kiss. These memories are as vivid now as their occurrence more than 68 years ago.

—*Ralph Hazelbaker,* B.S. BUSINESS, 1951

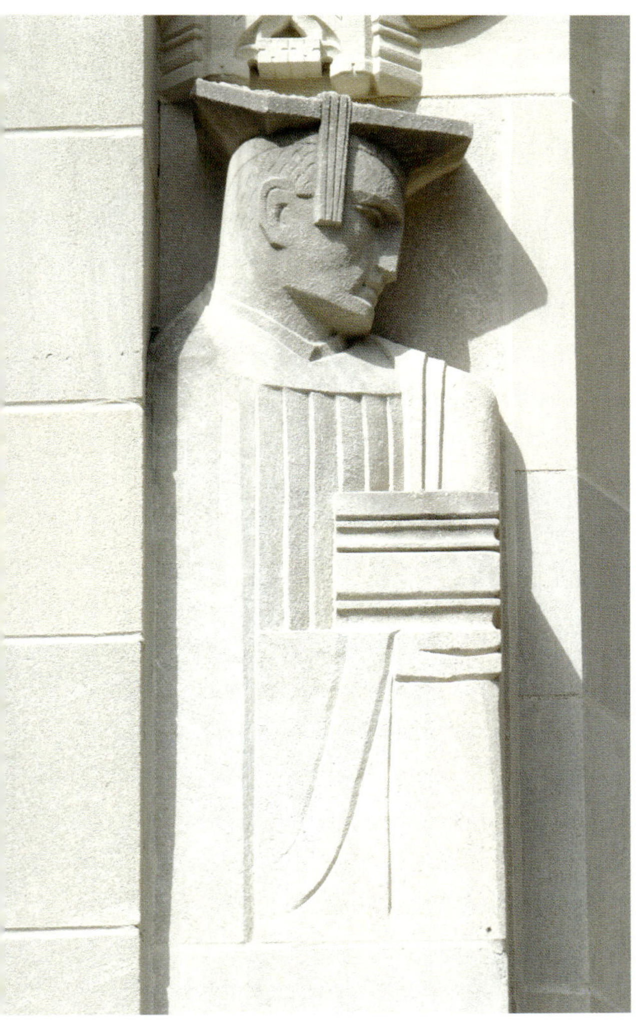

Limestone carving.

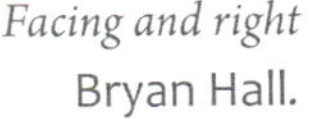

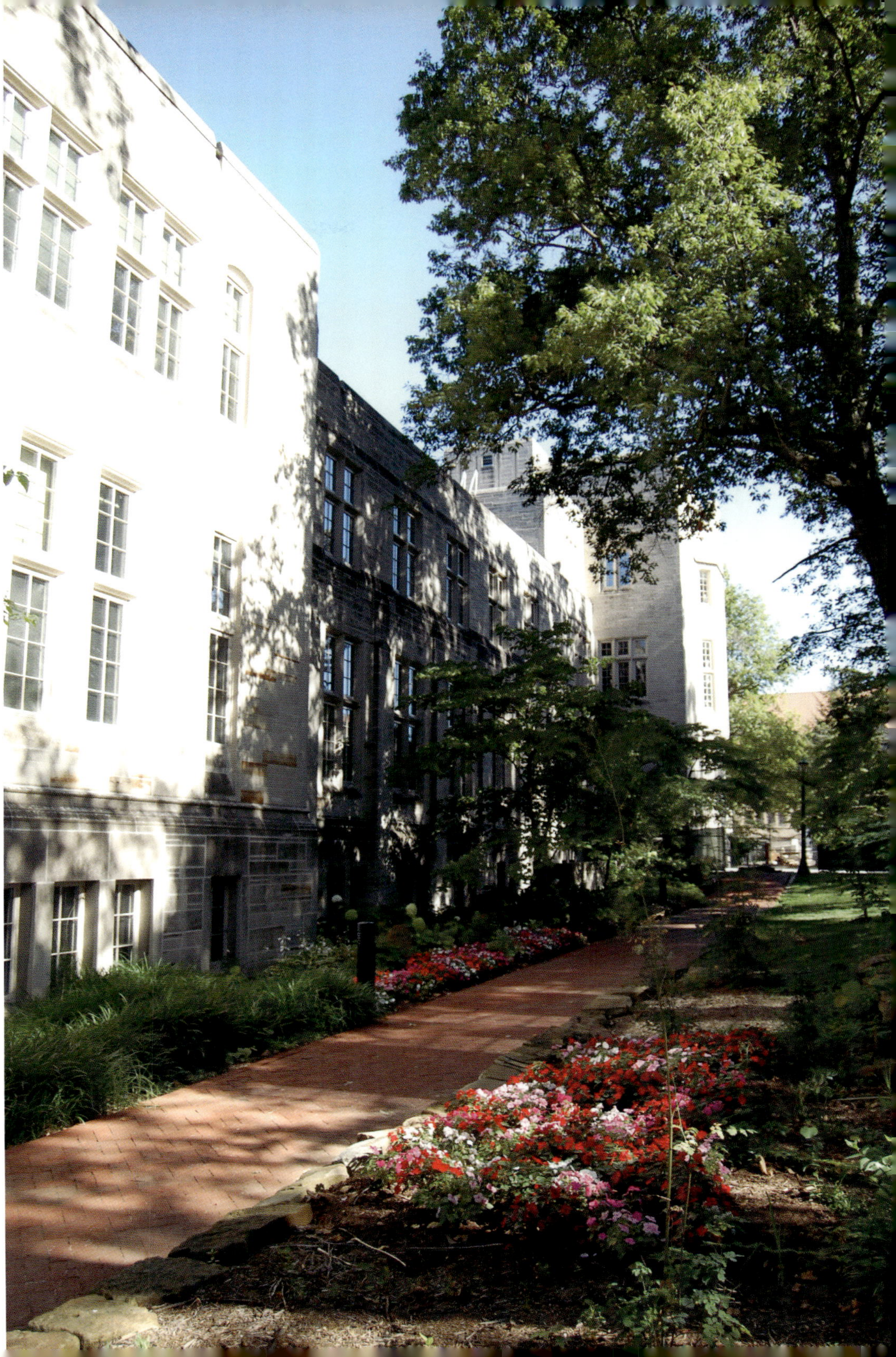

Facing and right
Bryan Hall.

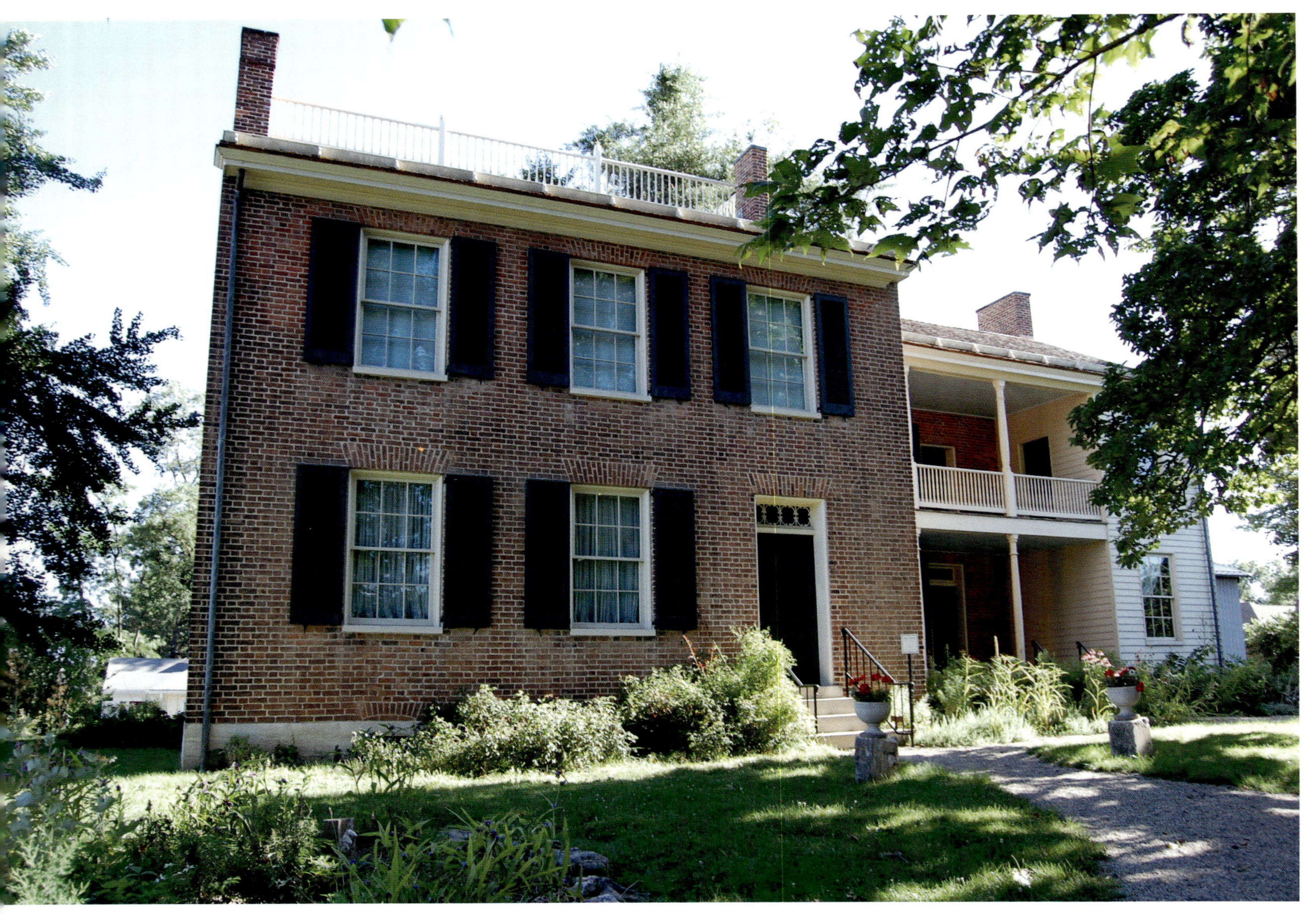

Above
Wylie House Museum.

Facing
Old-fashioned bearded iris with garden sage in bloom. *Sherry Wise*

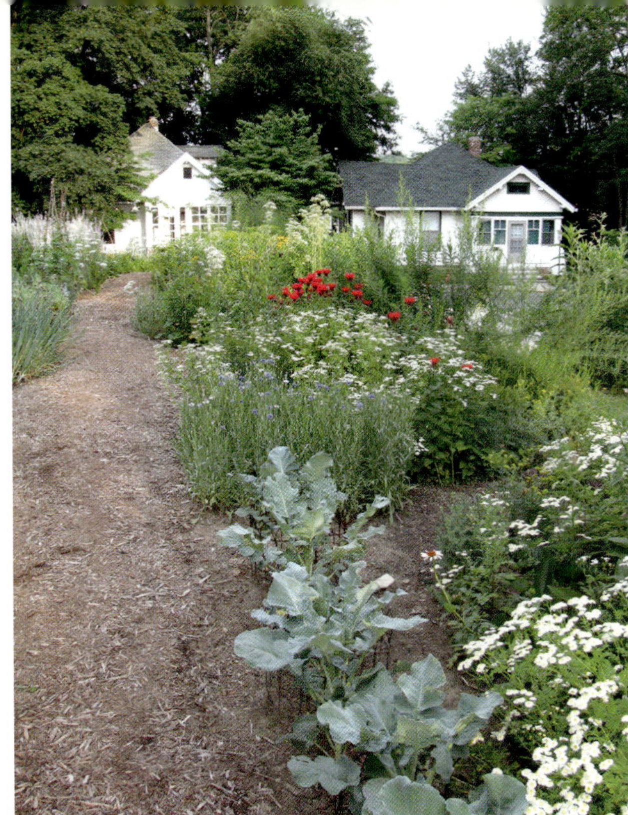

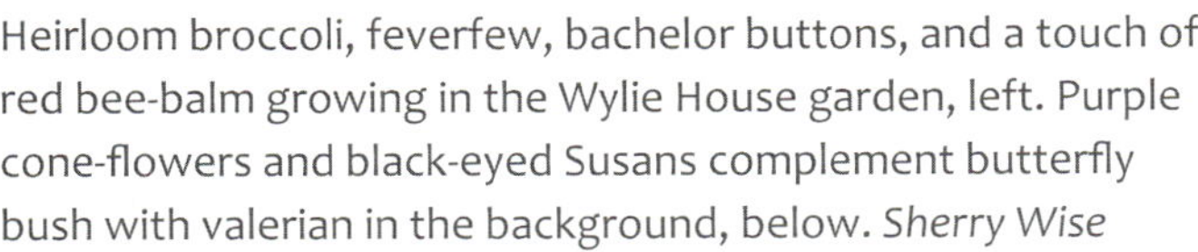

Heirloom broccoli, feverfew, bachelor buttons, and a touch of red bee-balm growing in the Wylie House garden, left. Purple cone-flowers and black-eyed Susans complement butterfly bush with valerian in the background, below. *Sherry Wise*

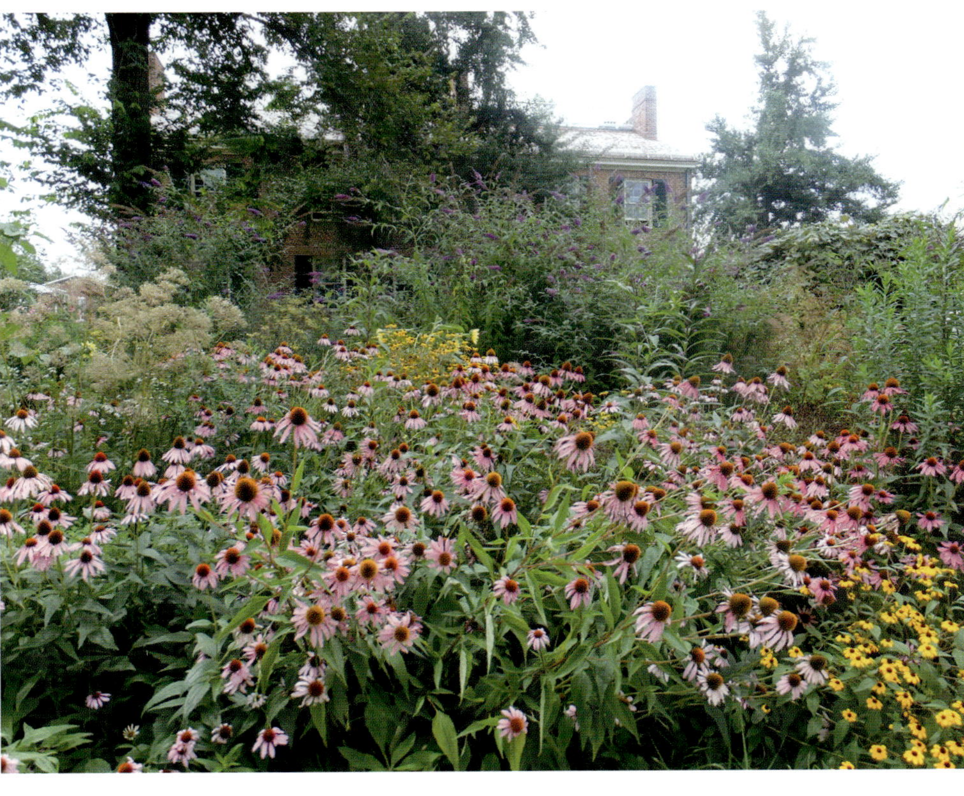

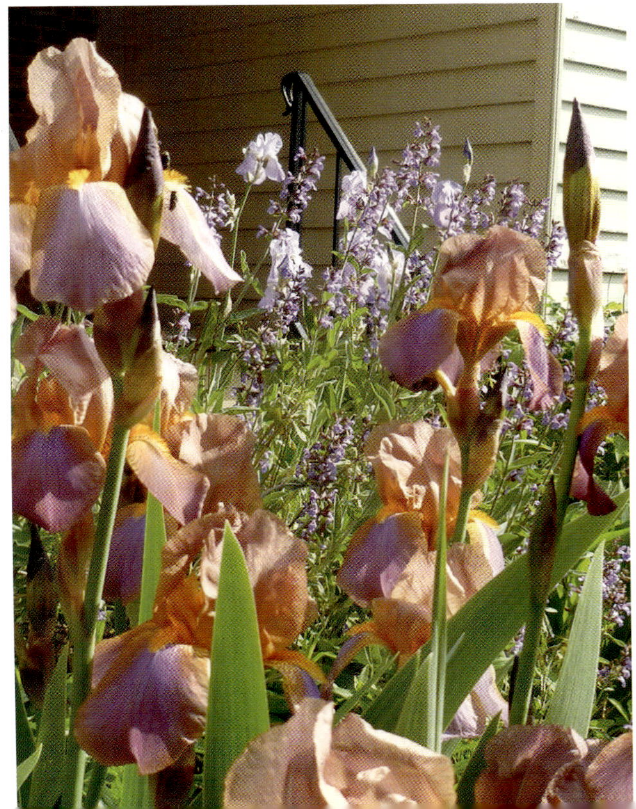

Wylie House, home of the first president and his large family, is one of the university's treasures. Its ongoing restoration to the early 19th century transports us to the era and culture of those early days when the university was founded. We are so grateful to be patrons of this historical site.

—*Sue Robinson*, B.S. EDUCATION, 1955
Murray Robinson, B.S. BUSINESS, 1955; M.B.A., 1957

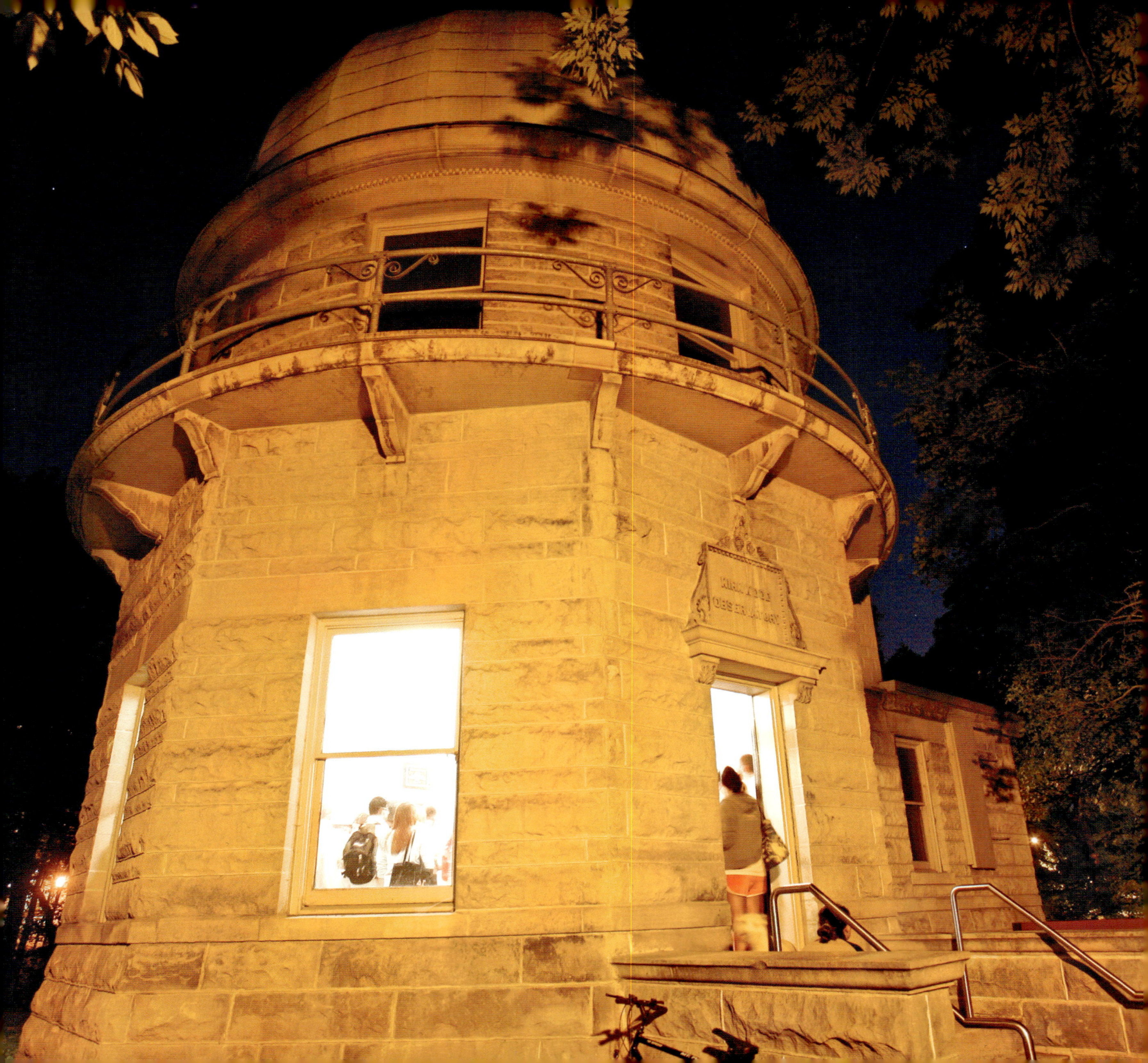

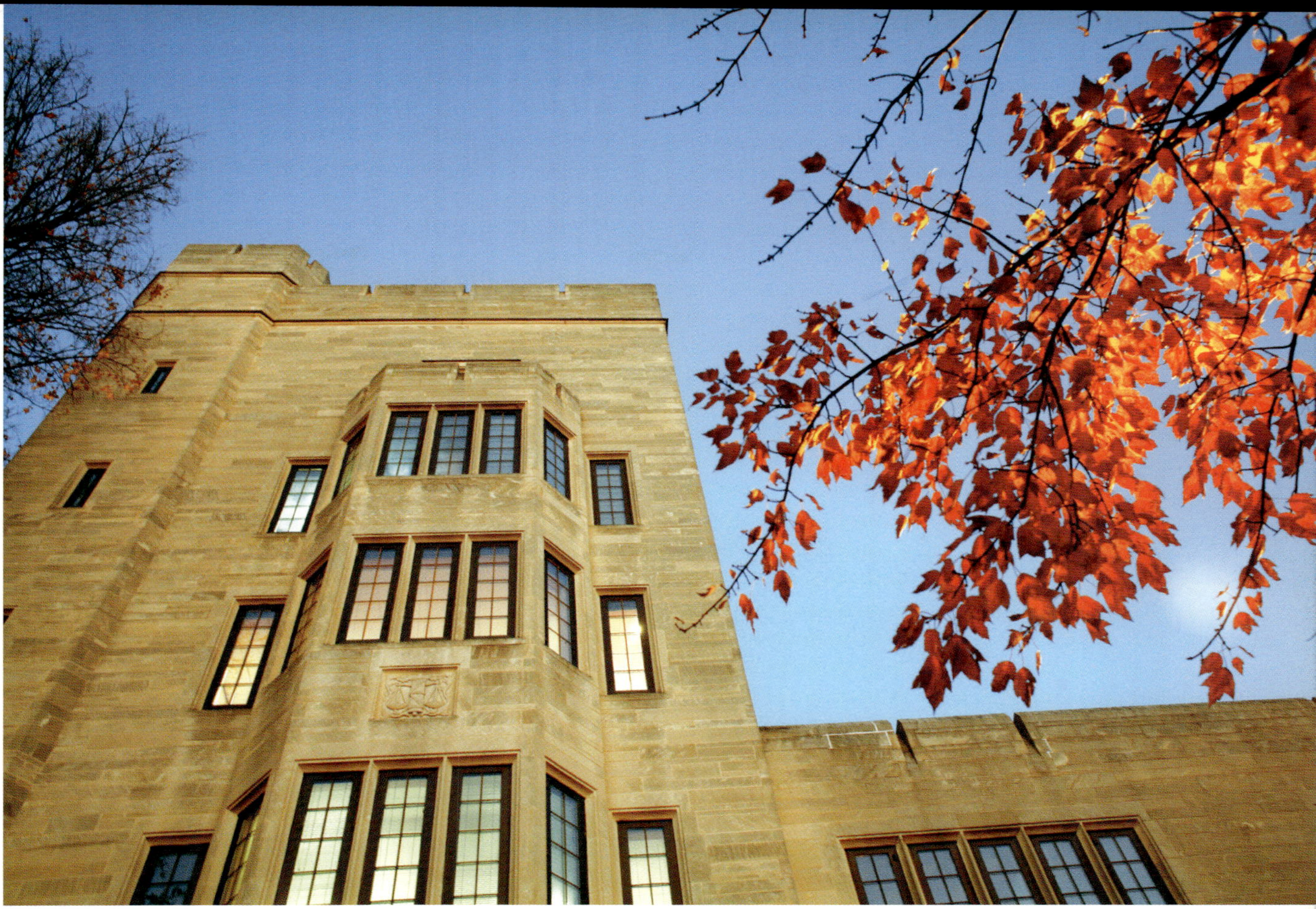

Kirkwood Observatory.

Maurer School of Law.

indiana memorial union

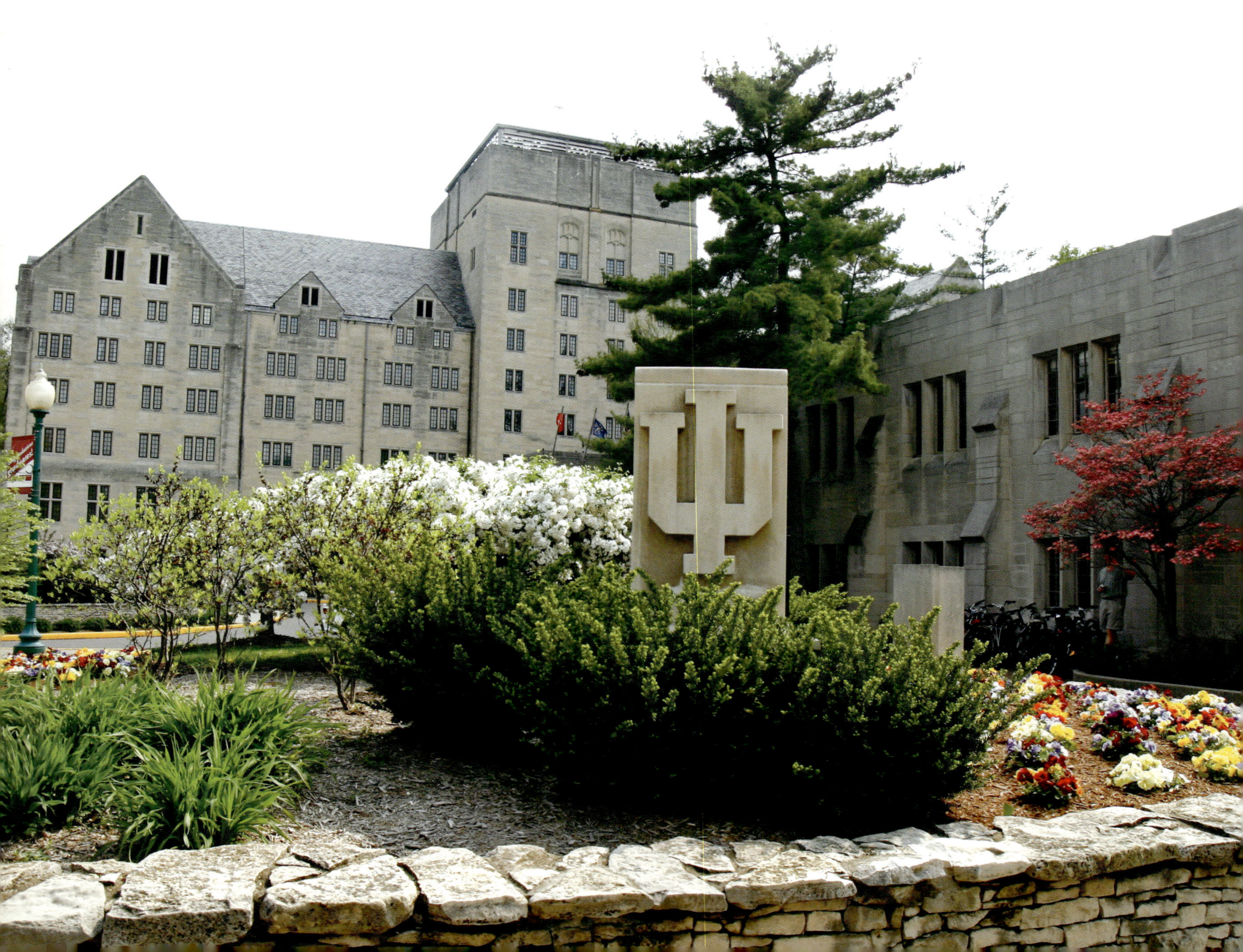

I enjoyed walking along the sidewalk bordering the hotel wing of the Indiana Memorial Union and taking in the fascinating blend of visual textures, full of contrasts but always in harmony. The gentle incline of the stairs heading south encouraged slowing down and savoring the Jordan Creek ravine, followed by the intimate Dunn Cemetery and Beck Chapel on the left, set against the massive limestone wall of the Union building hotel to the right. Emerging onto East Kirkwood, the old world touches gave way to glimpses of the earliest modernist architecture on campus, the Chemistry Building and Ballantine Hall, still graced by restrained ornamental carvings and tied together by those wonderful Hoosier trees!

—*Frank W. Hoffmann*

B.A. HISTORY, 1971; M. LIBRARY SCIENCE, 1973

Facing
Indiana Memorial Union.

Tudor Room, Indiana Memorial Union.

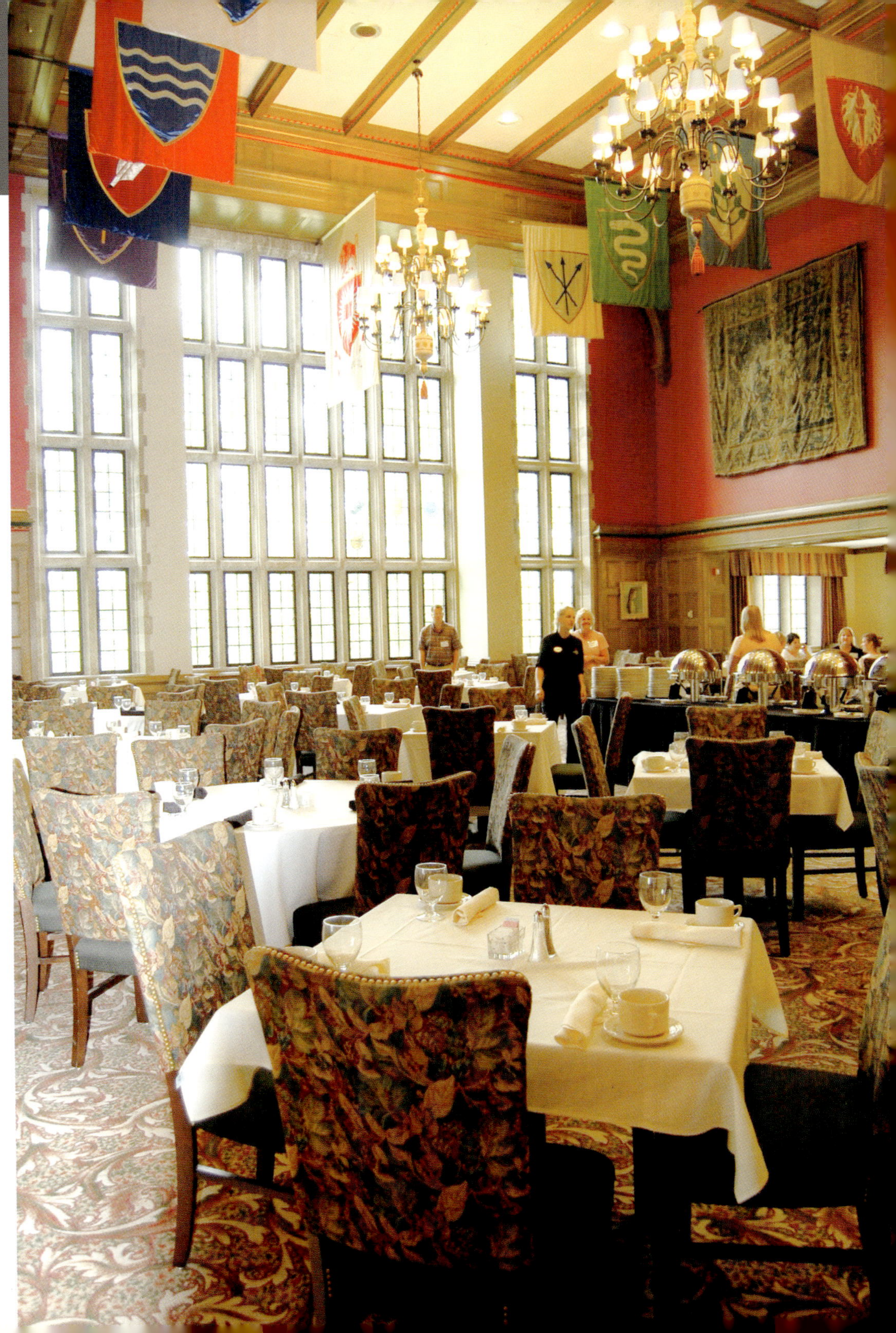

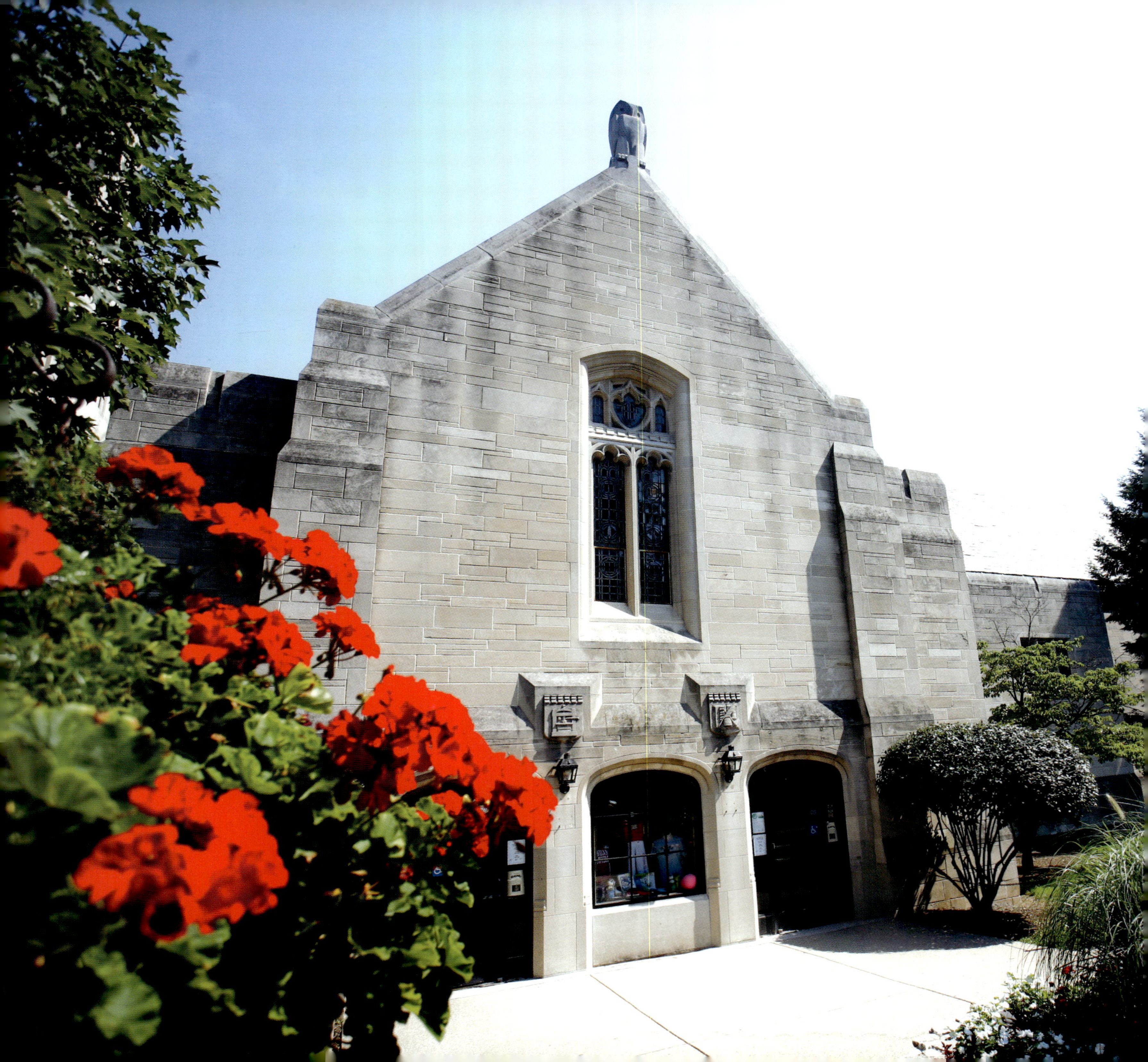

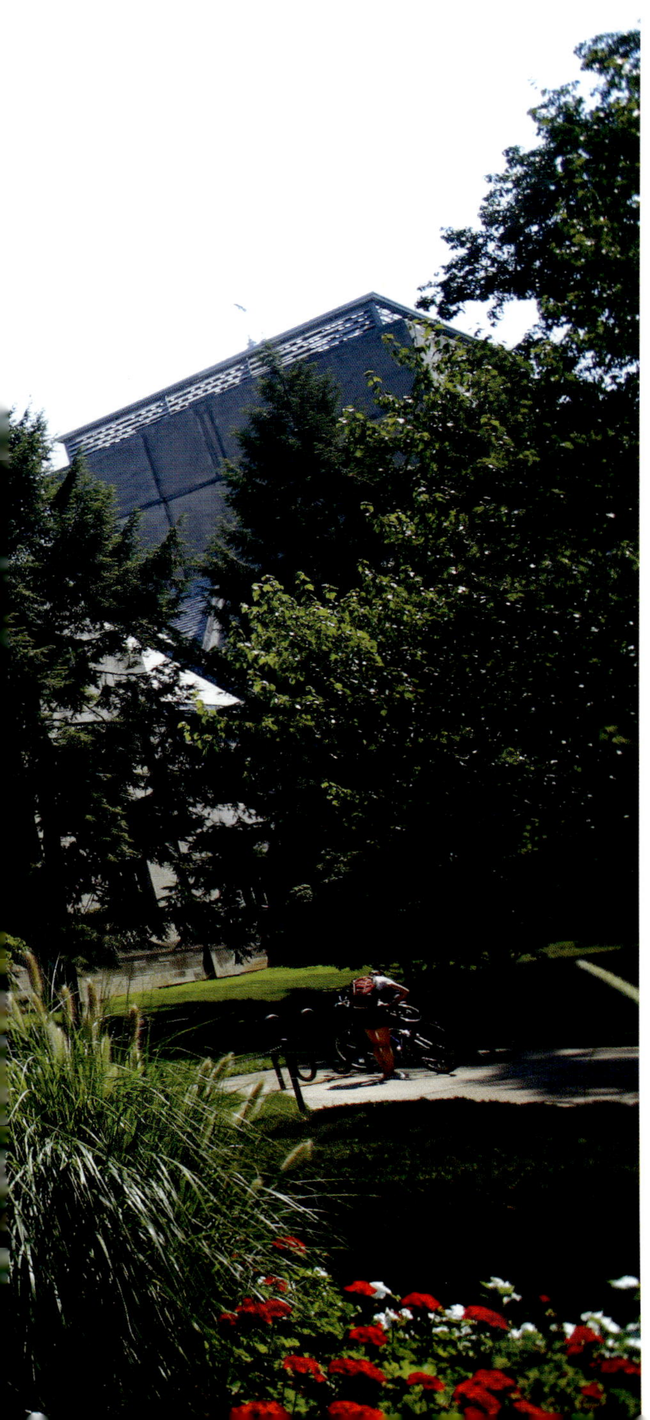

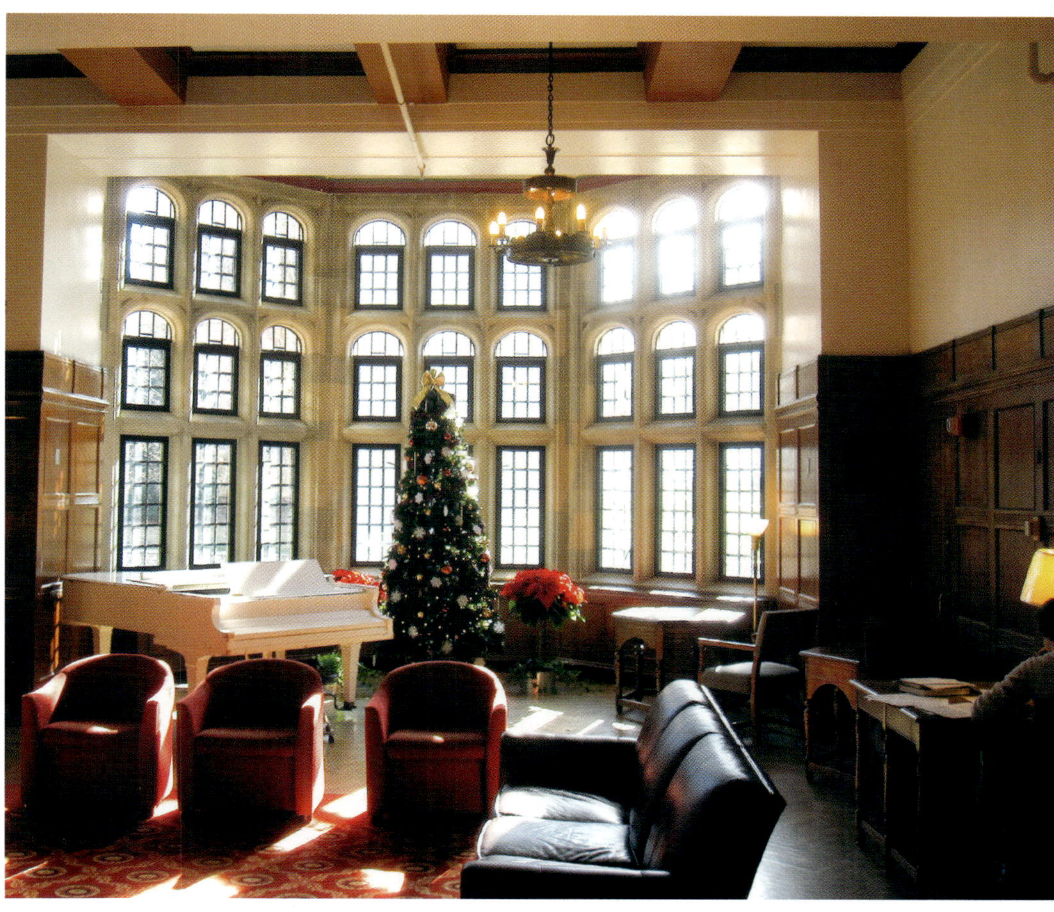

Facing
Indiana Memorial Union, bookstore entrance.

South Lounge, Indiana Memorial Union. *Rob Guillen*

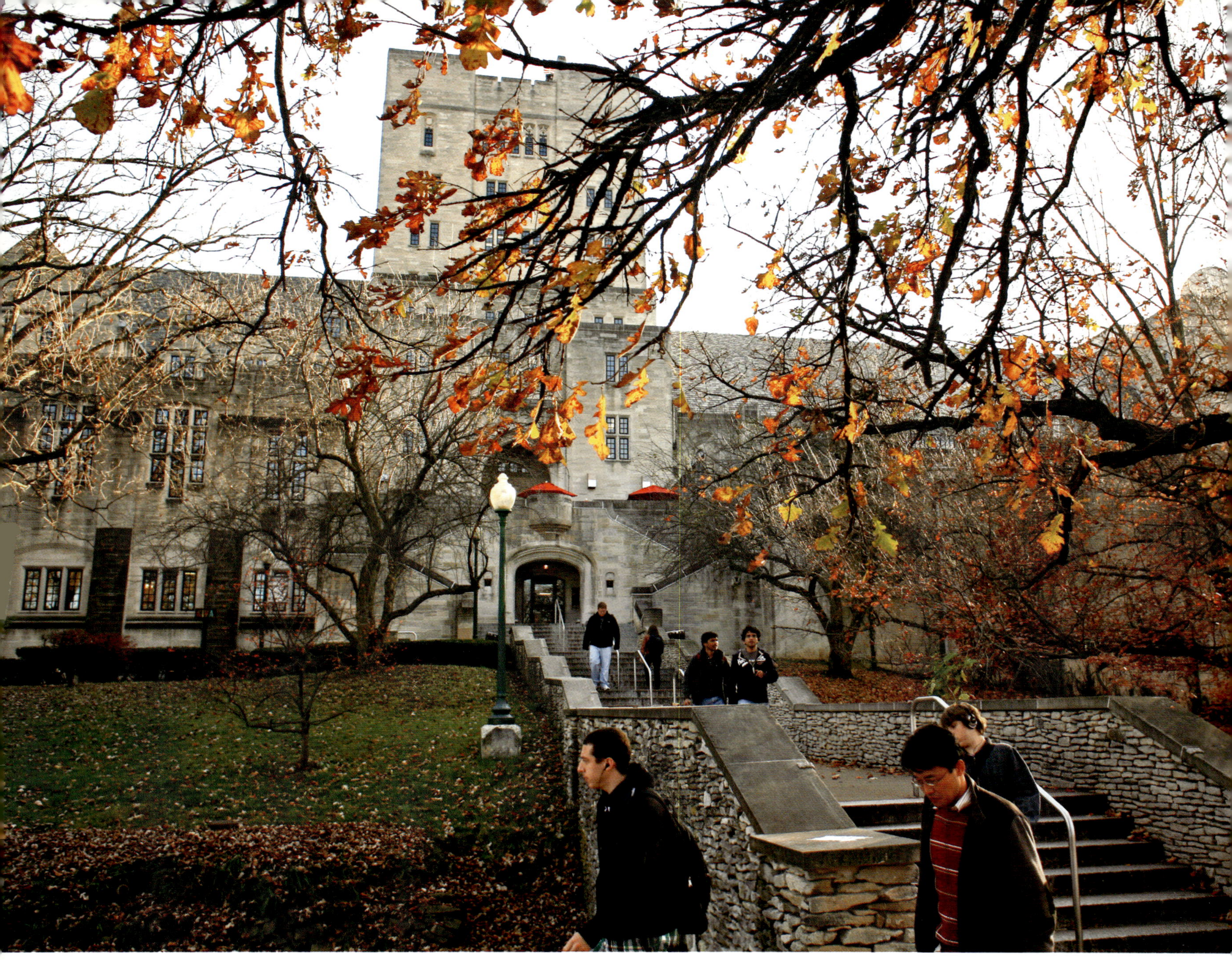

Indiana Memorial Union.

Towering over a game of Frisbee in Dunn Meadow.

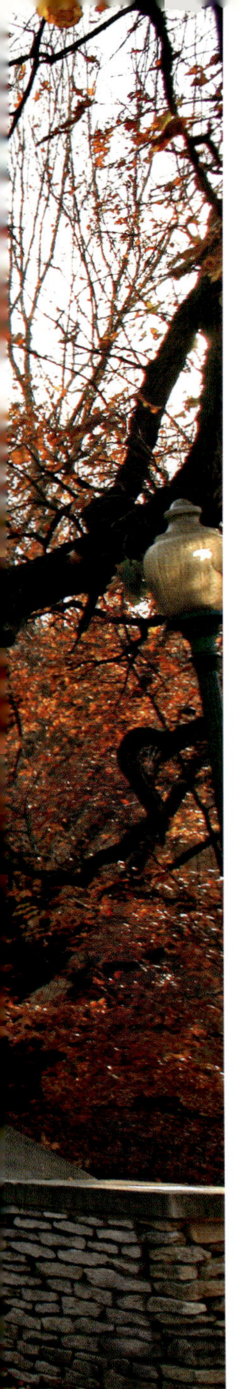

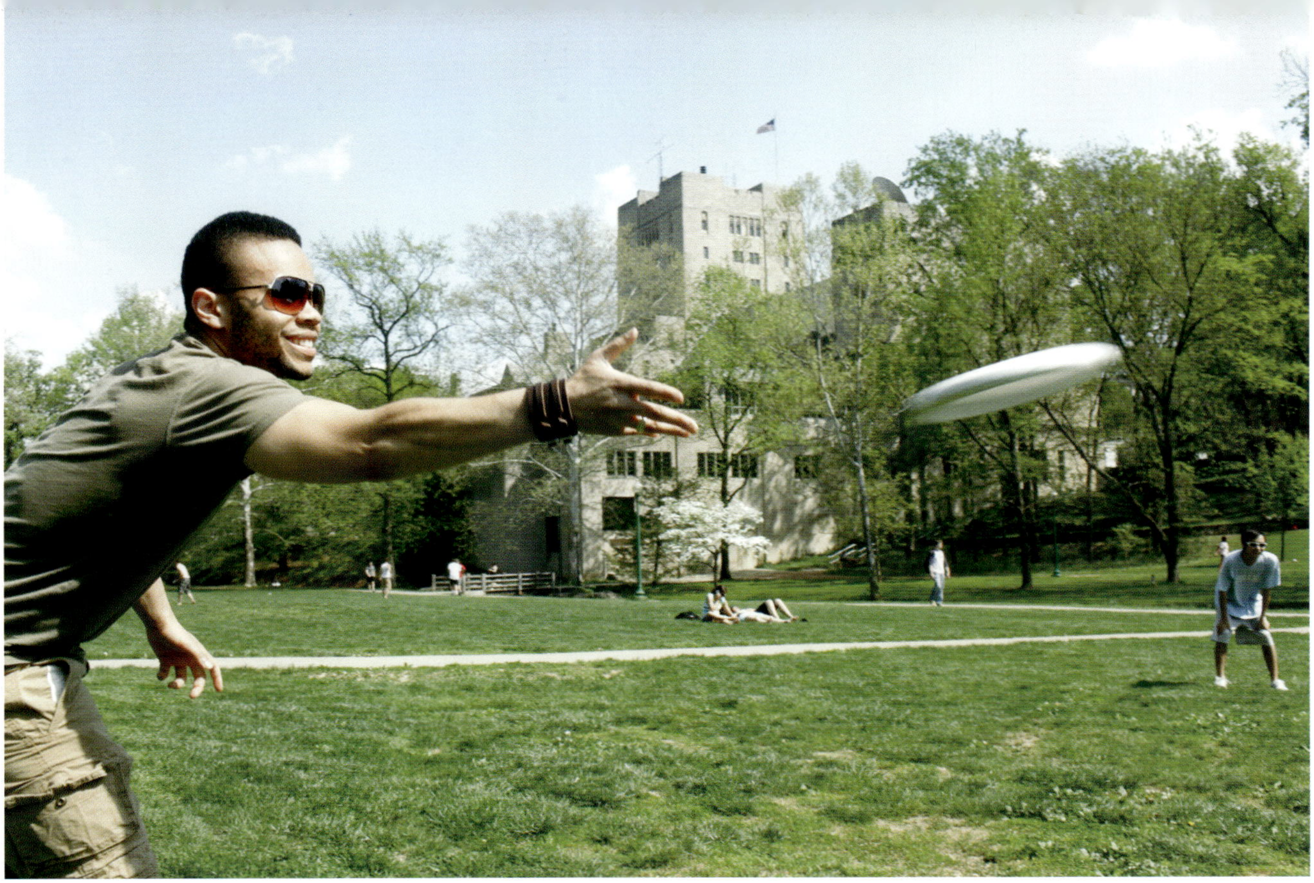

I was on campus during the turbulent '60s when many pressing issues surfaced. Dunn Meadow was a special place for a wide range of activities—both politically and socially. There was an ongoing debate whether to allow students to use Dunn Meadow to gather to protest, but because freedom of expression was so important to our administration, there was a sense of responsibility and no gathering ever got out of hand. The meadow was also a laid-back place to throw a Frisbee or spread blankets and rest along the Jordan River, adding to the tranquility and openness of the university. As a Sigma Chi, I was able to look out my window and enjoy one of the gems of this university every day.

—*Mike Shumate,* B.S. BUSINESS, 1967

During my 38 years at IUB, I always appreciated the high level of student engagement in campus activities and issues. Dunn Meadow is one of my favorite places because it was the site of so many student-initiated events, from festivals to concerts to protests to memorial gatherings. Dunn Meadow provided the stage for student voices to be heard.

—*Dr. Richard N. "Dick" McKaig*

DEAN OF STUDENTS, IU BLOOMINGTON 1991–2009

beck chapel

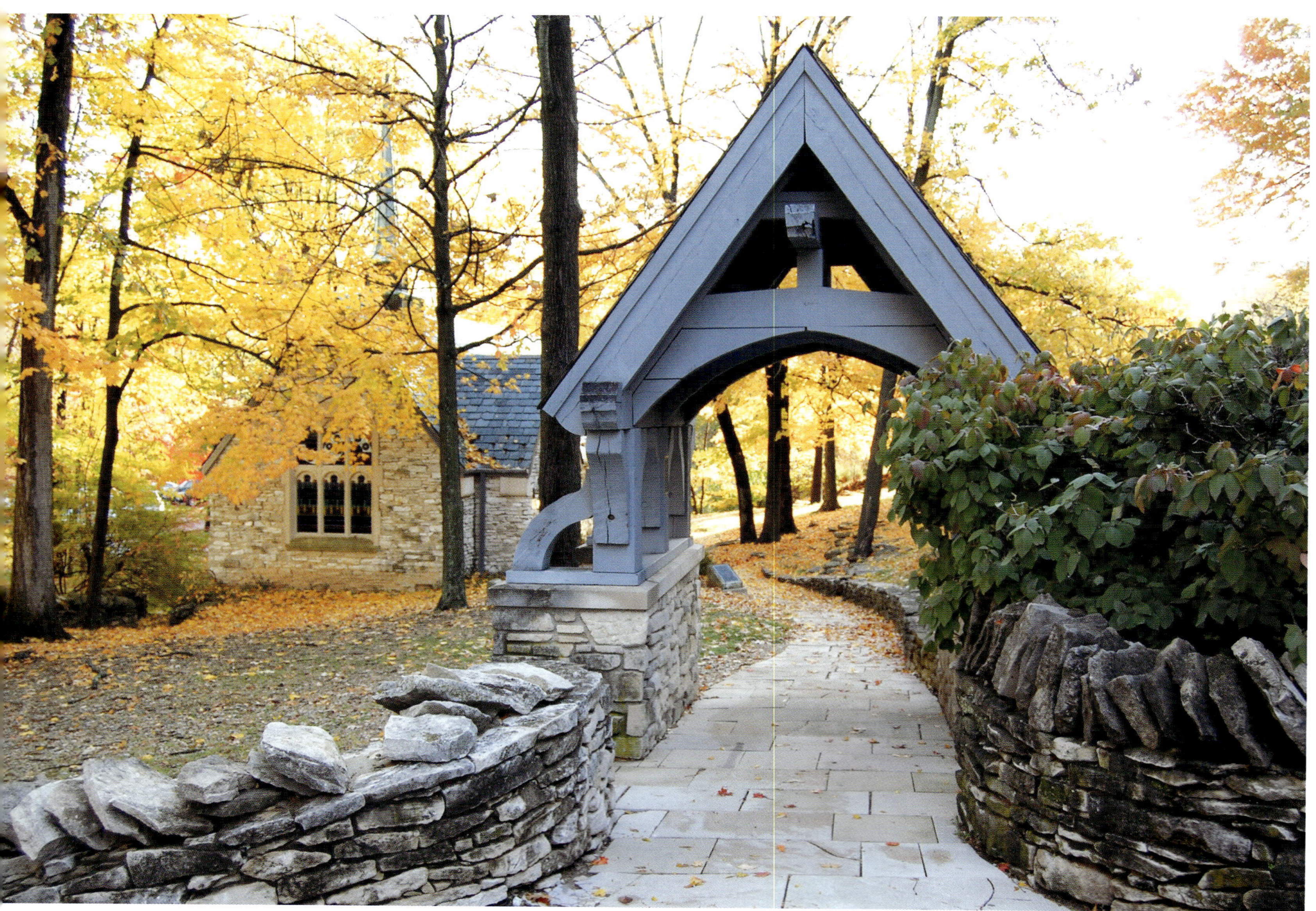

Beck Chapel.

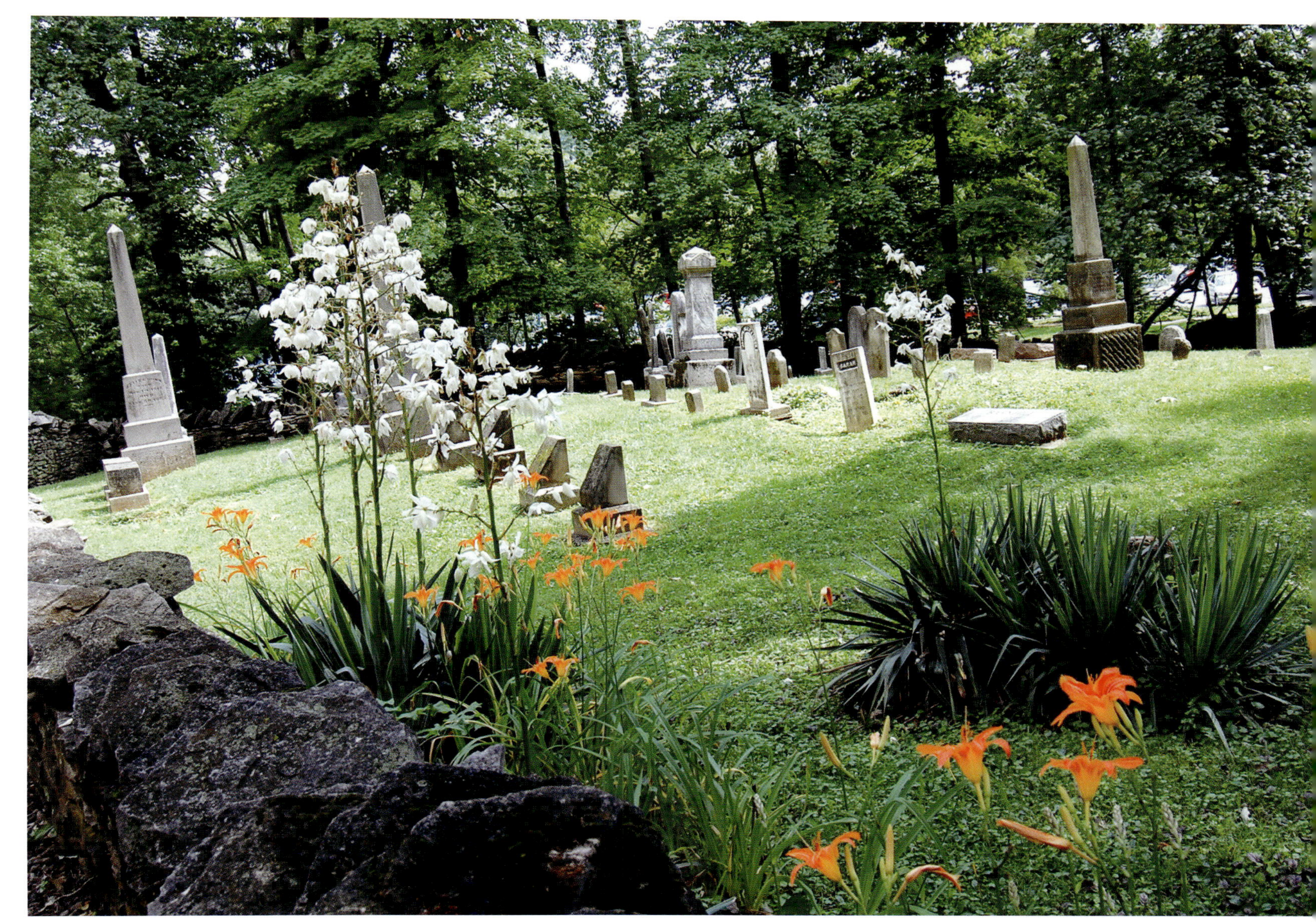

Dunn Cemetery.

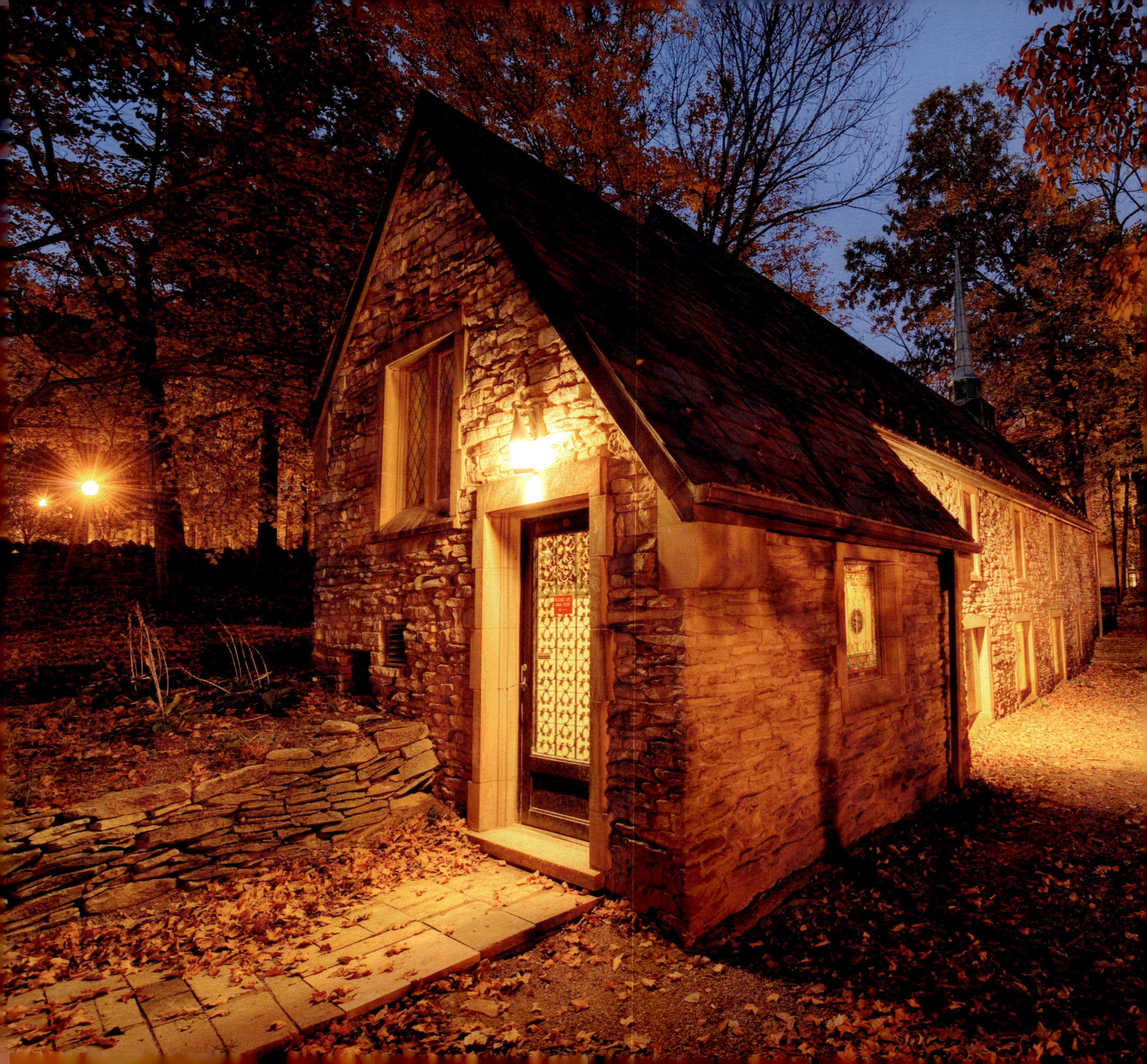

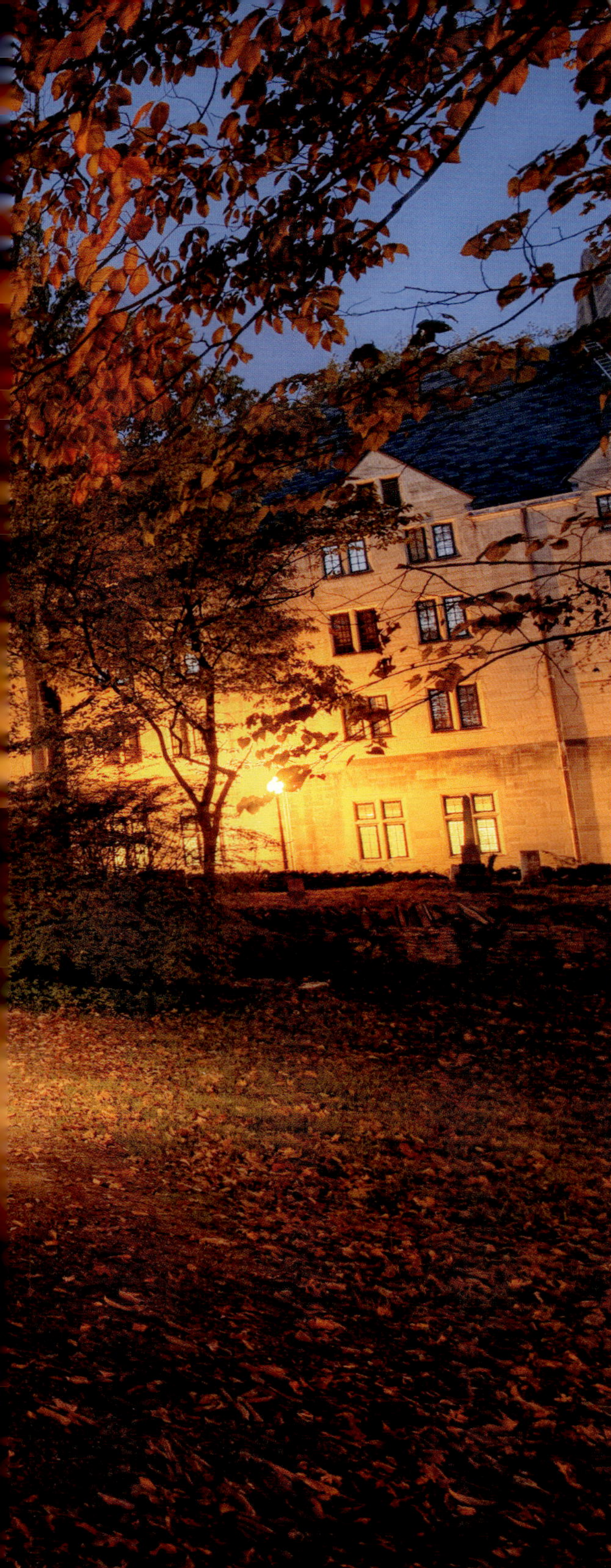

When I was looking for a peaceful place, not necessarily to pray but to be calm during the often tumultuous hippie era, I would spend my time inside the wonderful and restful Beck Chapel. It was in the center of campus, and although everybody was rushing by, the chapel remained calm in the middle of chaos.

—*Jane Jorgensen,* B.S. EDUCATION, 1972

Beck Chapel illuminates a fall evening. *Justin Kern*

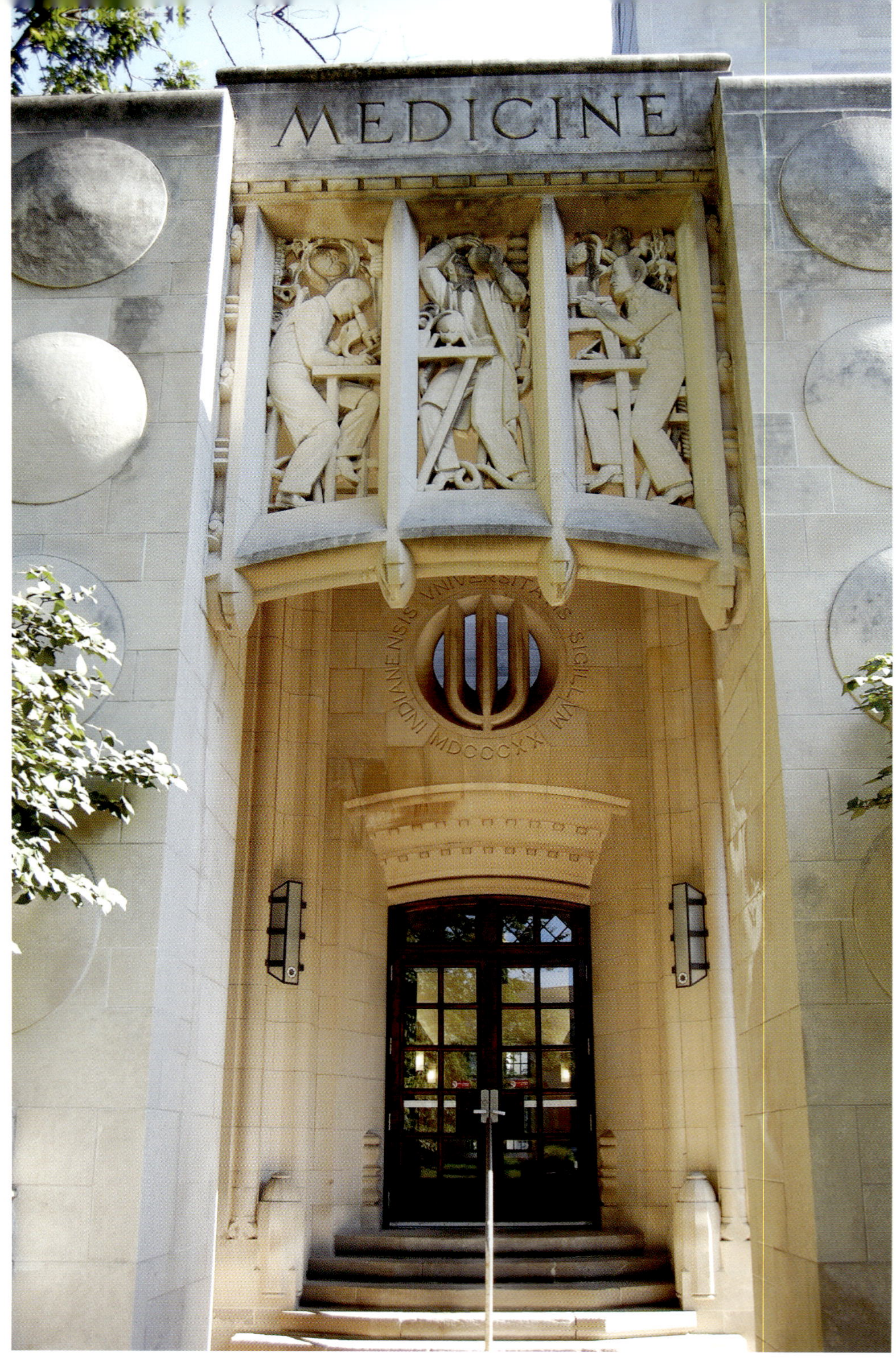

Limestone carving on Myers Hall.

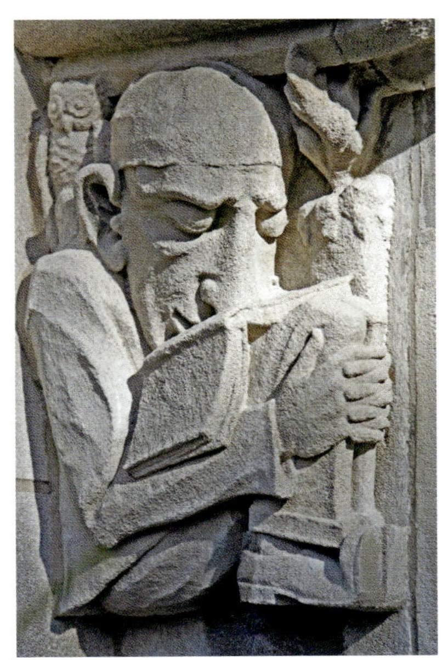

On the arched entrance to Memorial Hall: a carving of a sleeping student with his nose in a book, a candle burning at his side, and an owl on his shoulder is paired with a carving of a professor ringing a bell while calling out to the student with a morning songbird.

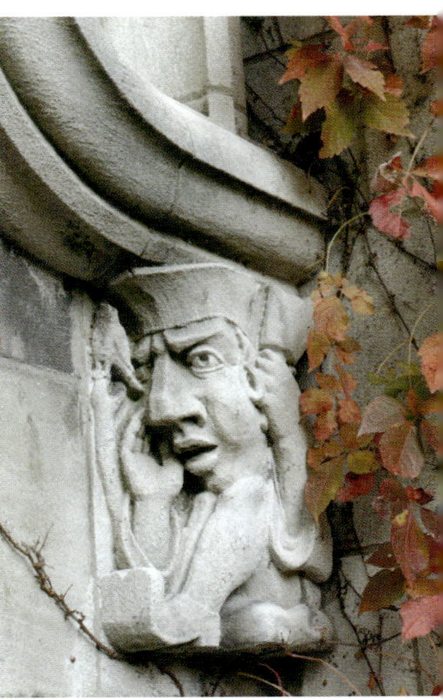

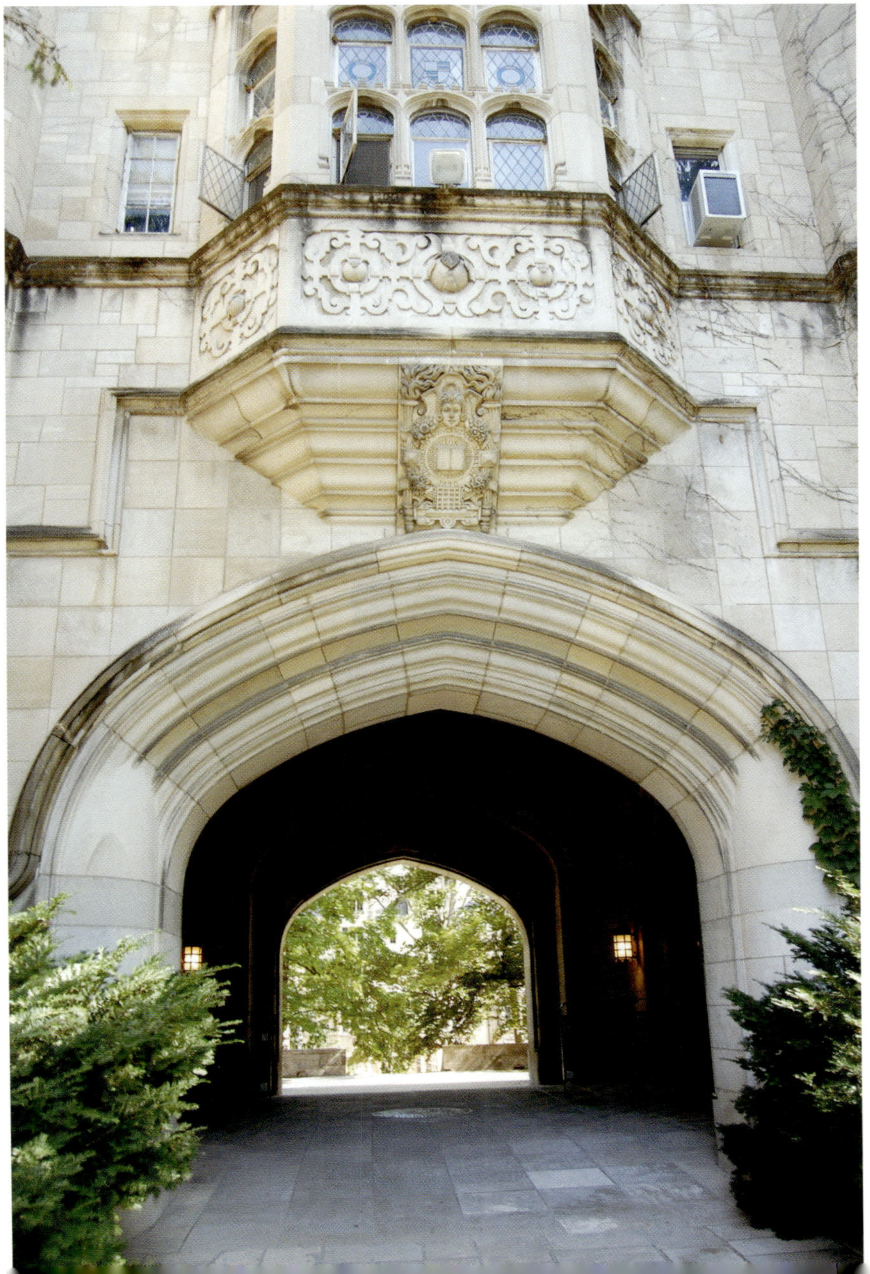

Memorial Hall.

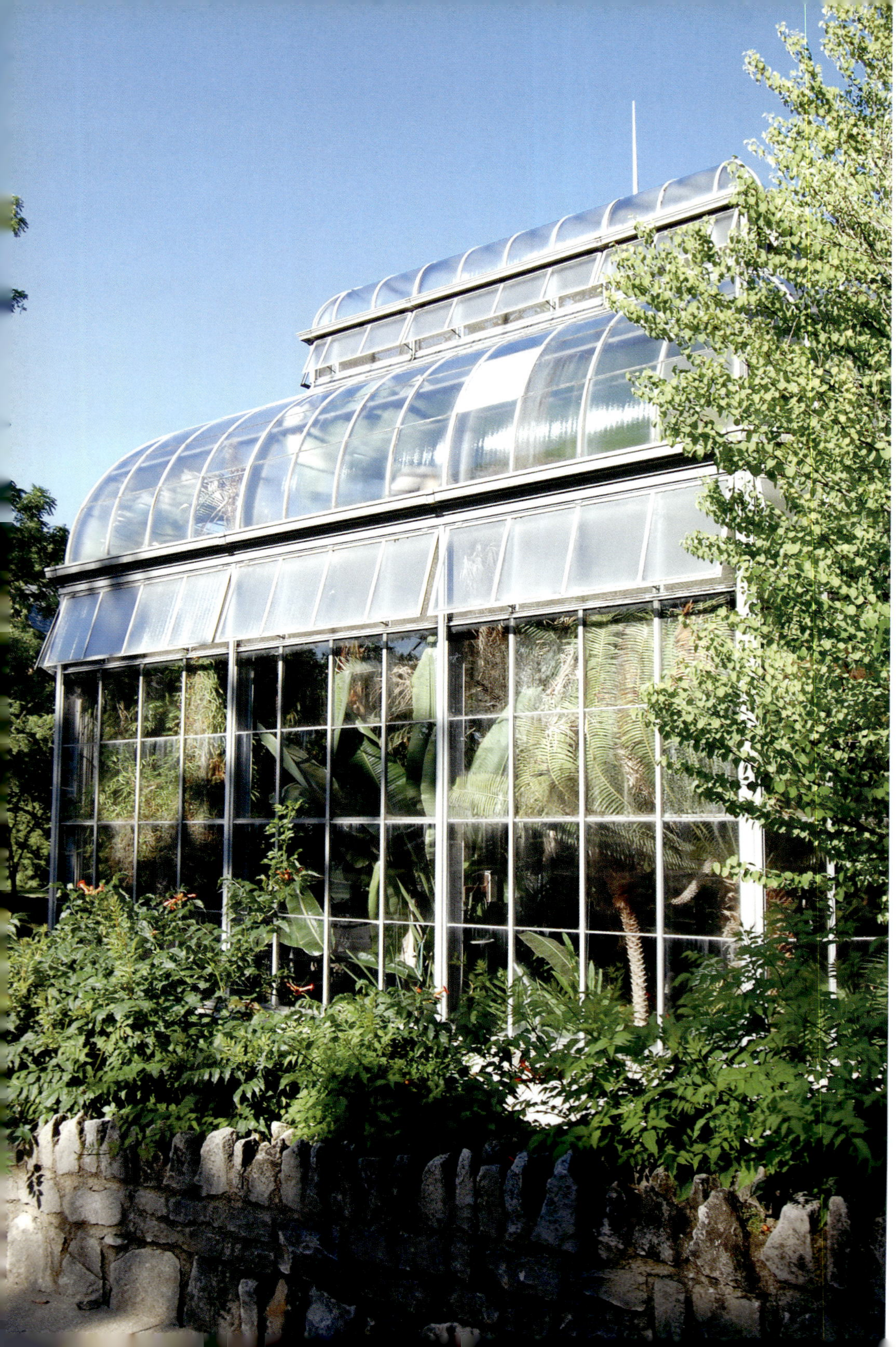

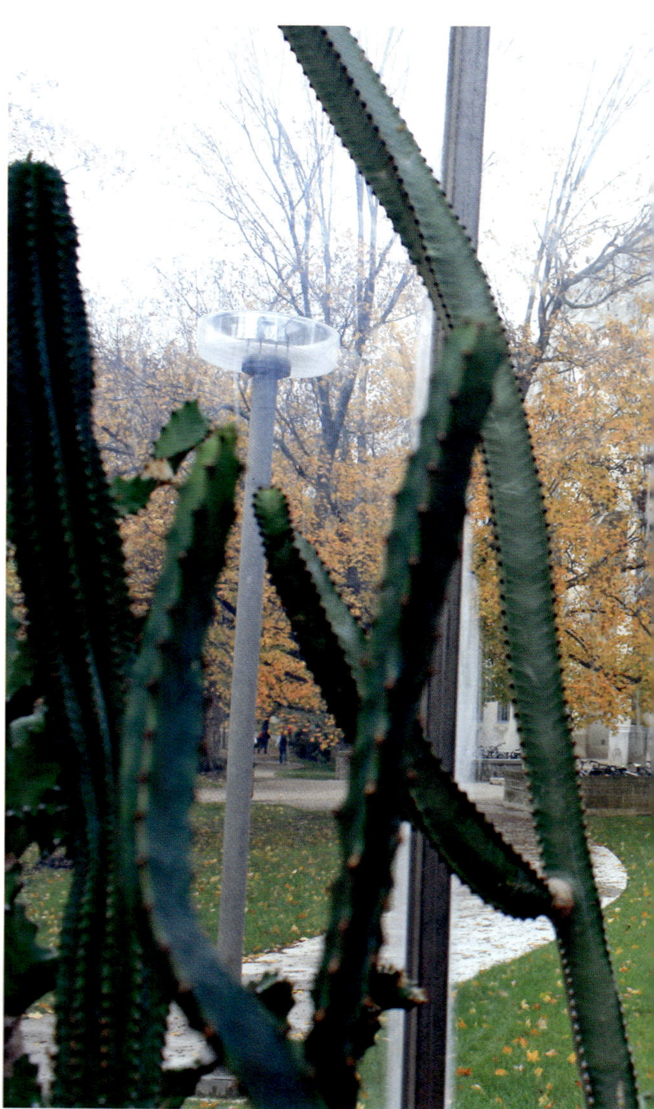

Greenhouse.

jordan hall greenhouse

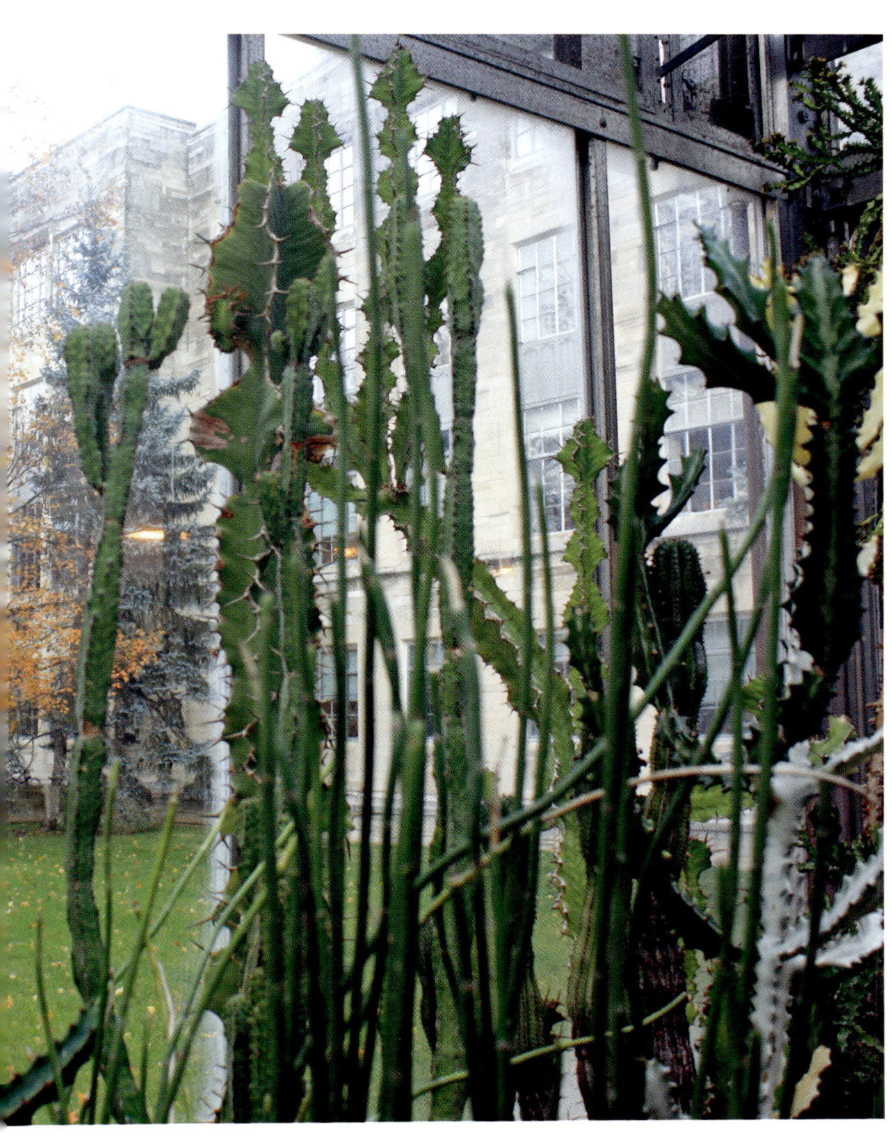

Cacti and Jordan Hall. *Mandy Hussey*

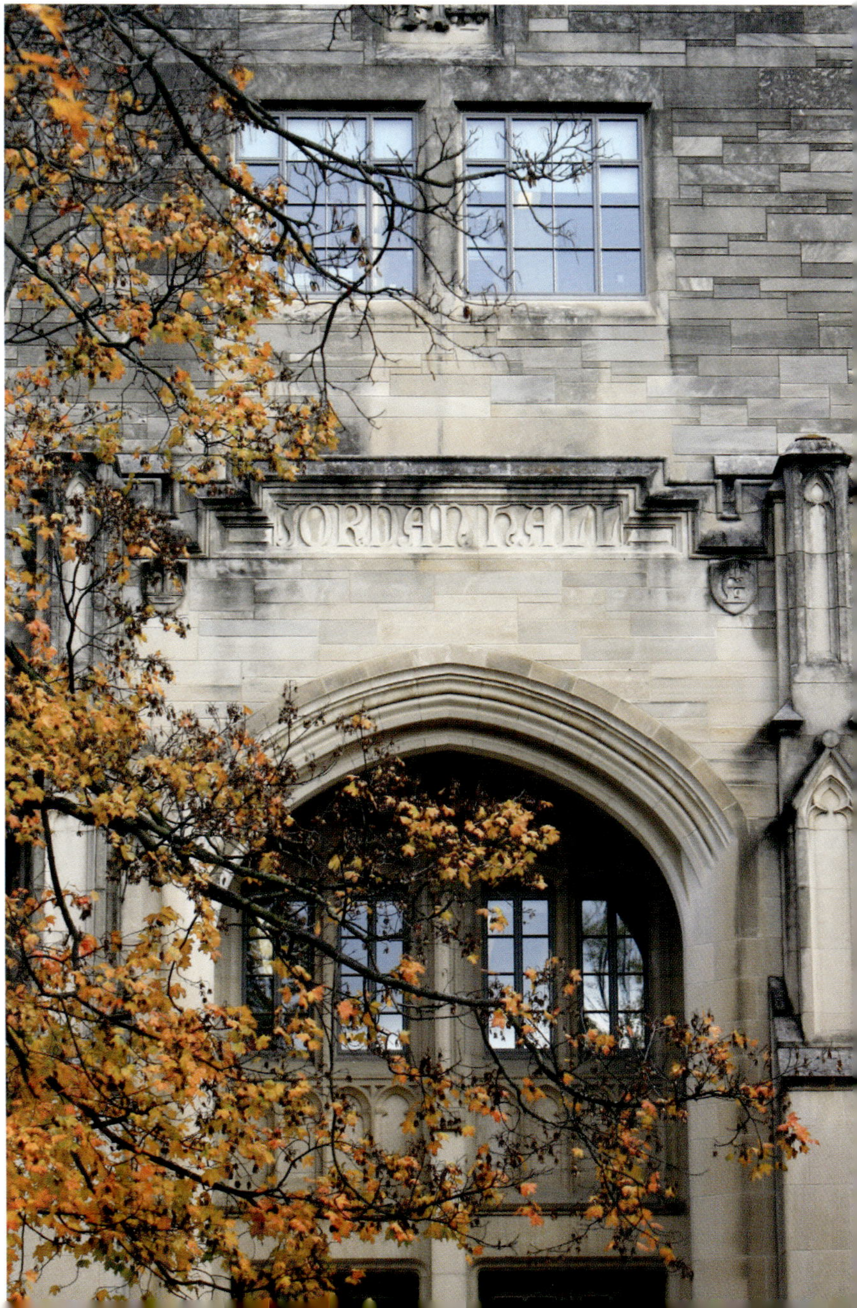

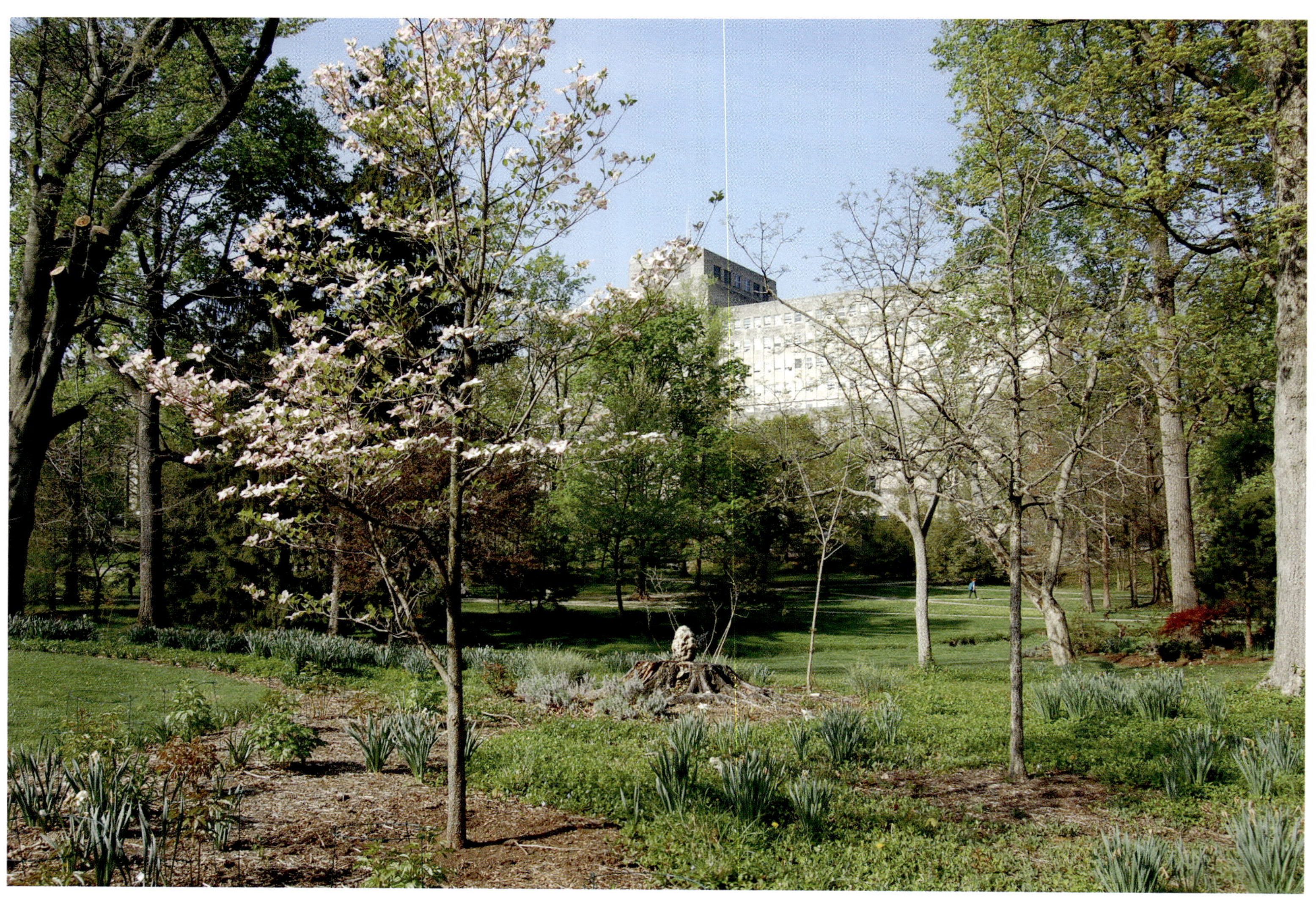

I've obtained three degrees from IU Bloomington, so I have many memories of wonderful times on this campus. I feel so lucky to live in Bloomington, Indiana, and I still visit the campus on a regular basis. I love walking through the woods between the president's home, Ballantine Hall, and Woodburn. A beautiful, calming green space, it brings back wonderful memories of walking to and from class. . . . I have had the good fortune to visit many campuses, both in the US and abroad, yet I haven't seen a more beautiful campus than IUB.

—*Roberta Trattner Sherman*

B.A. SOCIOLOGY, 1972; M.A. SOCIOLOGY, 1974;
PH.D. COUNSELING, 1982

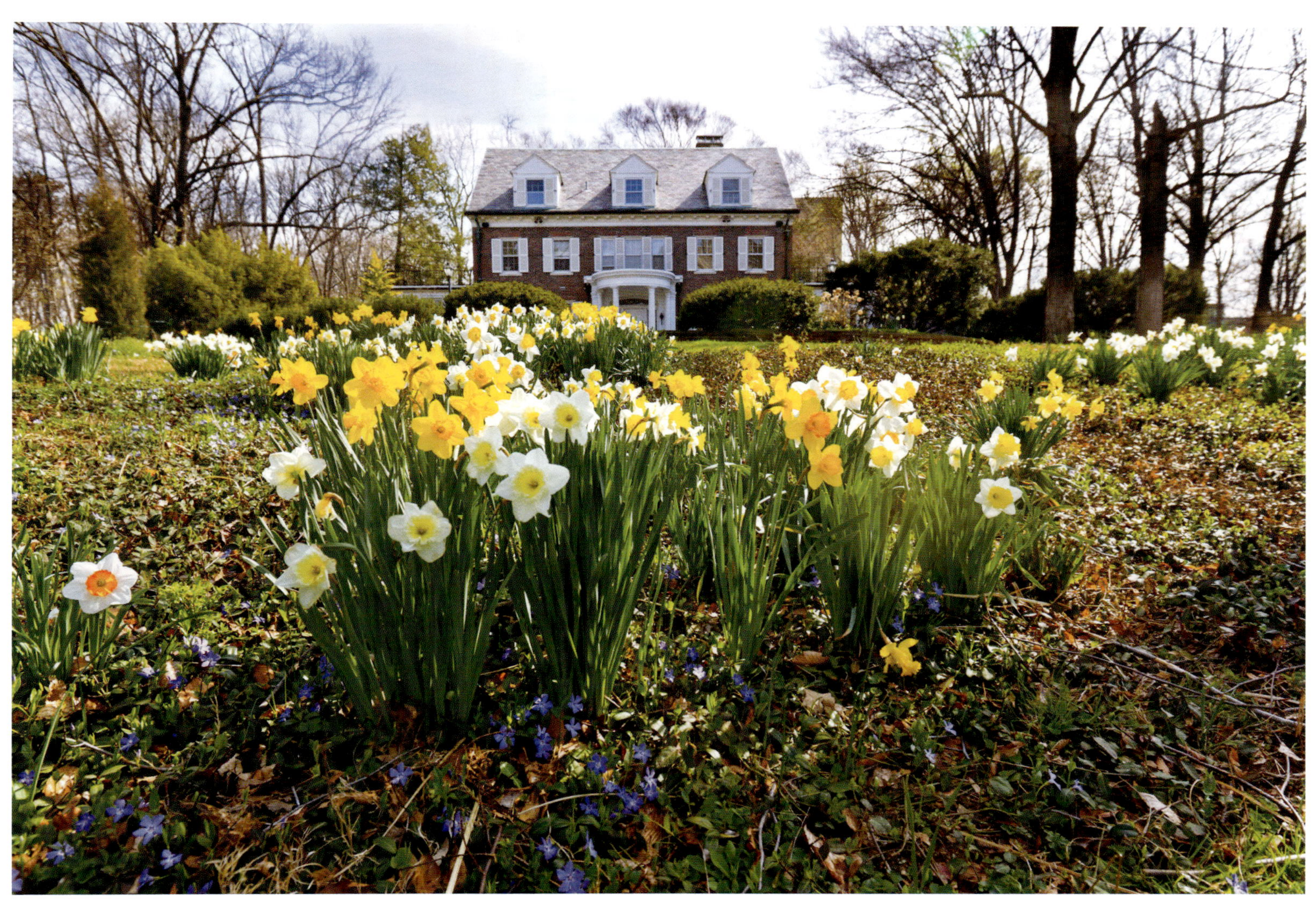

Ballantine Hall.

Bryan House.

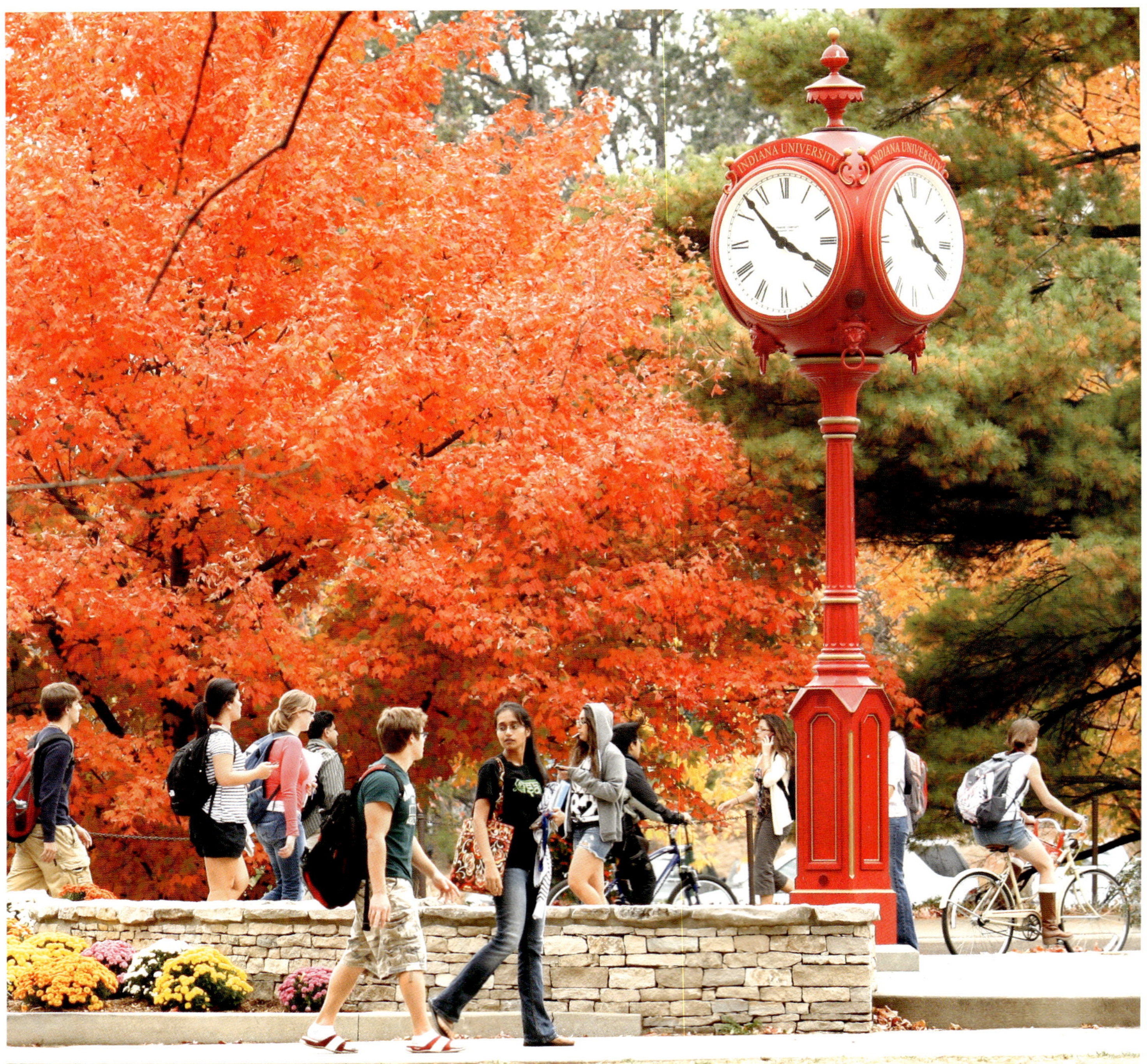
INDIANA UNIVERSITY
INDIANA UNIVERSITY

Standing between Morrison and Sycamore halls is a tiny, courtyard-like area lined by benches. At its center is the most beautiful tree on IU's campus—a young, unassuming Japanese maple. Nestled away from the hubbub of the Student Union and Ballantine Hall, this small getaway was the perfect retreat when I wanted to dive into a good book or get some homework done. In the spring, the tree comes alive—appearing as though its leaves are on fire. IU has many serene places with majestic natural scenery, but for me, this little-known arboreal haven has a sort of quiet, aesthetic perfection.

—*Nico Perrino*, B.A. JOURNALISM, 2012

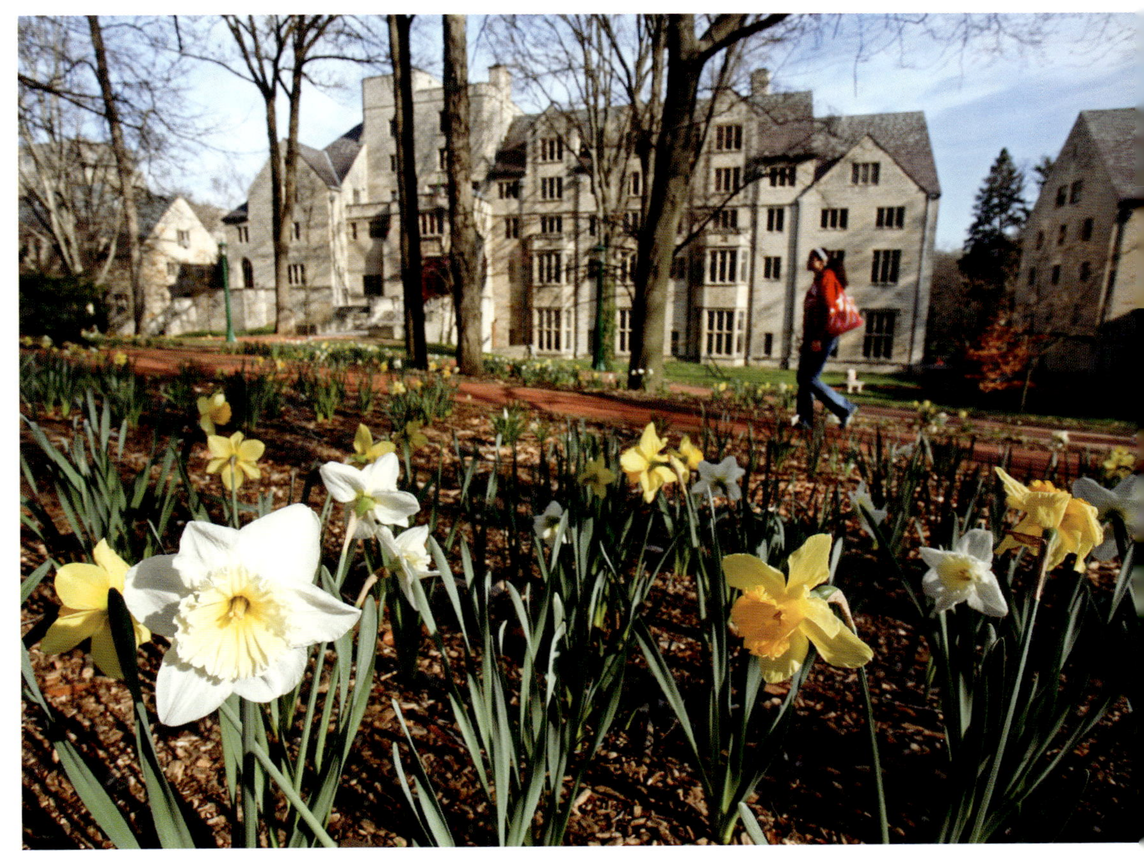

The red clock keeps students on time for class.

A flowery path near Morrison Hall.

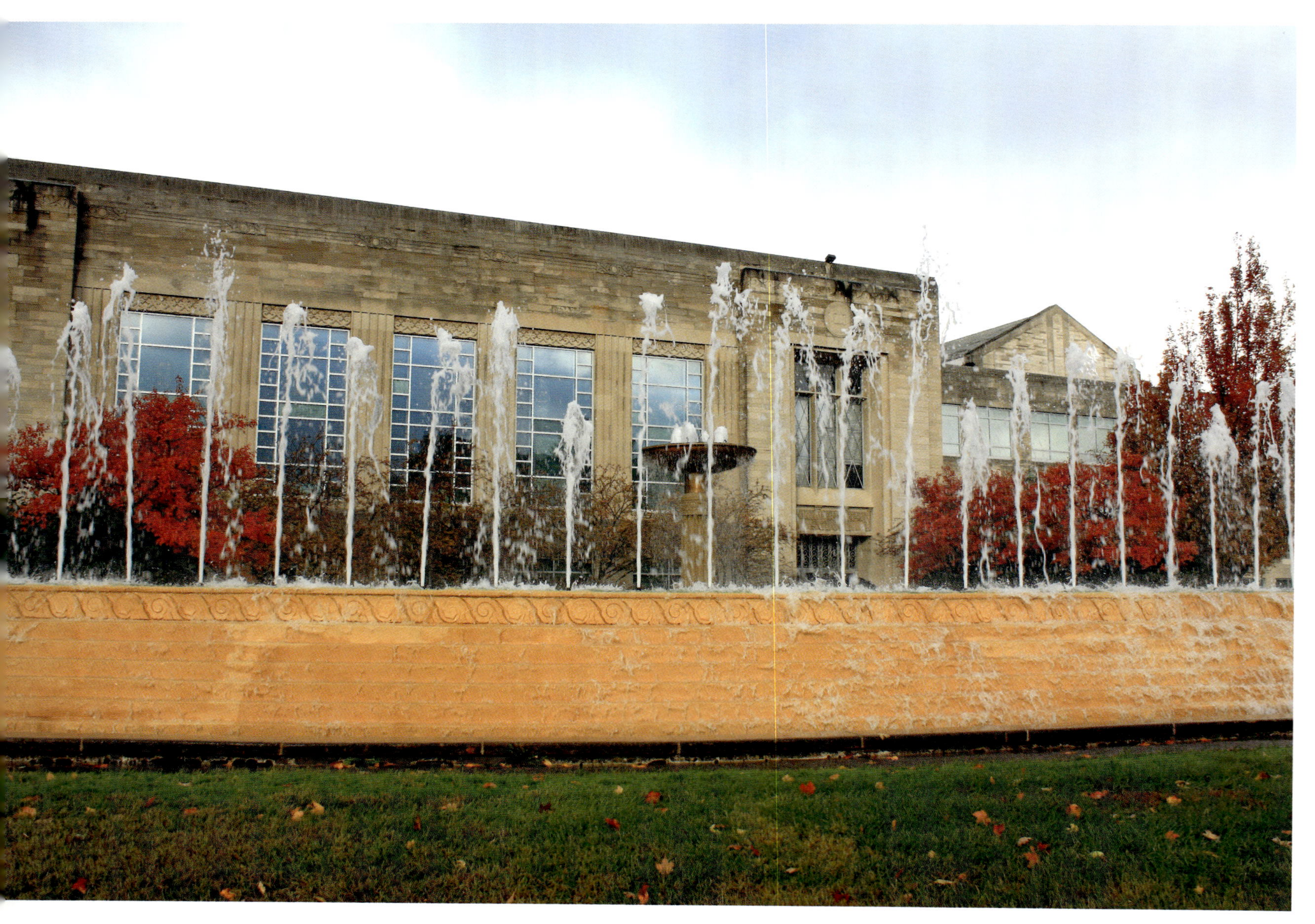

Jacobs School of Music. *Mandy Hussey*

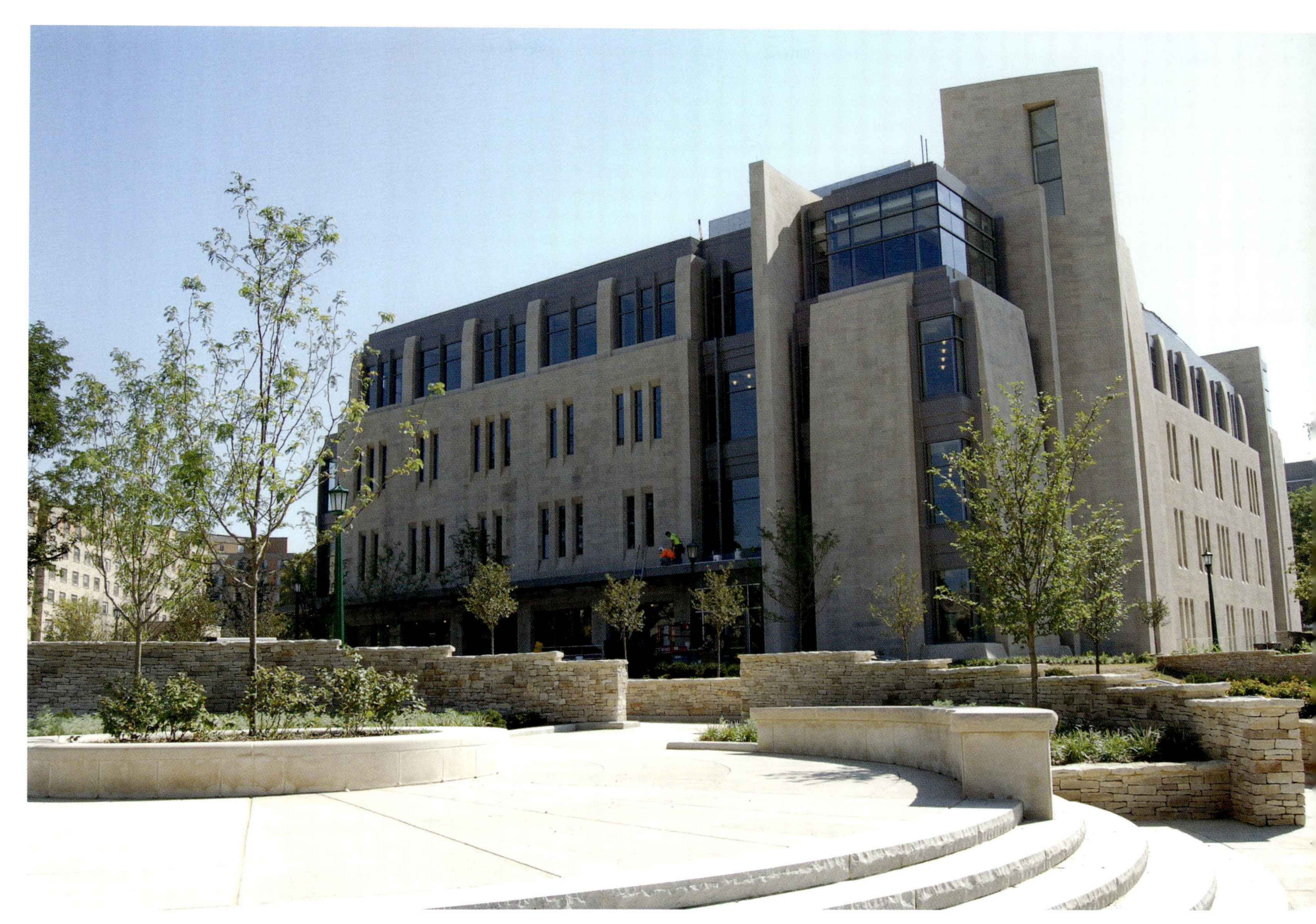

Jacobs School of Music East Studio Building.

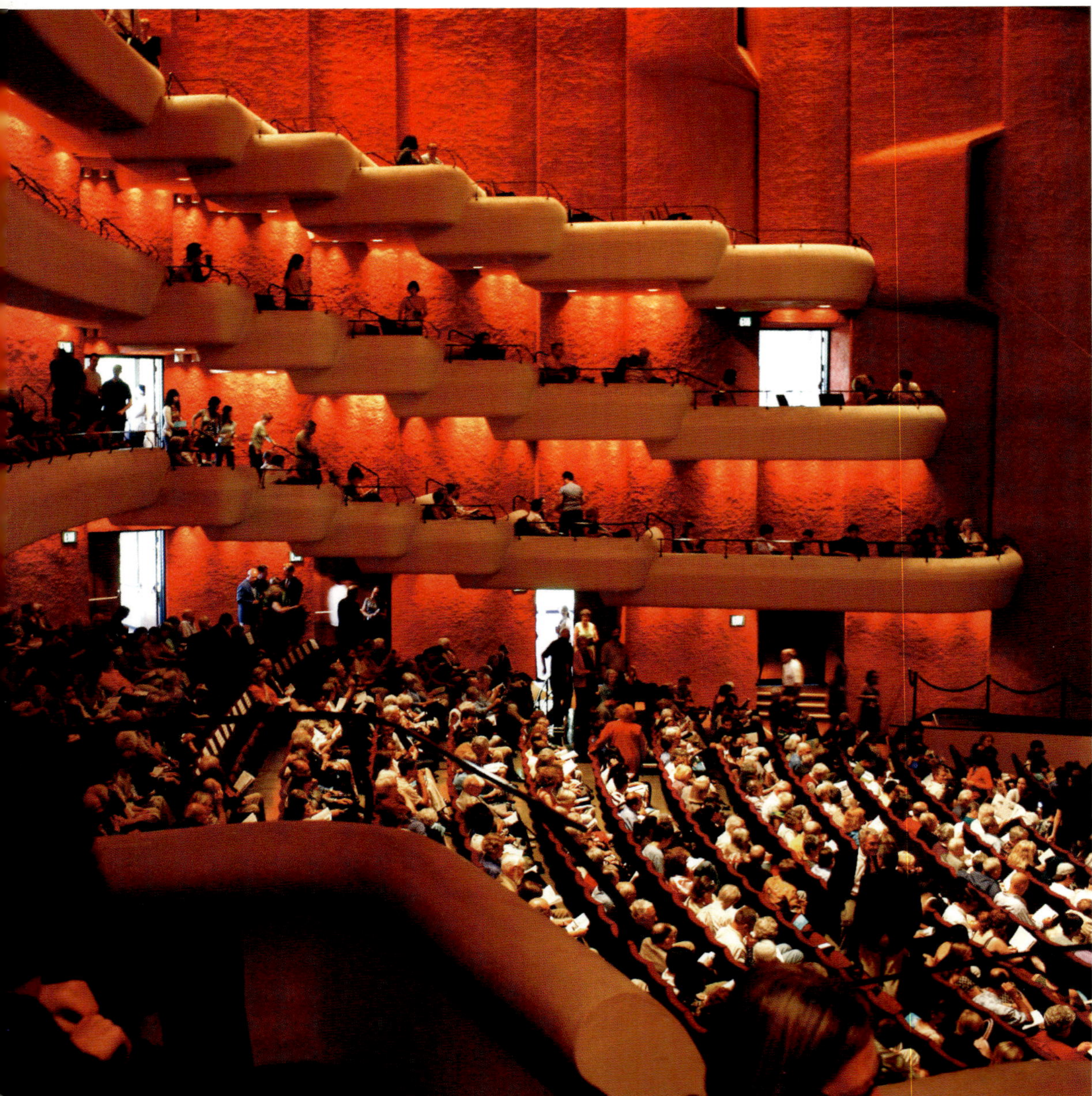

I had the privilege of serving Indiana University Bloomington as a music professor for 26 years and as Dean of Students for ten of those years. The IU Bloomington campus is not ONE of the most beautiful campuses in the US, it is the MOST beautiful campus in the world. Generations of students, faculty, staff, alumni, parents, donors, and public servants have conscientiously over decades made it so. The buildings, woods, meadows, streams, and bridges have made it visually so. And it is the deeply held feelings and close personal interconnections and accessibility that make it so, spiritually. It is "The Spirit of Indiana University" that keeps it unmatched!

—*Dr. Michael V. W. Gordon*

DEAN OF STUDENTS,
IU BLOOMINGTON 1981–1991

Musical Arts Center during a performance.

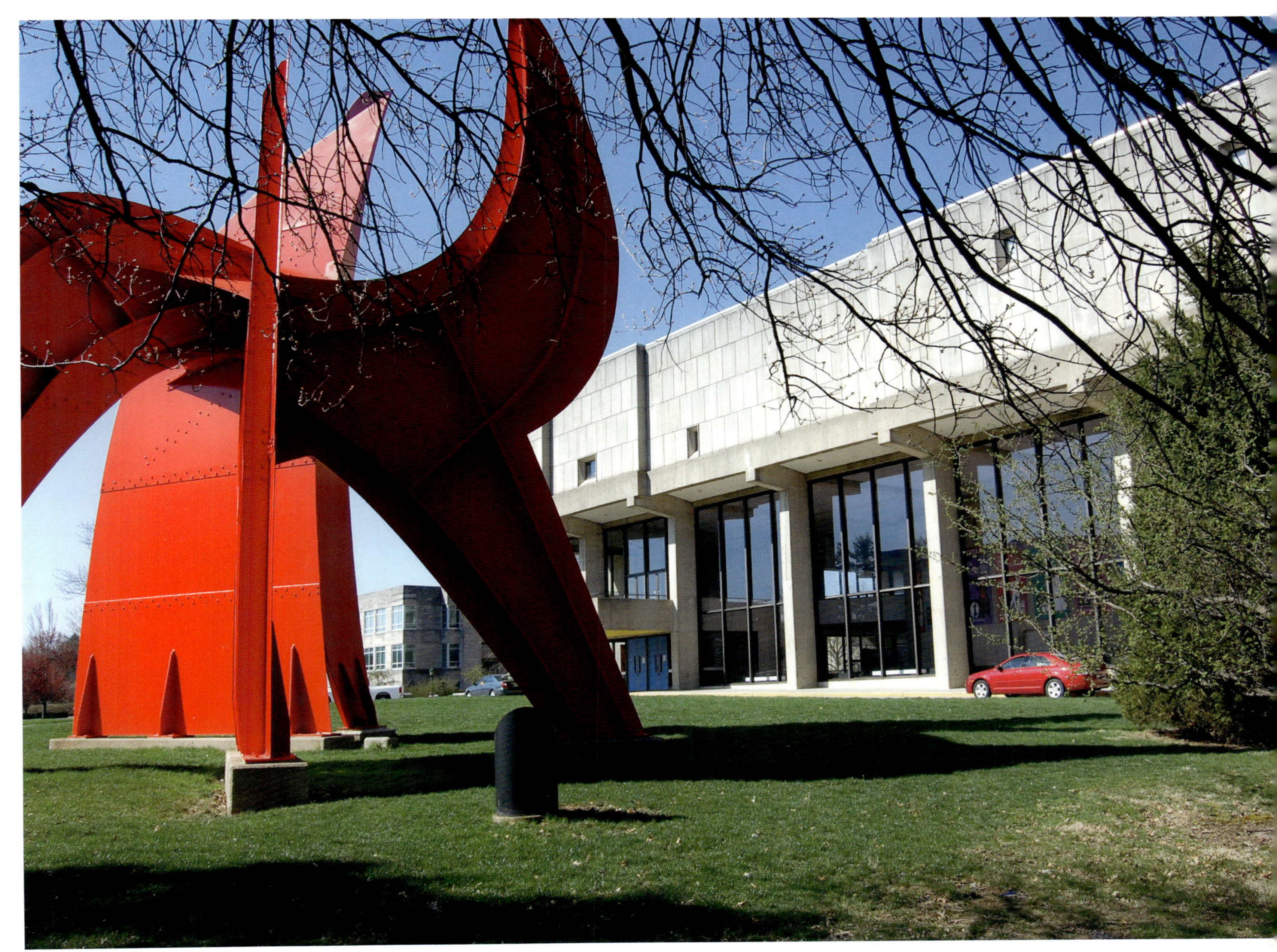

Musical Arts Center (MAC).

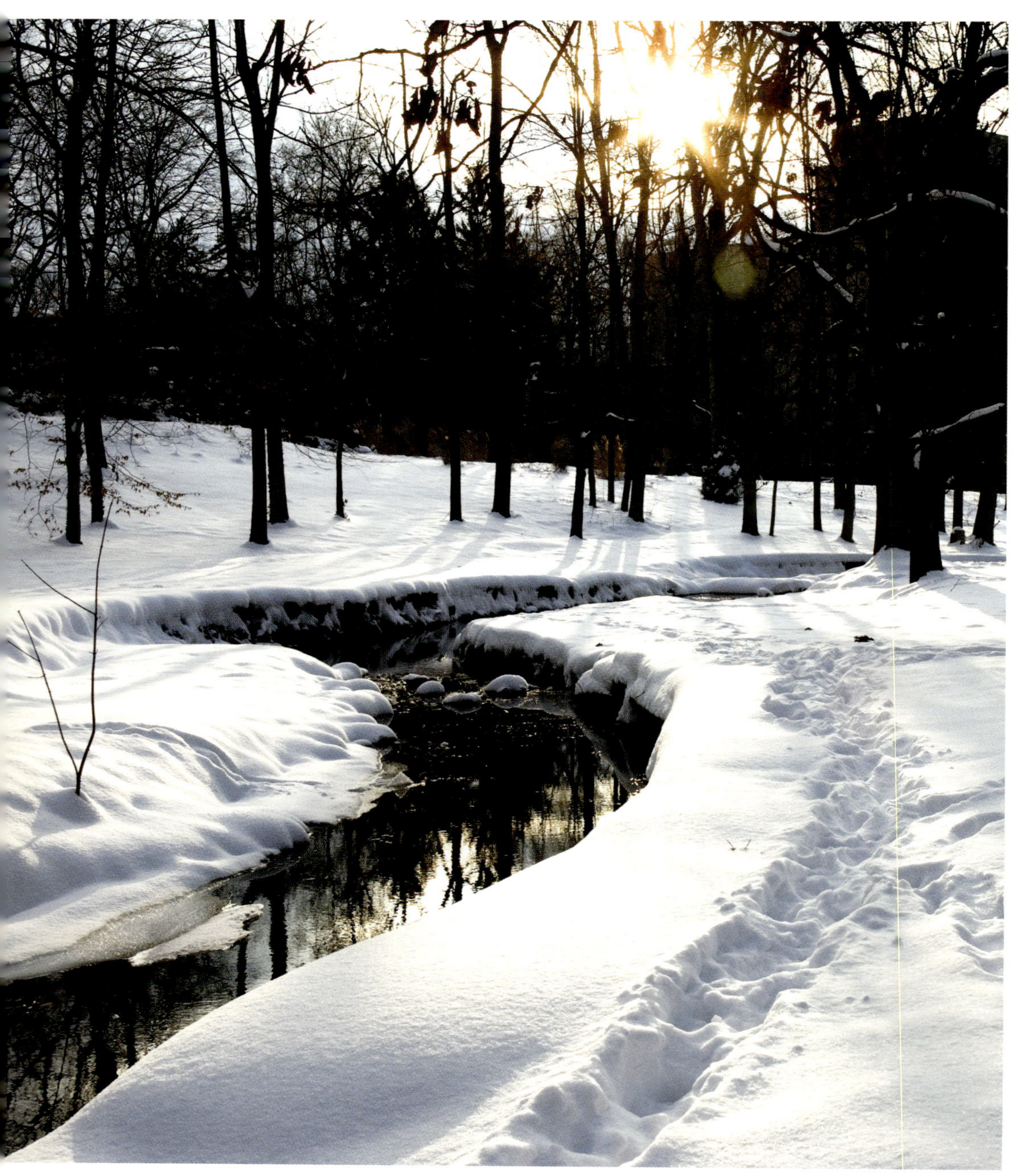

I lived at the Delta Gamma house on Jordan Avenue in the heart of campus. It was always so amazing and transformative to walk out my front door into the pretty woods—both uplifting and inspiring. The path to my classes was through these woods along the Jordan River. Even now I can remember the sun peeking through the trees as I headed to class—and thinking to myself: "Aren't I lucky I get to be here!"

—Kay Ryan Booth

B.A. FINE ARTS, 1972

The path next to the Jordan River through the woods from the Auditorium to Ballantine Hall is special to me. My future wife and I walked it to and from class, and on weekends we visited our favorite spot next to the river with a view of Bryan House. Depending on the season, we spread our blanket on the ground or wrapped ourselves in it to stay warm. In 1997 after Nan passed to a better place, I returned to the location and subsequently worked with the University for the placement of a bench. A plaque on the bench reads "To young love and in memory of Nancy C. Steiner, BS 1966. At the Jordan we cuddled, dreamed, and planned our future."

—Richard C. Steiner

B.A. POLICE ADMINISTRATION AND SOCIOLOGY, 1965

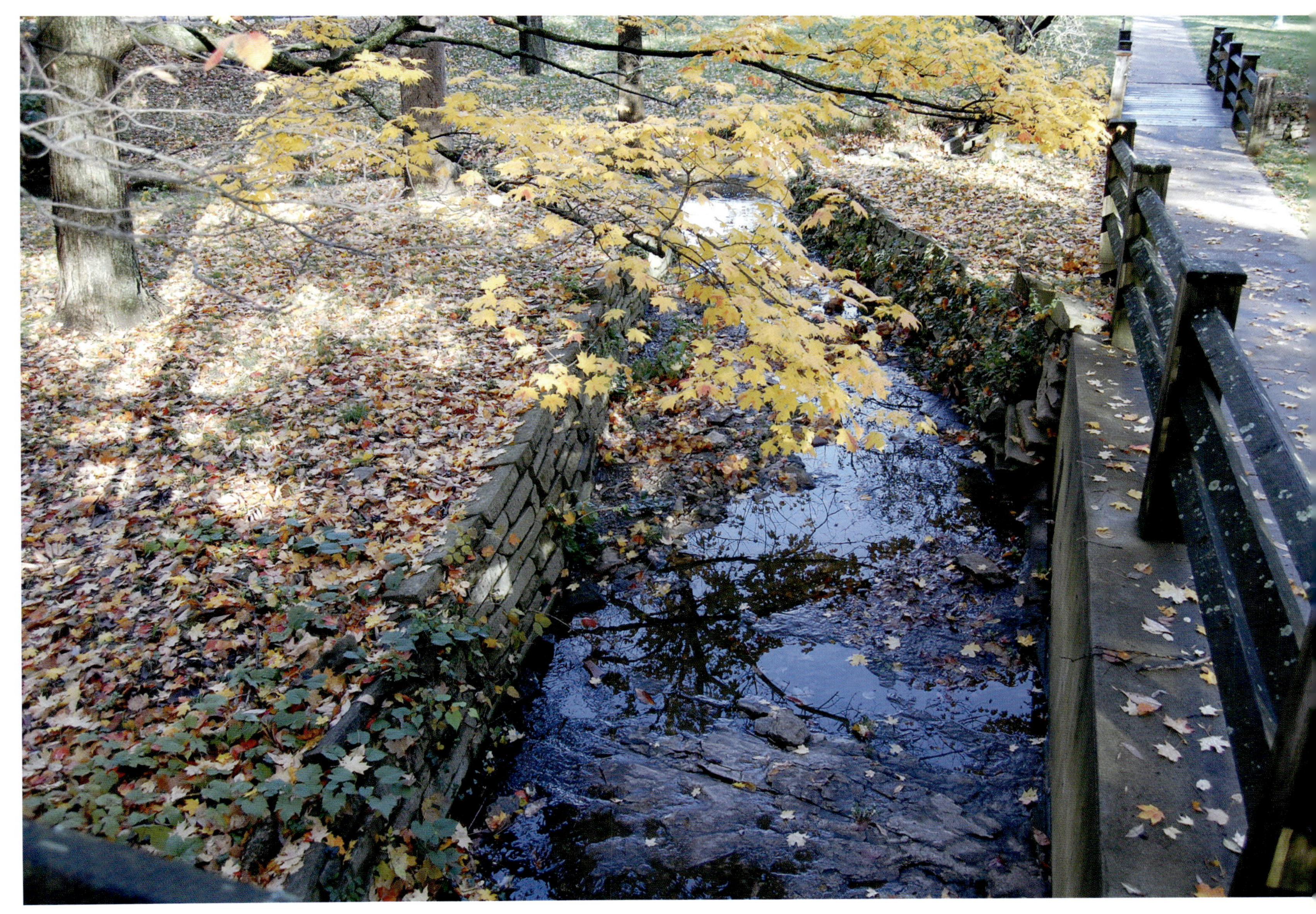

Snow on the banks of the Jordan River. *Chris Robb*

Jordan River in the fall.

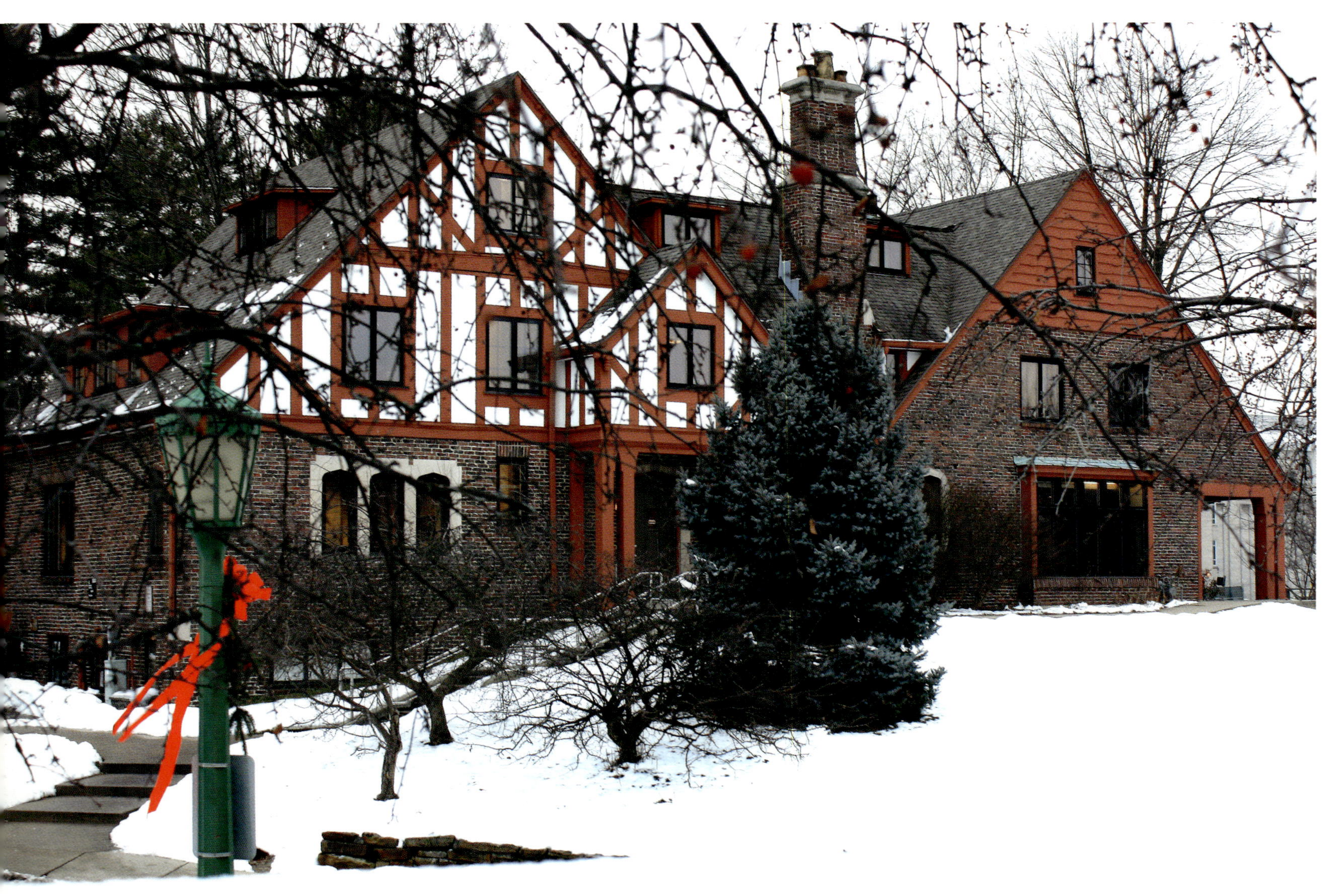

Leo R. Dowling International Center. *Mandy Hussey*

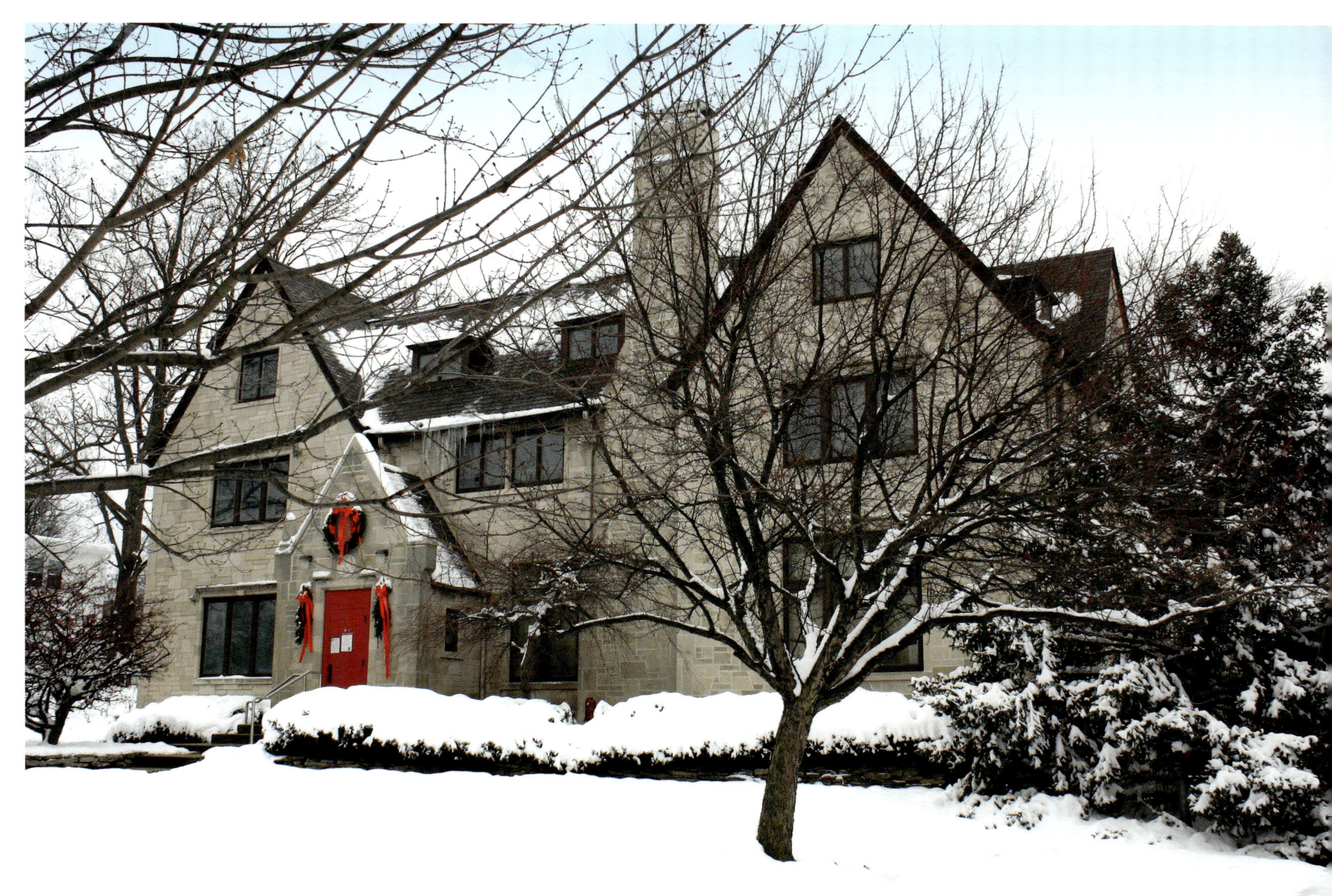

Office of Admissions adorned for the holidays. *Mandy Hussey*

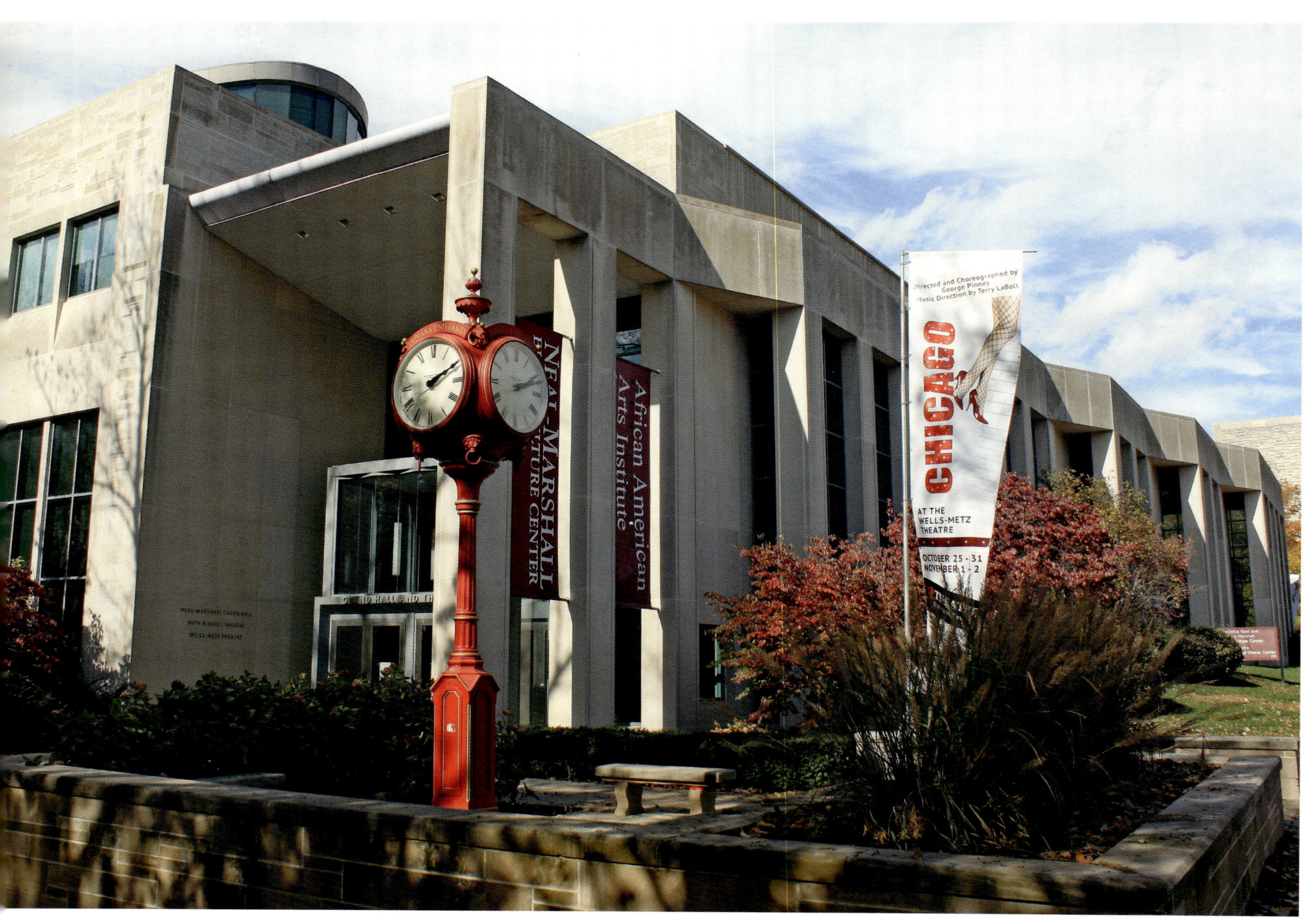

Lee Norvelle Theatre and Drama Center/Marcellus Neal and Frances Marshall Black Culture Center. *Mandy Hussey*

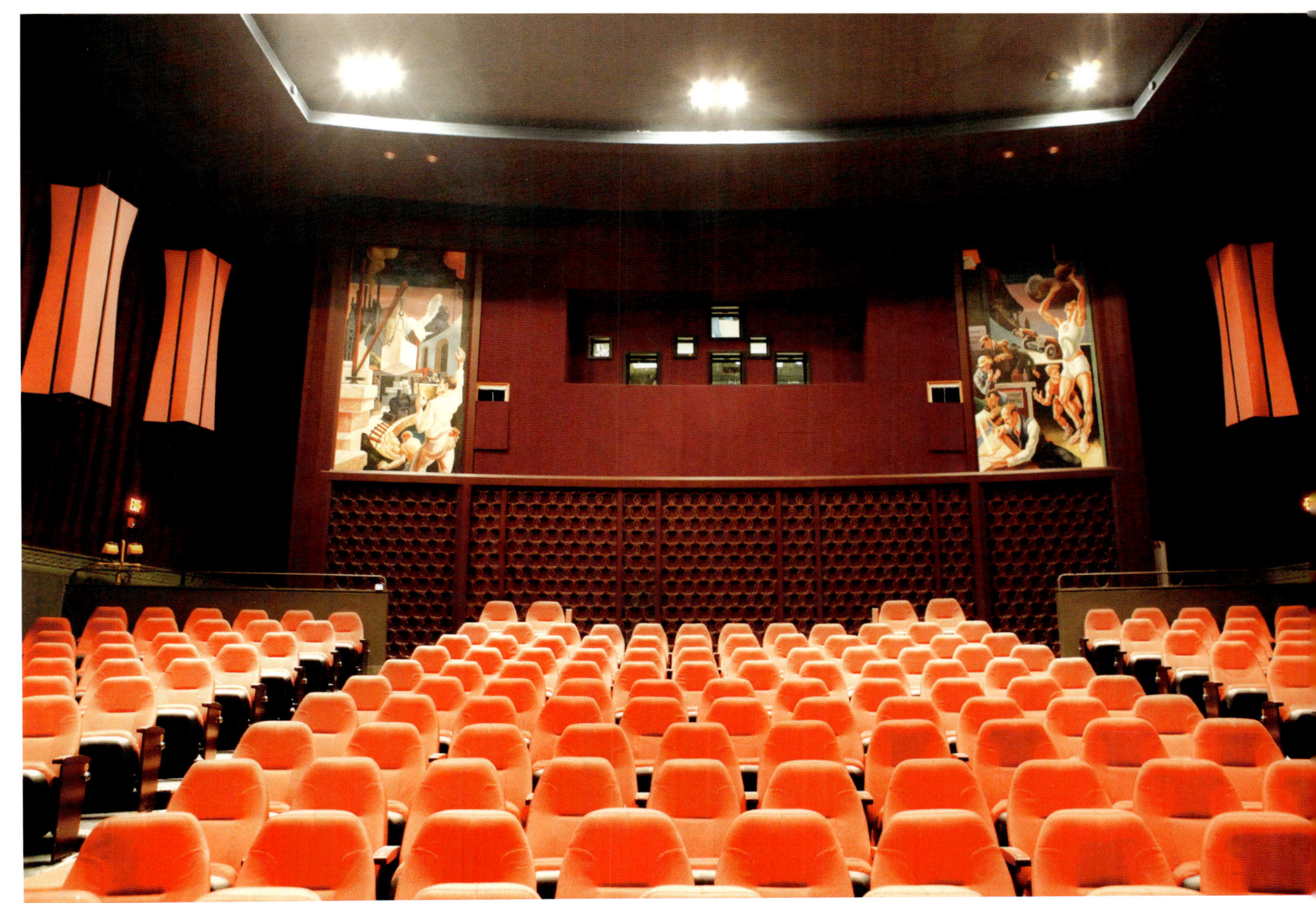

IU Cinema.

Chimes of Indiana

WORDS AND MUSIC BY HOAGY CARMICHAEL

Sing these chimes of Indiana,
Hail to the crimson hue;
Sing her praise to Gloriana,
Hail to our old IU
Lift your voices, join in loyal chorus
Let your heart rejoice in praise of those before us,
Sing these chimes of Indiana,
Ever to her be true!

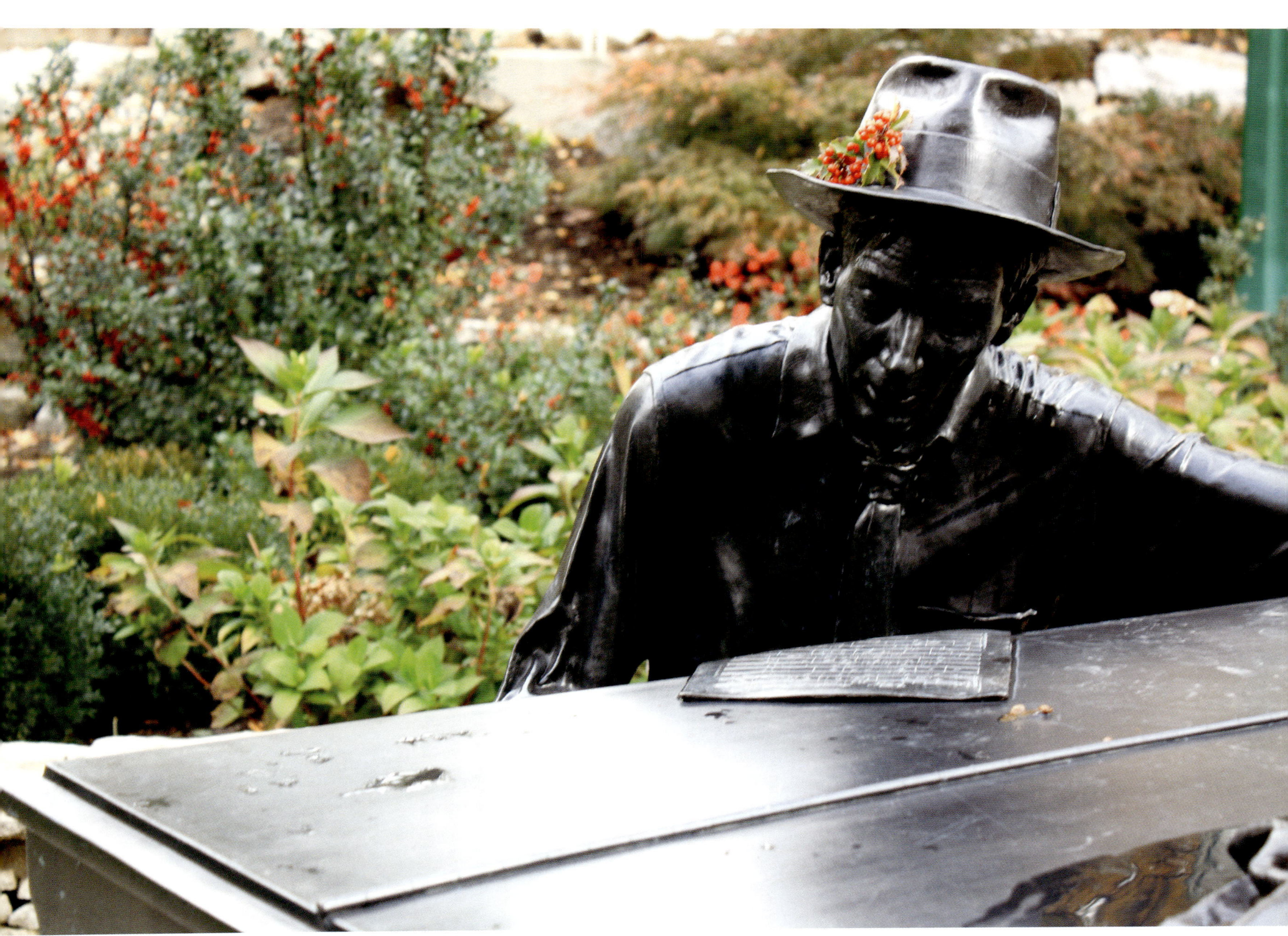

Hoagy Carmichael sculpture near the IU Cinema. *Mandy Hussey*

showalter fountain

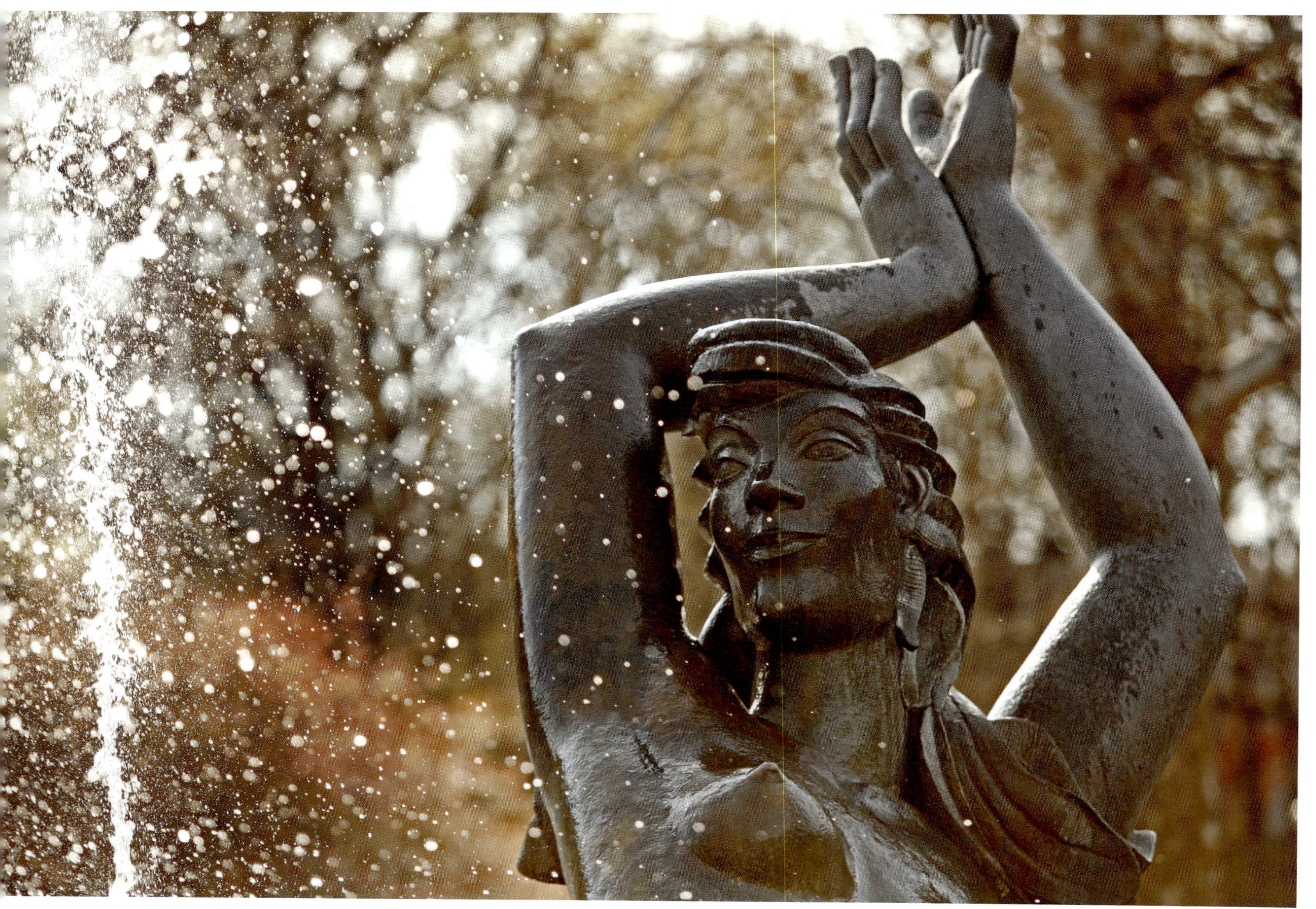

Water flowing from Showalter Fountain is a sure sign of spring.

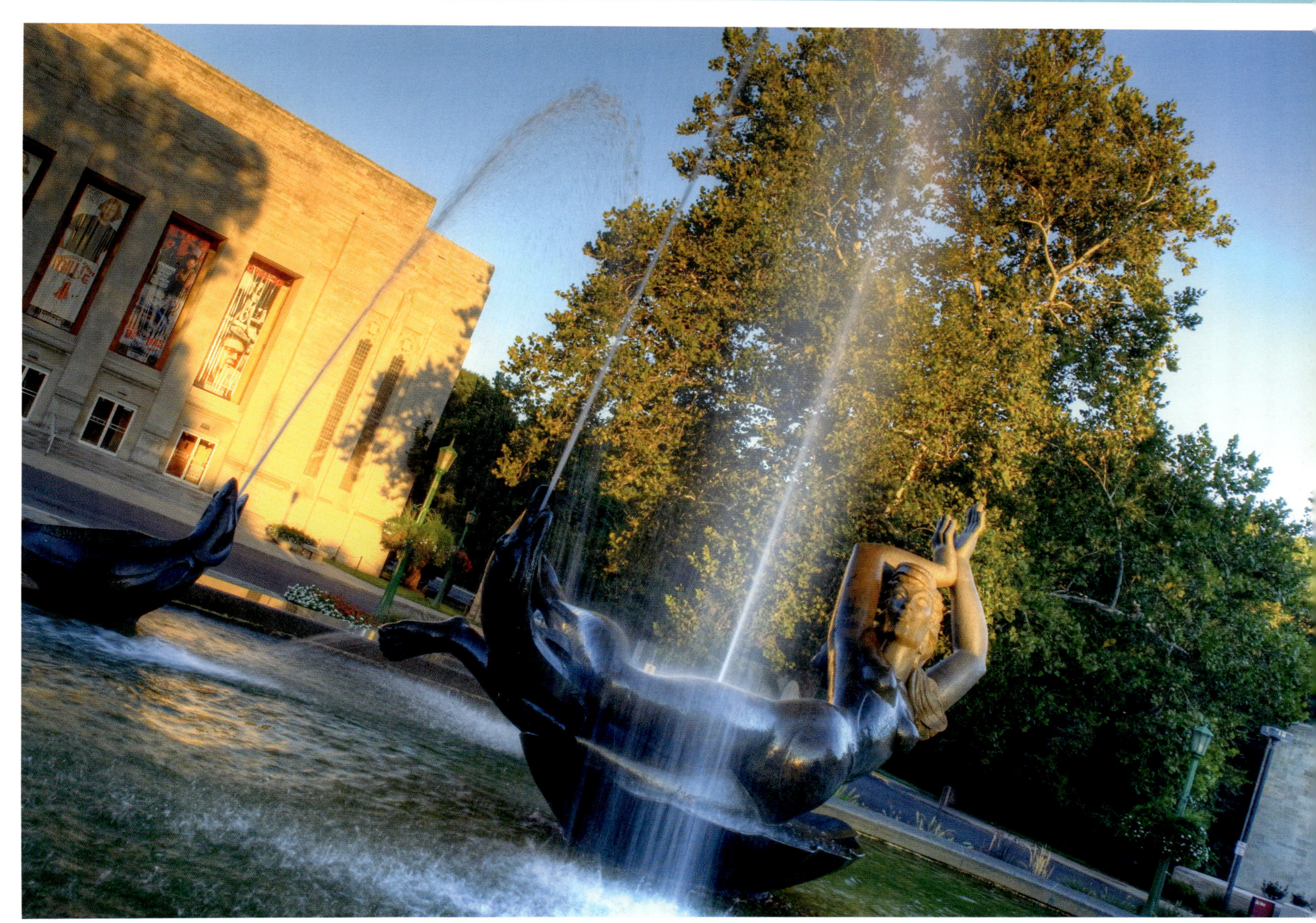

Showalter Fountain and the IU Auditorium. *Chris Robb*

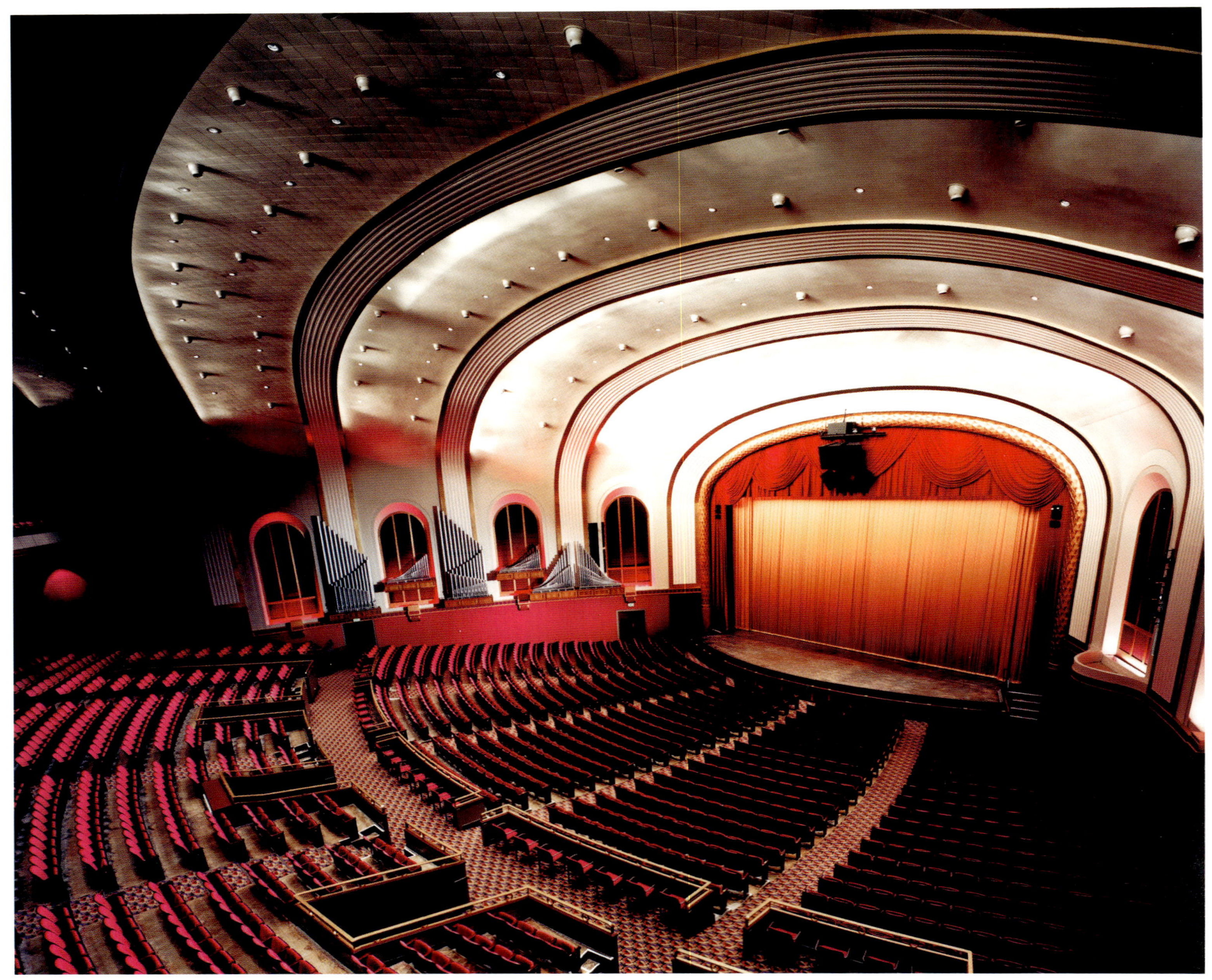

IU Auditorium.

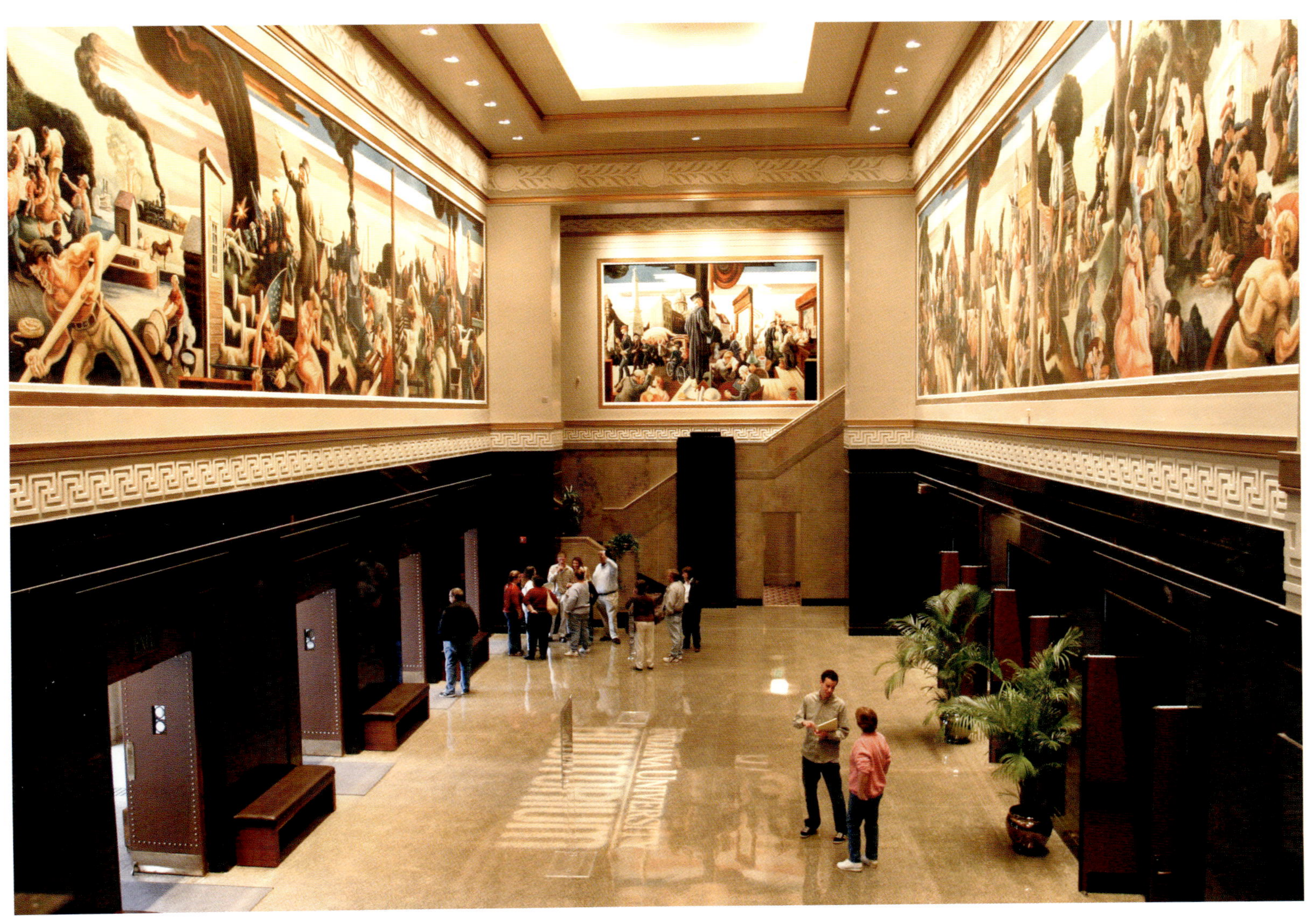

Thomas Hart Benton murals in the Hall of Murals, IU Auditorium.

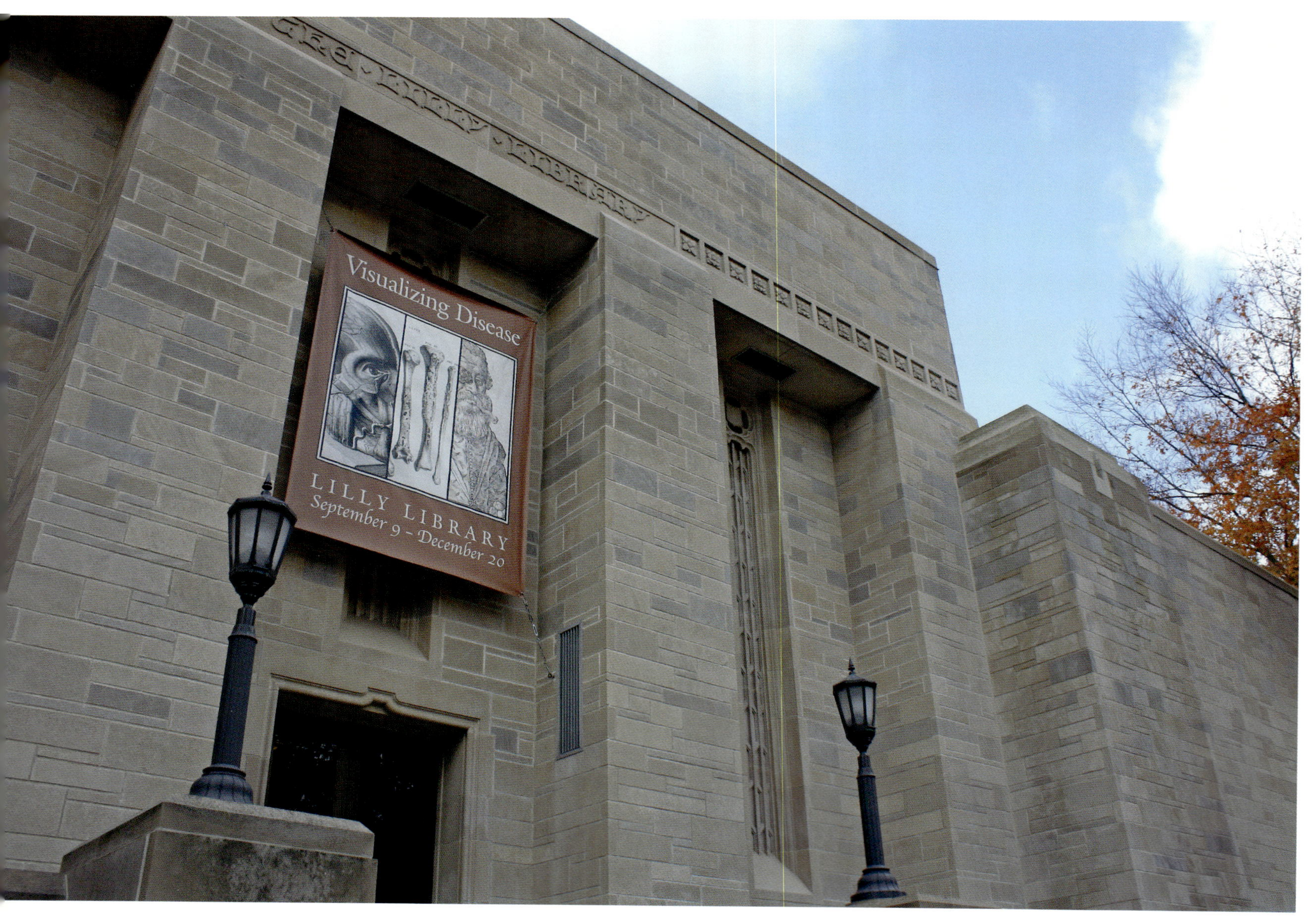

Lilly Library. *Mandy Hussey*

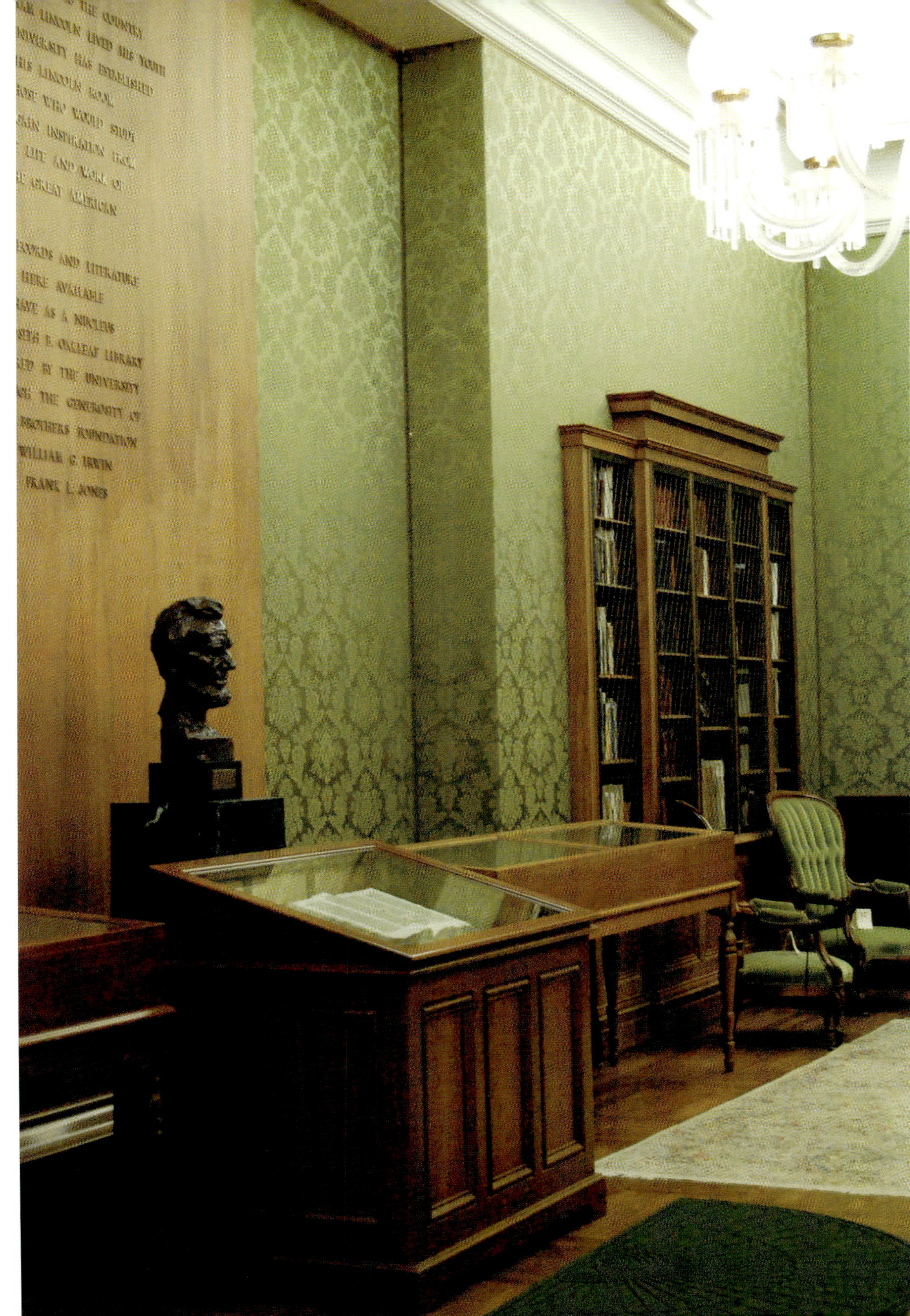

Lincoln Room, Lilly Library.

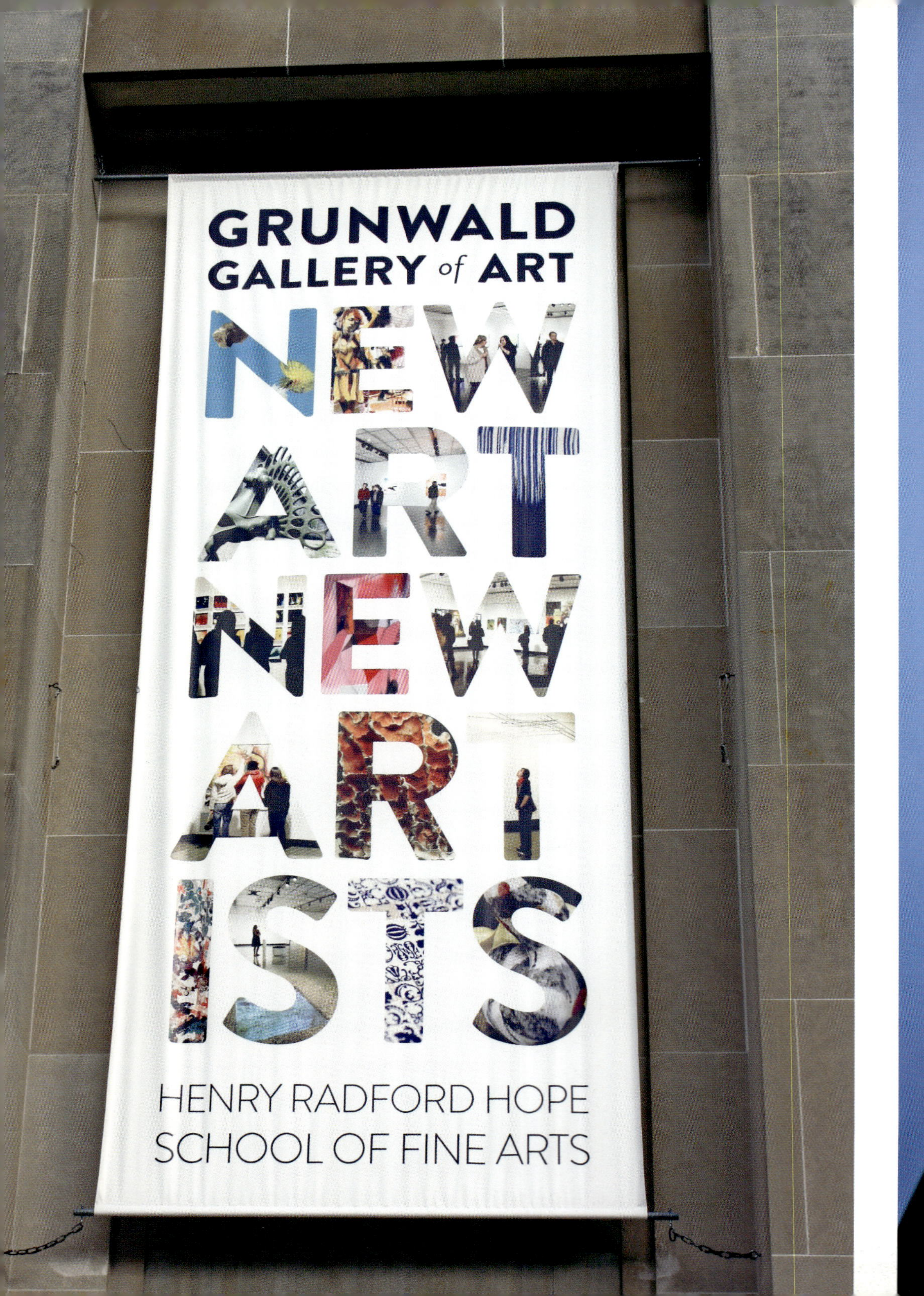

Grunwald Gallery banner. *Mandy Hussey*
Sculpture and IU Art Museum.

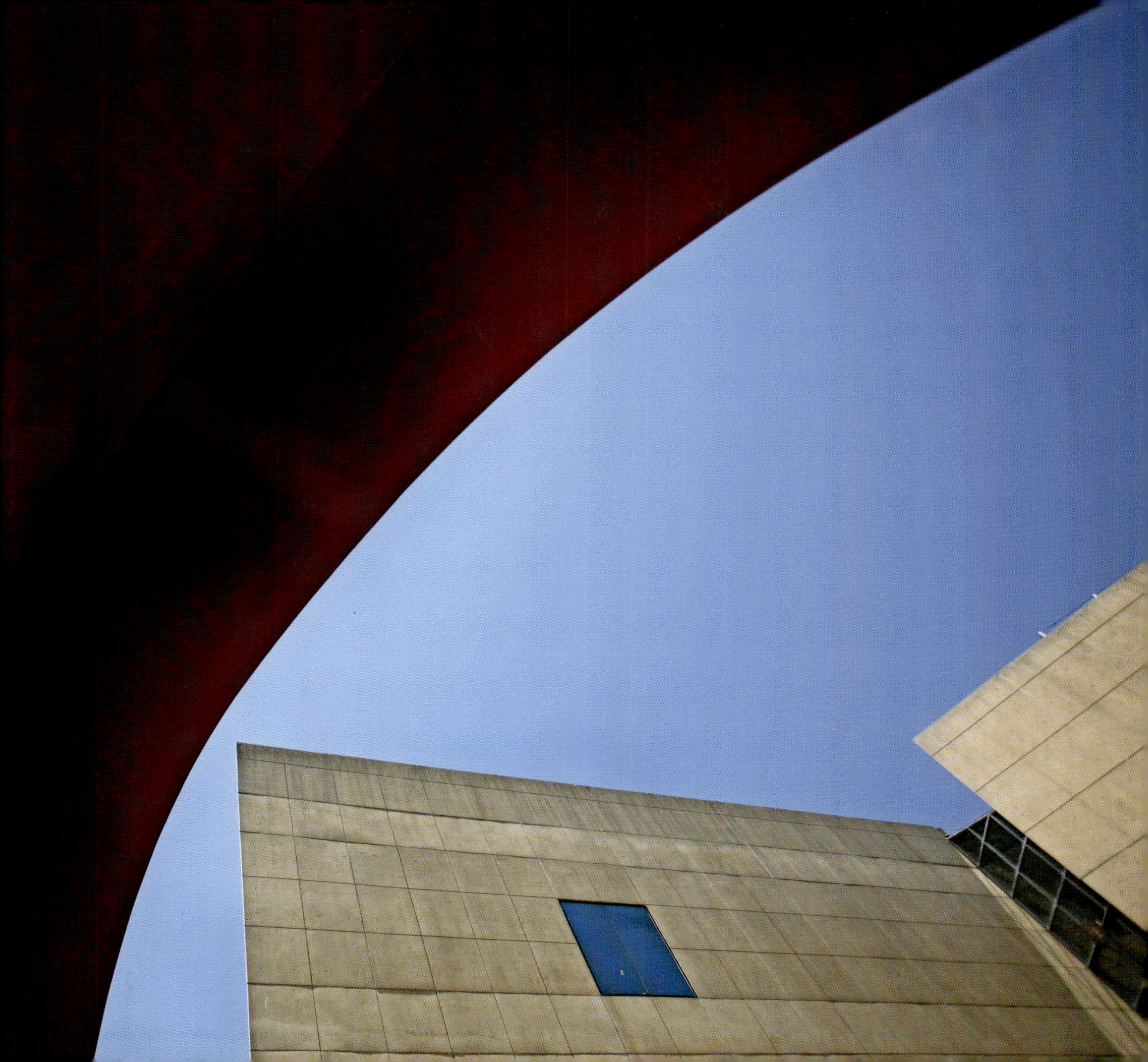

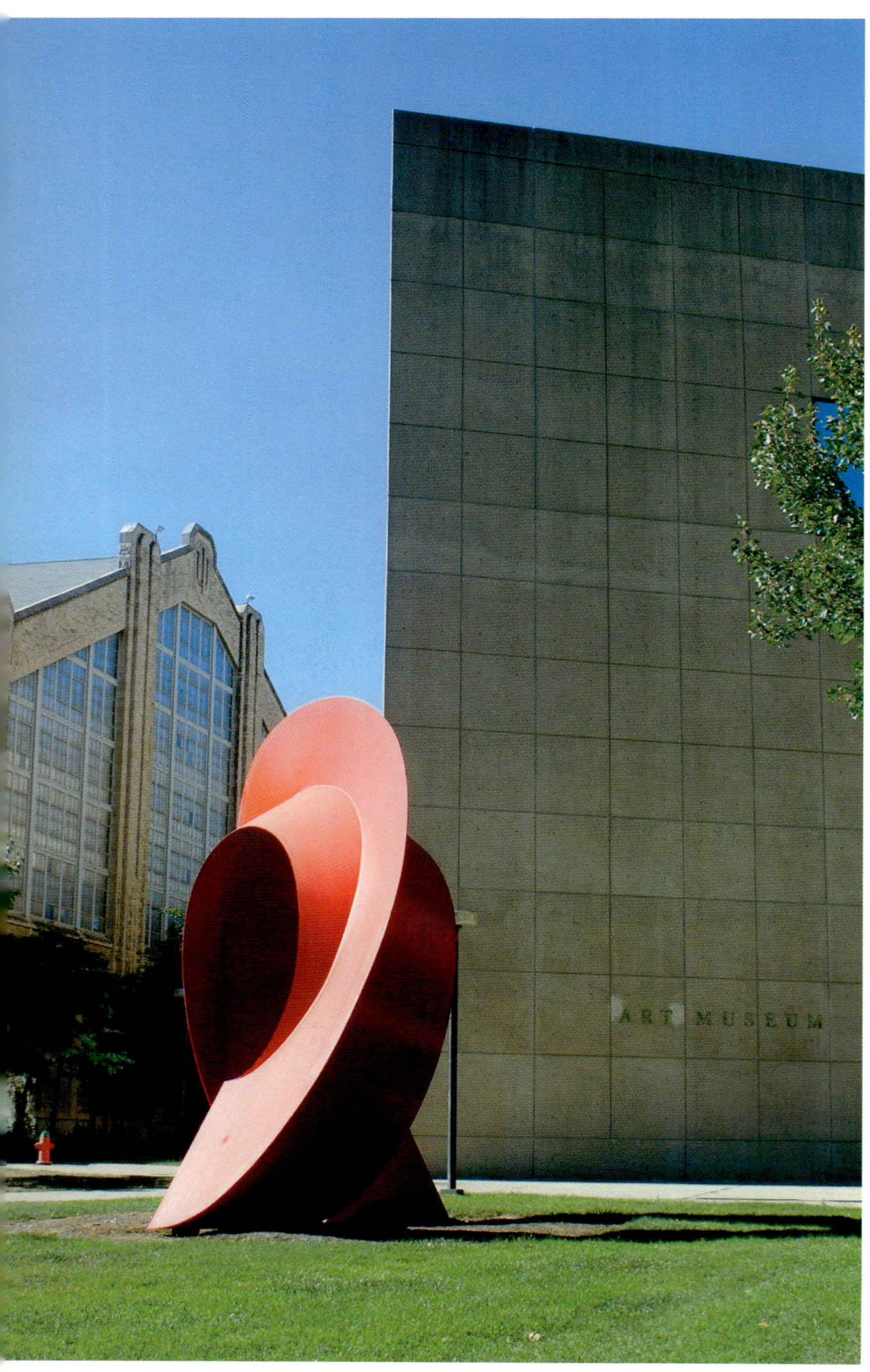

The IU Art Museum opens the world to its visitors geographically and chronologically in multiple media to answer questions and inspire further exploration into historical influences of time and place. The inspiration created by seeing wonderful works enriches my life in ways unlike any other visual experience.

—*Curt Simic*

PRESIDENT IU FOUNDATION, 1988–2008
B.S. PHYSICAL EDUCATION, 1964

The IU Art Museum is where Director Heidi Gealt and the other curators open eyes and minds to the full breadth of the visual arts.

—*Sara LeBien*
Bob LeBien, M.B.A., 1961

IU Art Museum.

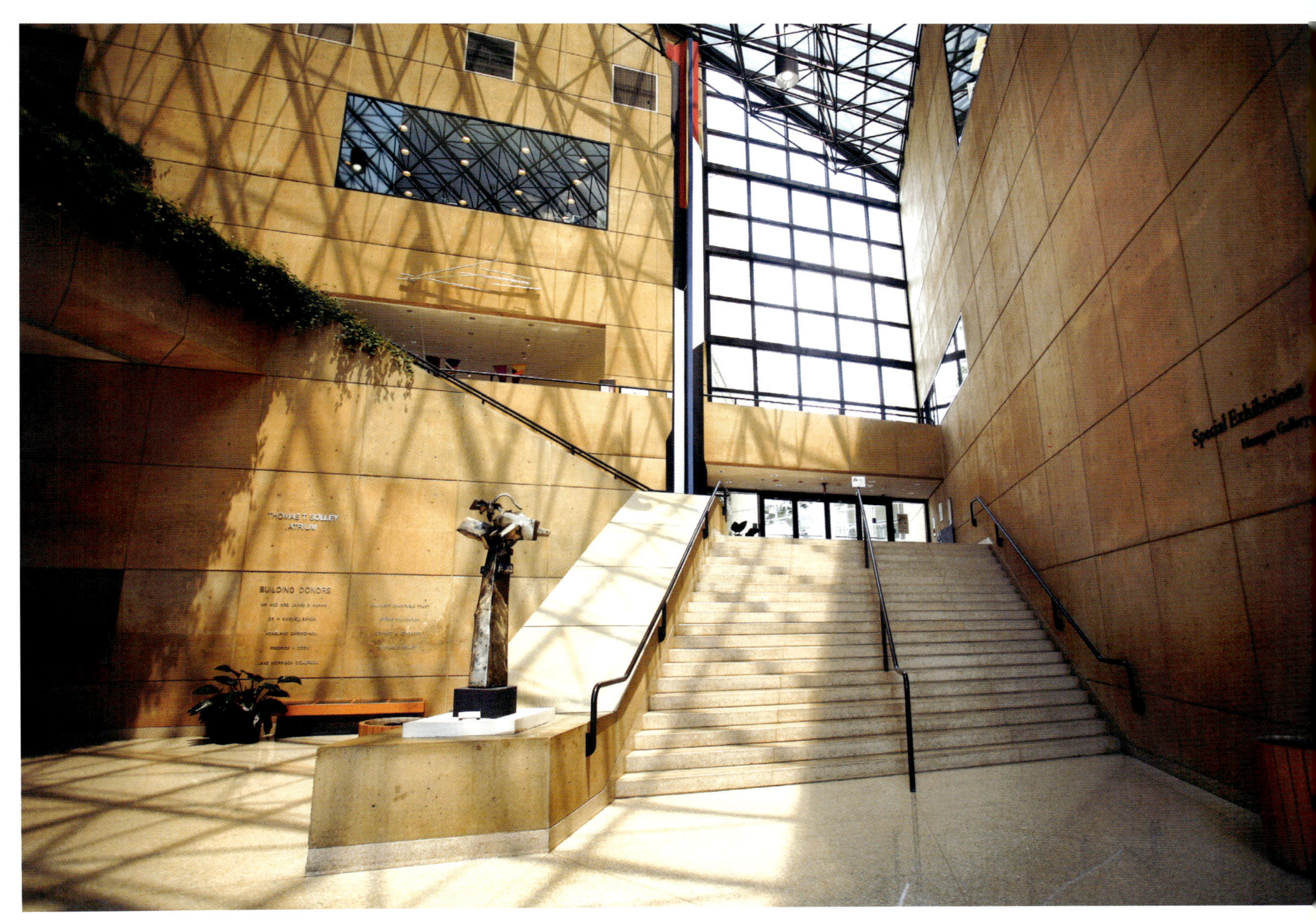

World-class architecture inside the IU Art Museum.

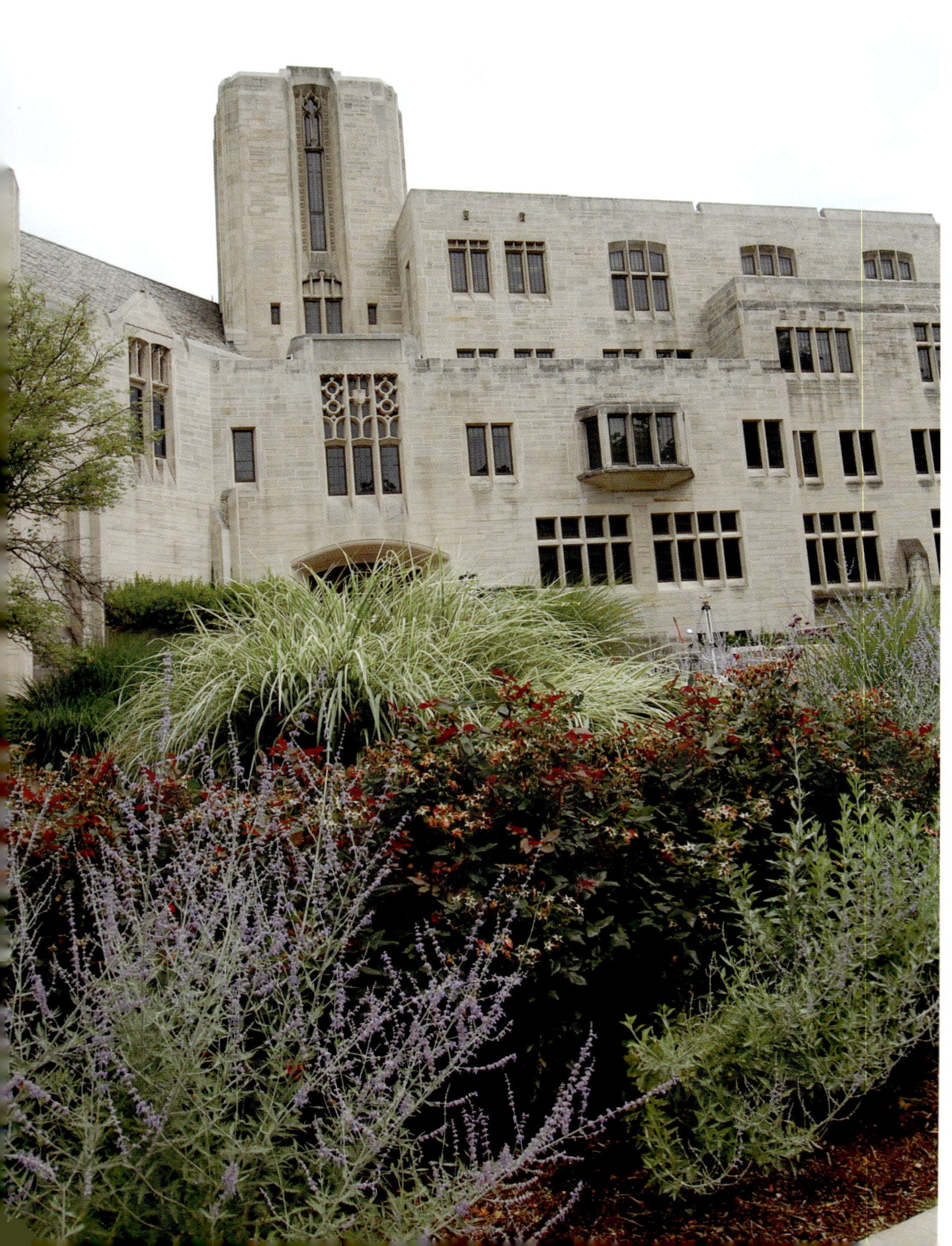

My favorite place on campus has to be the lawn in front of Woodburn Hall in the early fall. I have the best memories of sitting in the shade, reading my textbooks—whether for American Film or Spanish—just watching fellow classmates, buses, bikers, and professors pass by, energized with the inexplicable fervor of a new semester.
I will never forget the feeling of the bright October sun through the multi-colored leaves and of knowing, with gratitude, that IU was a very special place.

—Kim Cook

B.A. JOURNALISM, 2011

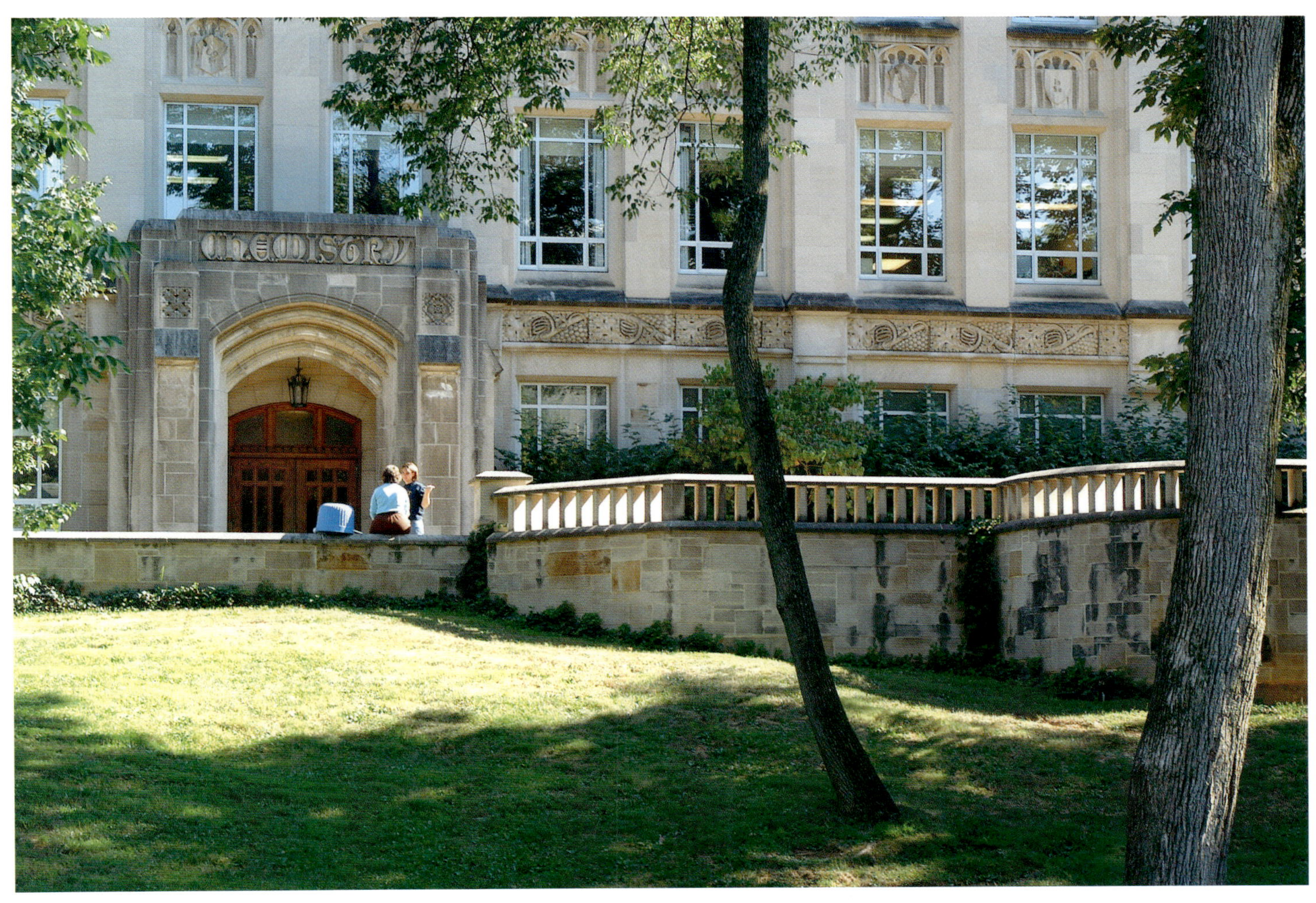

Woodburn Hall.

Chemistry Building.

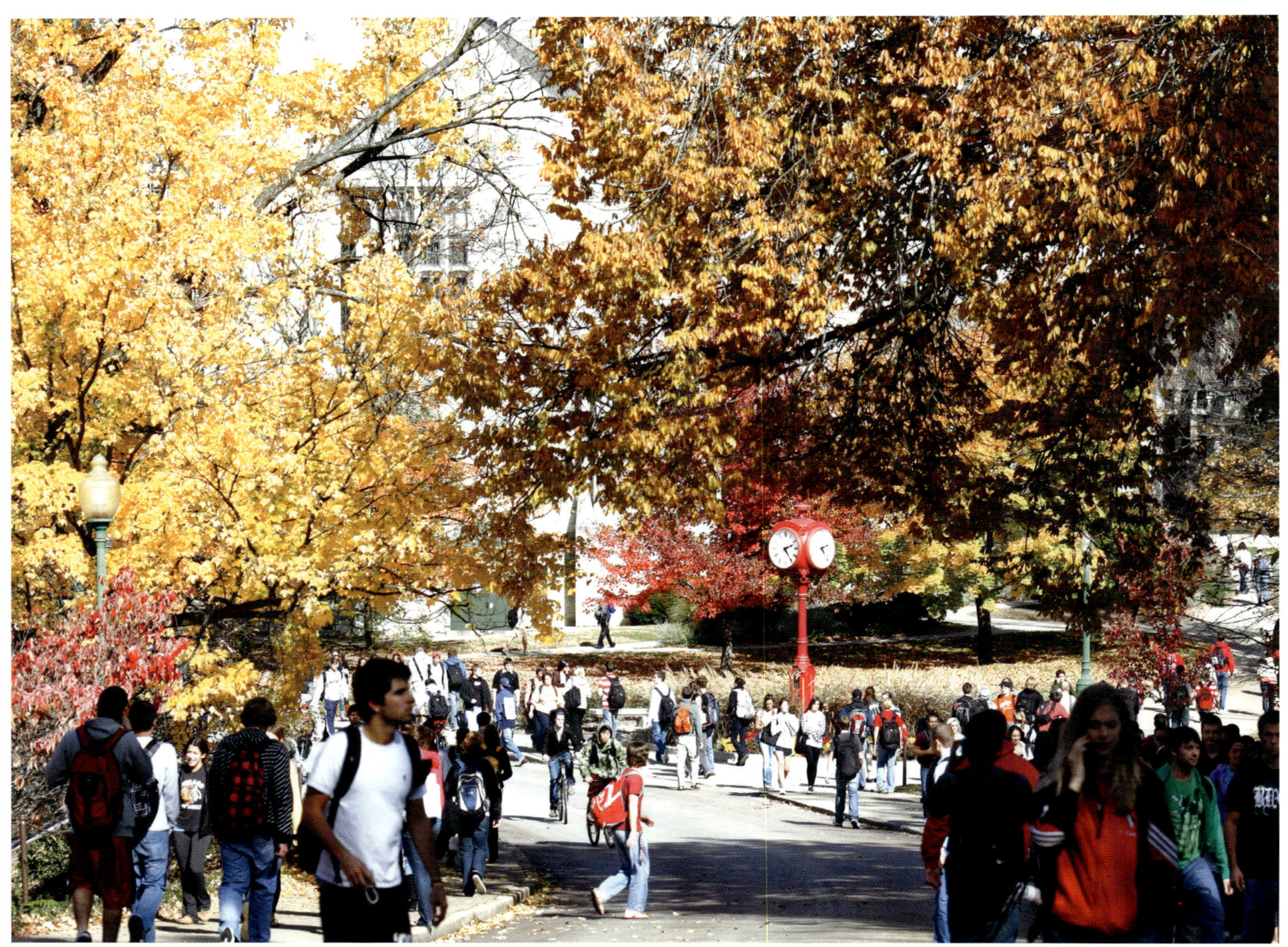

One of my favorite places is Forrest Avenue between Woodburn Hall and the Chemistry Building. The road is full of students of all personalities, upbringings, and perspectives on life; it brings color and life to campus. The beauty of diversity is most evident here, perfectly capturing why I fell in love with IU.

—*Kaitlyn Walker,* B.A. MATHEMATICS; B.S. POLICY ANALYSIS, 2013

Forrest Avenue.

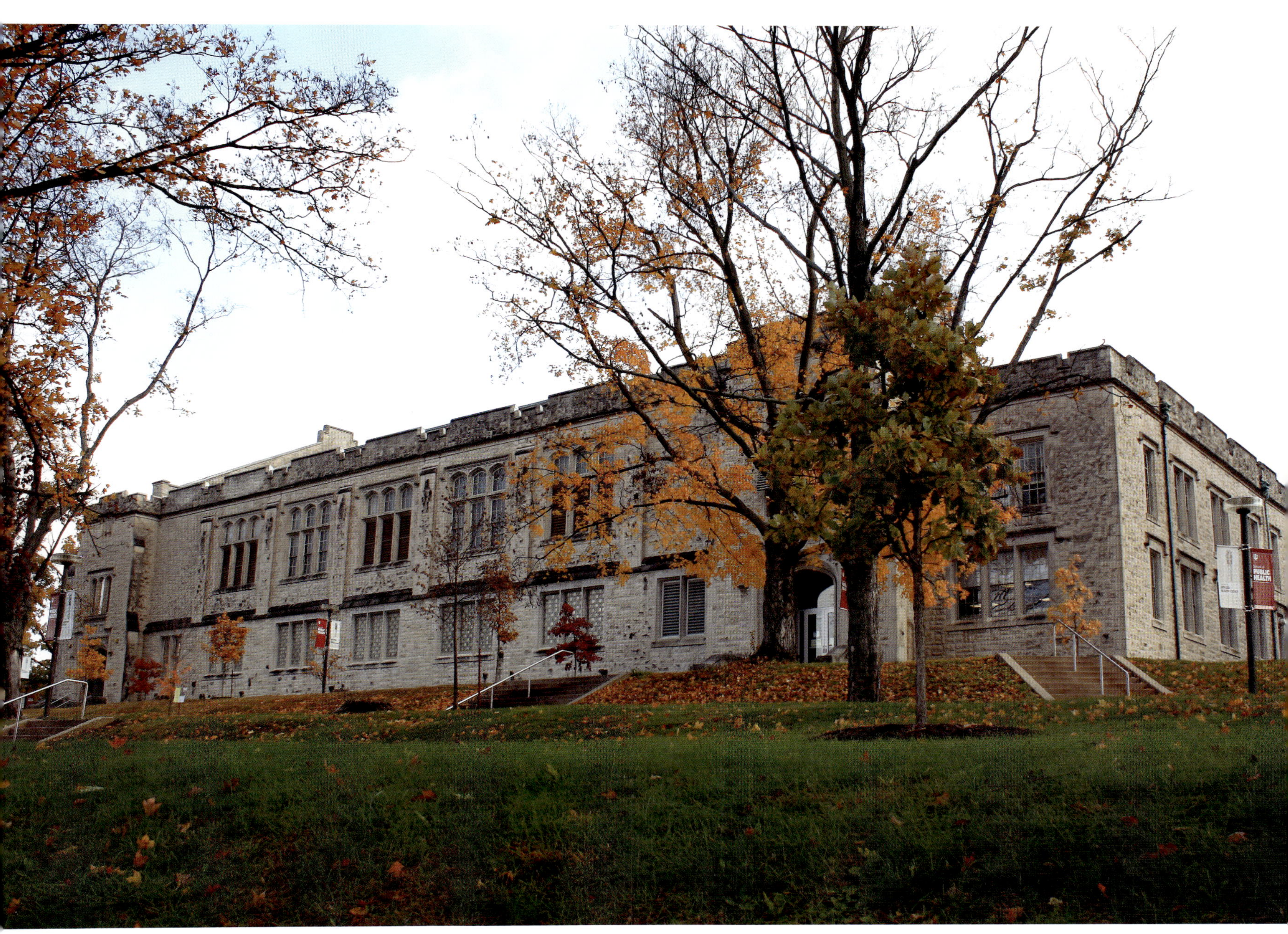

School of Public Health Building and Wildermuth Intramural Center. *Mandy Hussey*

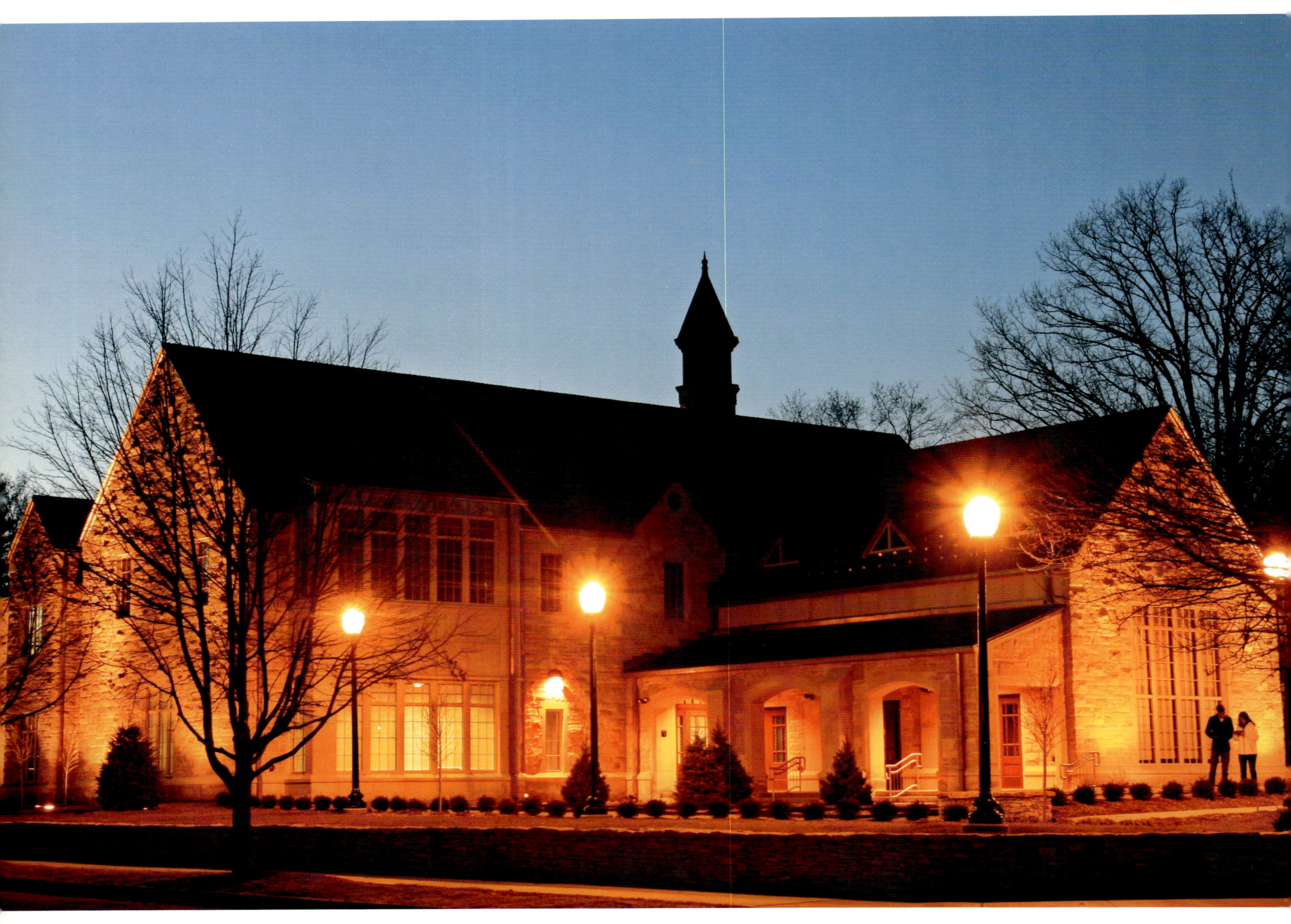

Hutton Honors College.

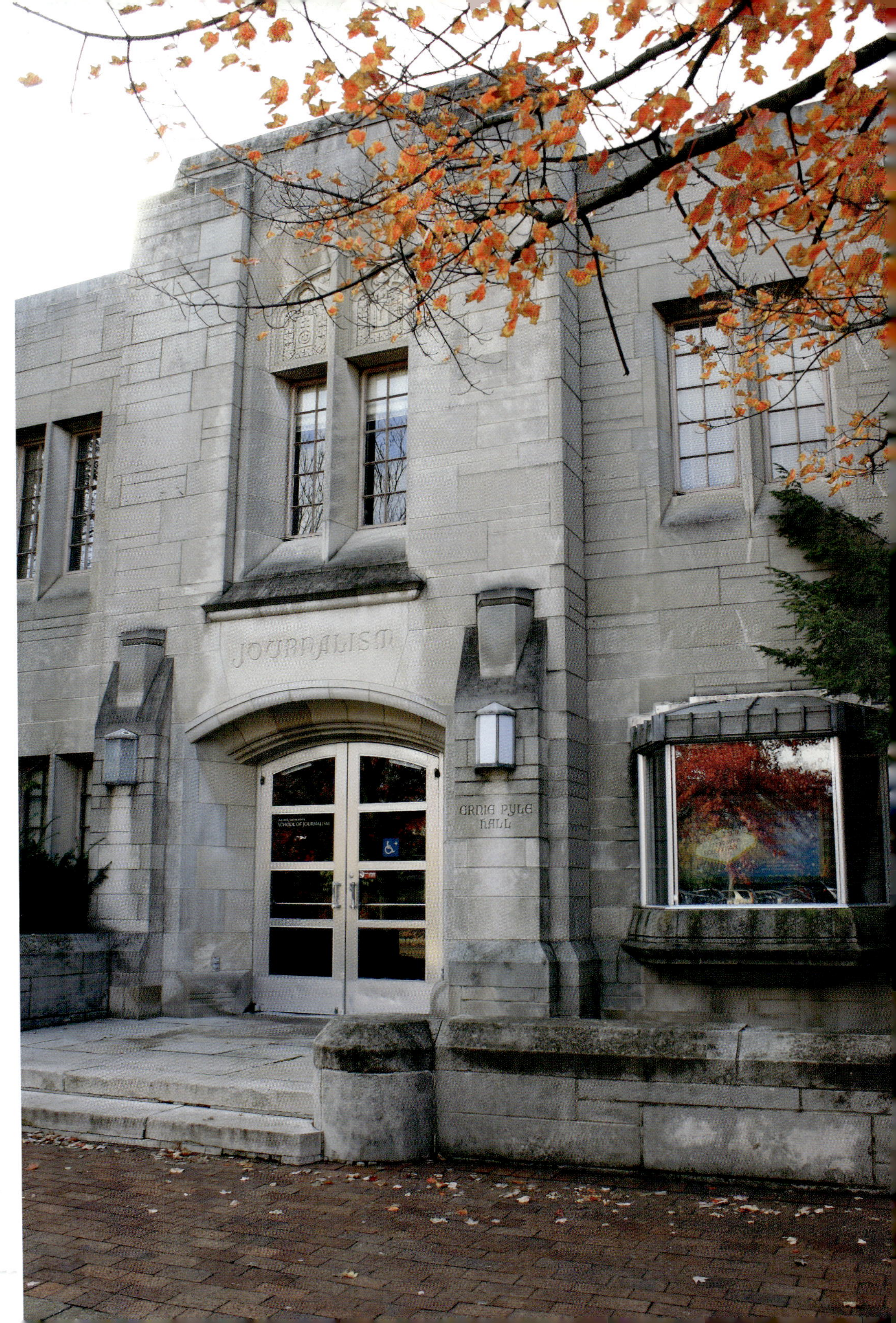

Ernie Pyle Hall (School of Journalism). *Mandy Hussey*

arboretum

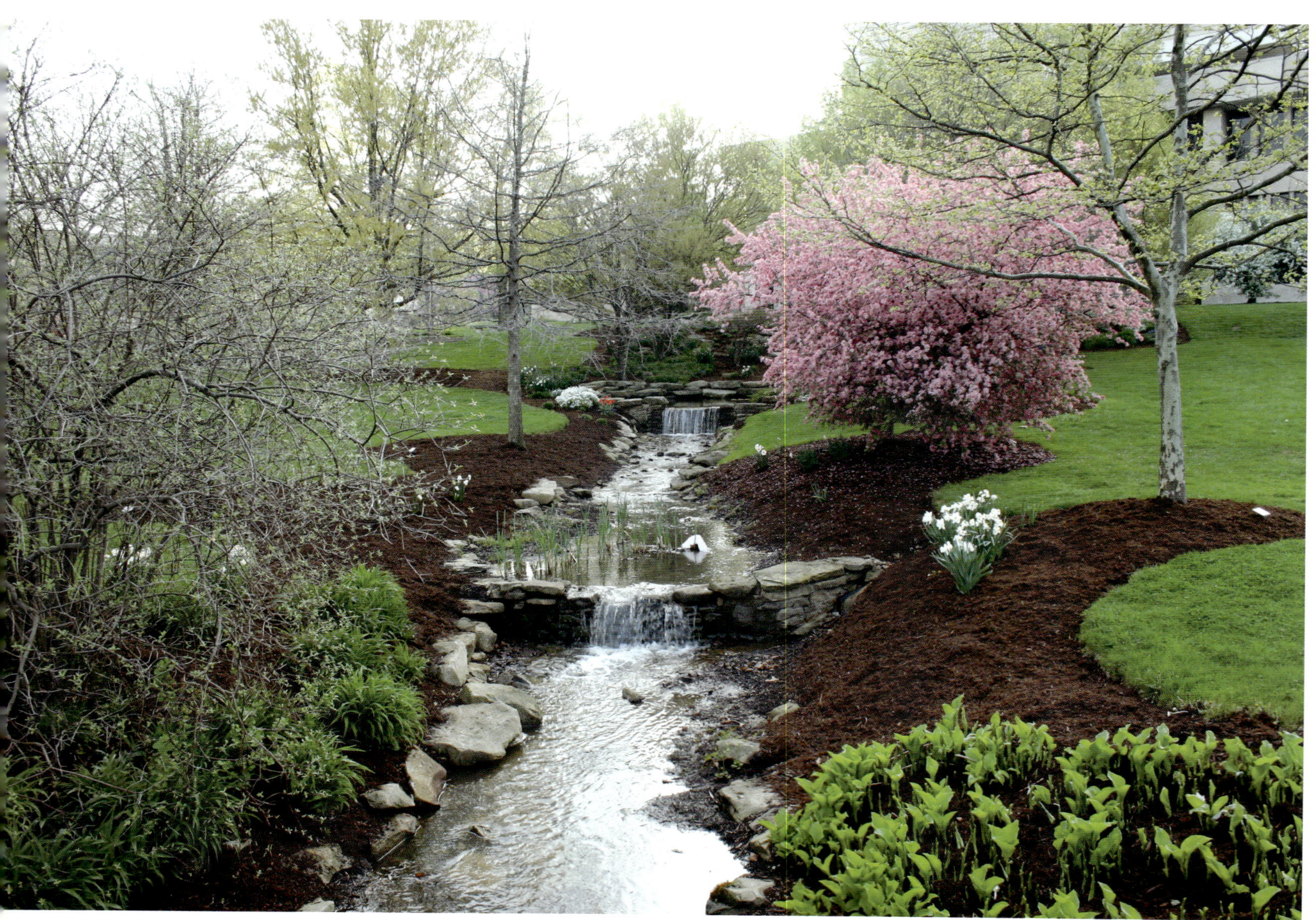

Waterscape, Jesse and Beulah Cox Arboretum. *Milton Hamburger*

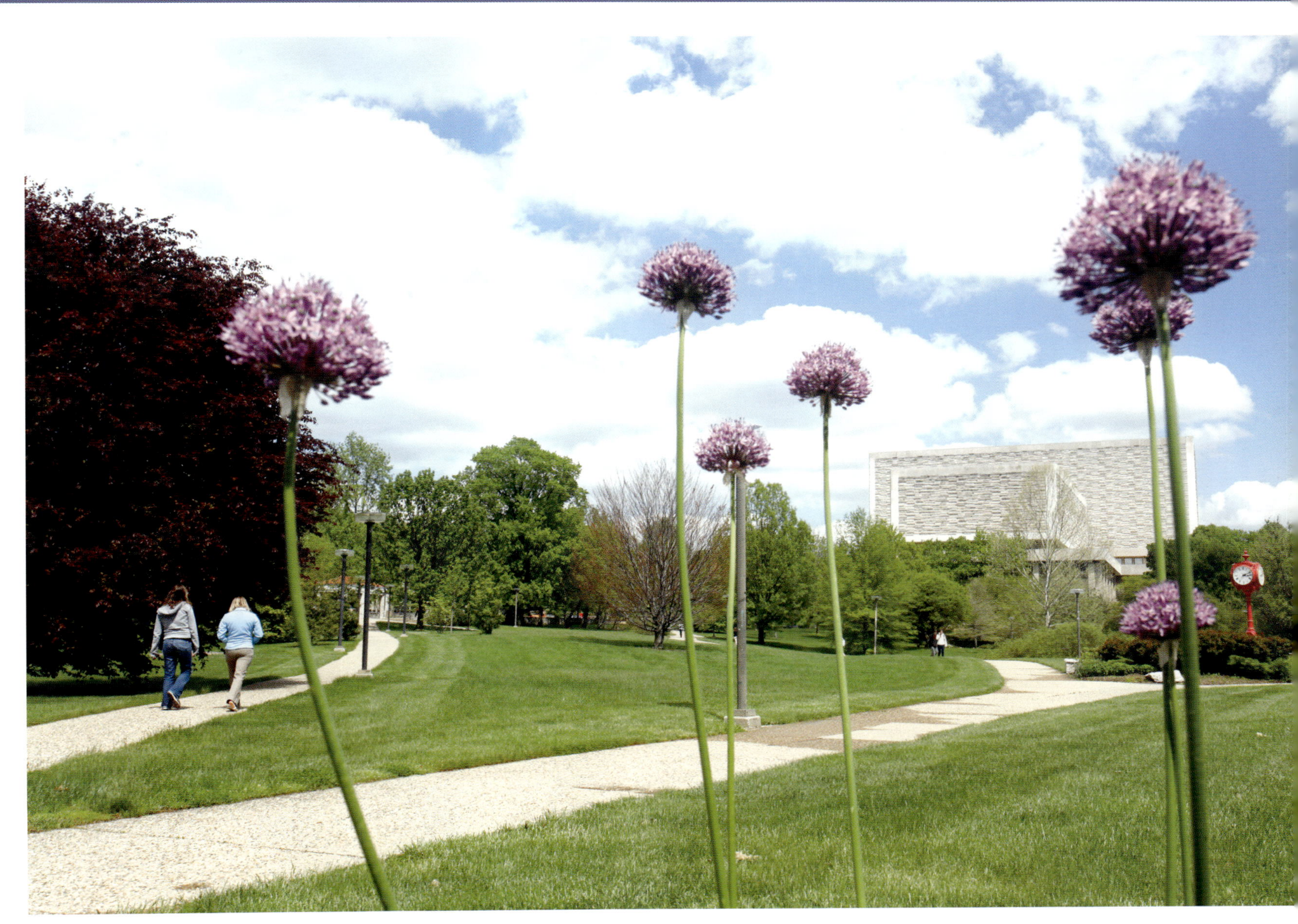

Arboretum paths lead to Herman B Wells Library.

arboretum gazebo

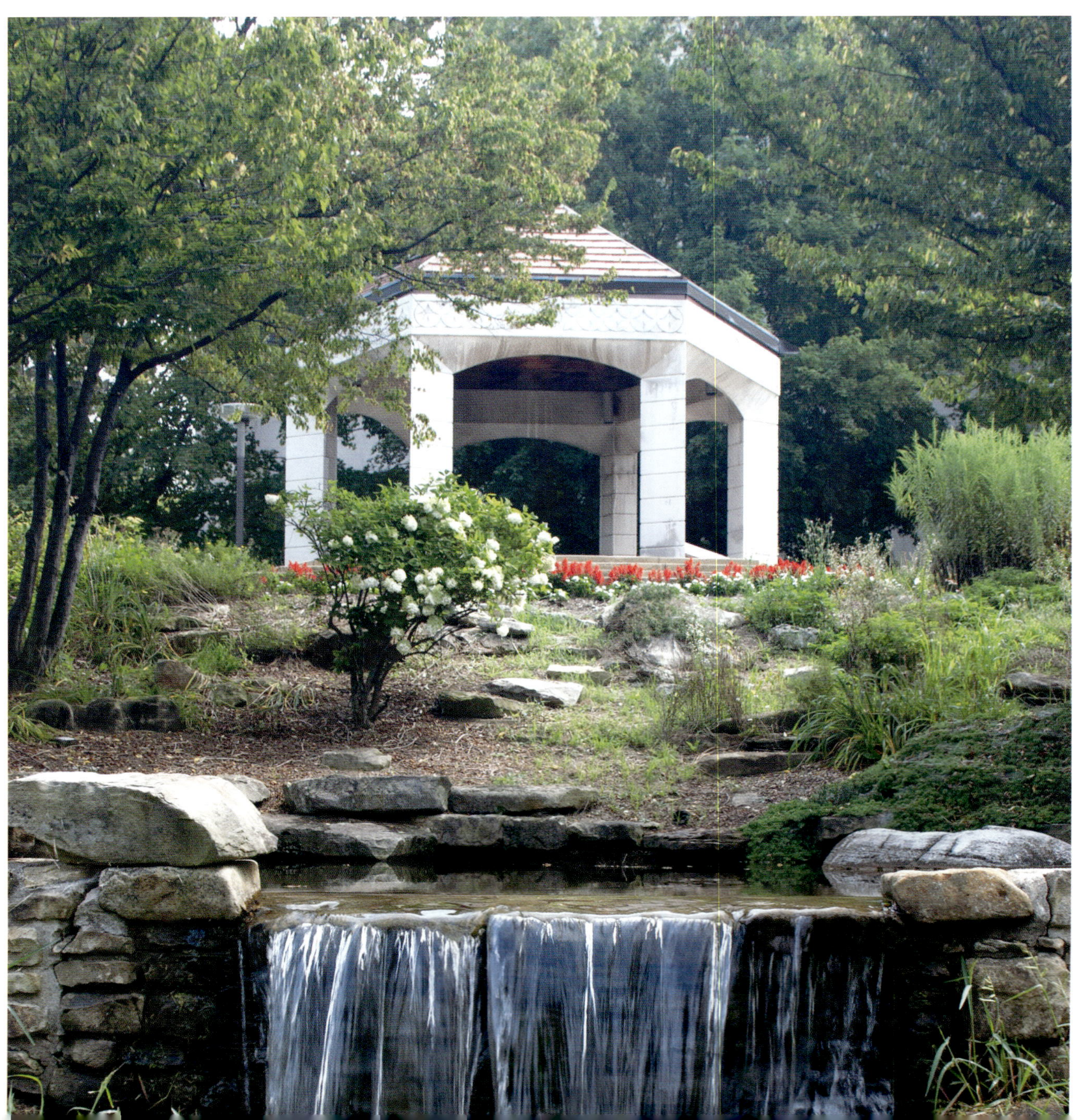

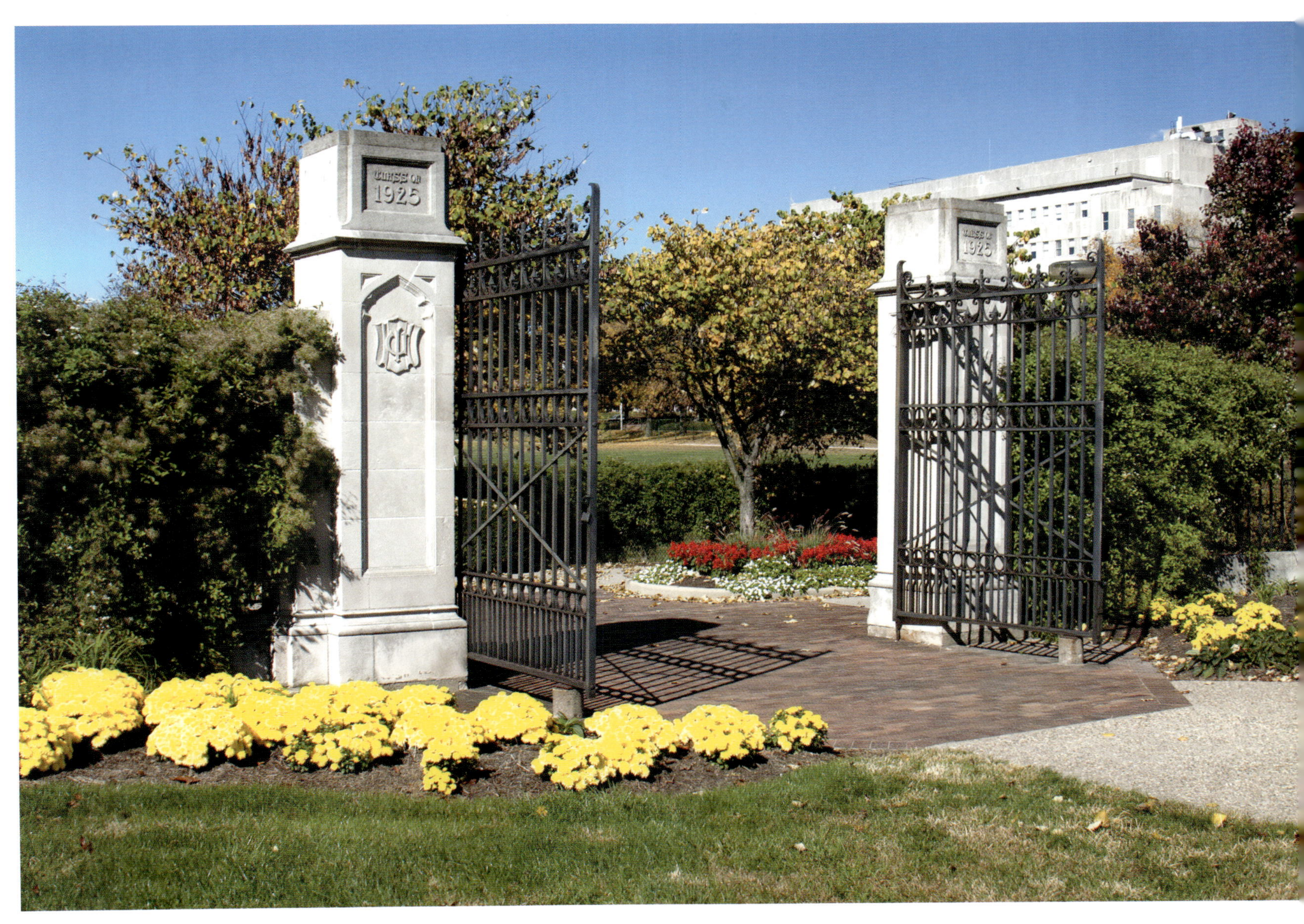

Arboretum Gazebo on a warm summer day. *Chris Robb*

Arboretum Gates. *Chris Robb*

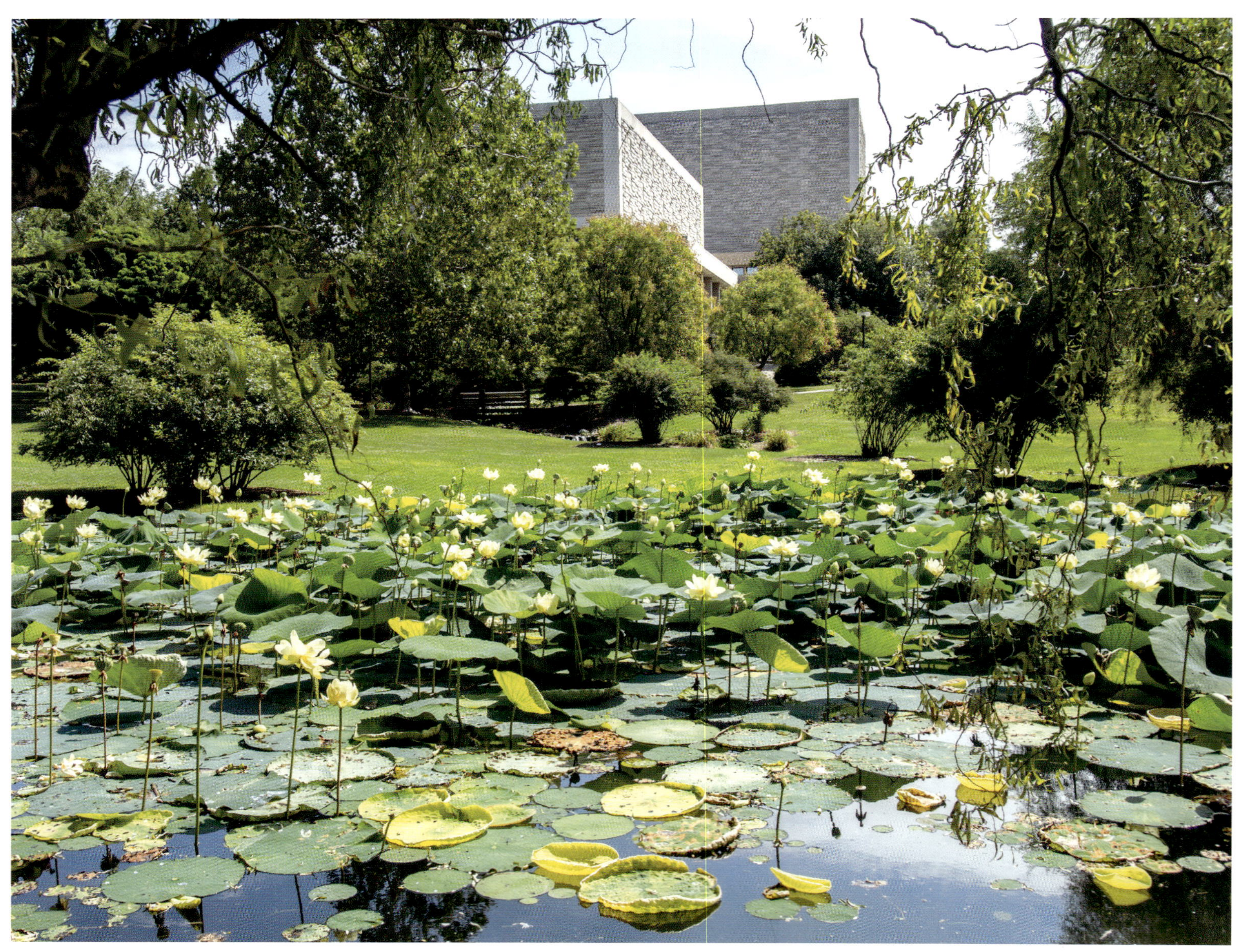

A lily pond in the Arboretum.

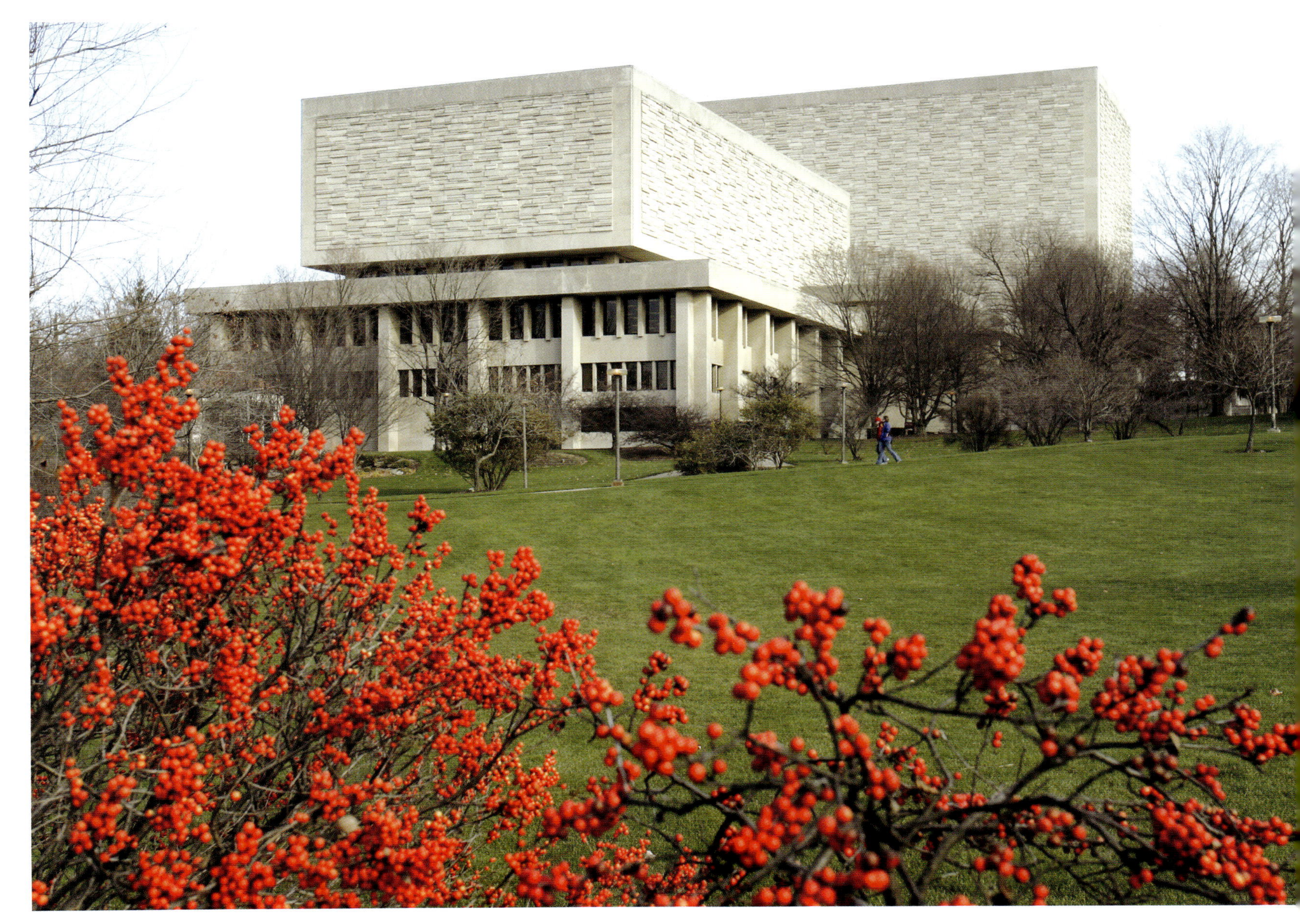

Herman B Wells Library.

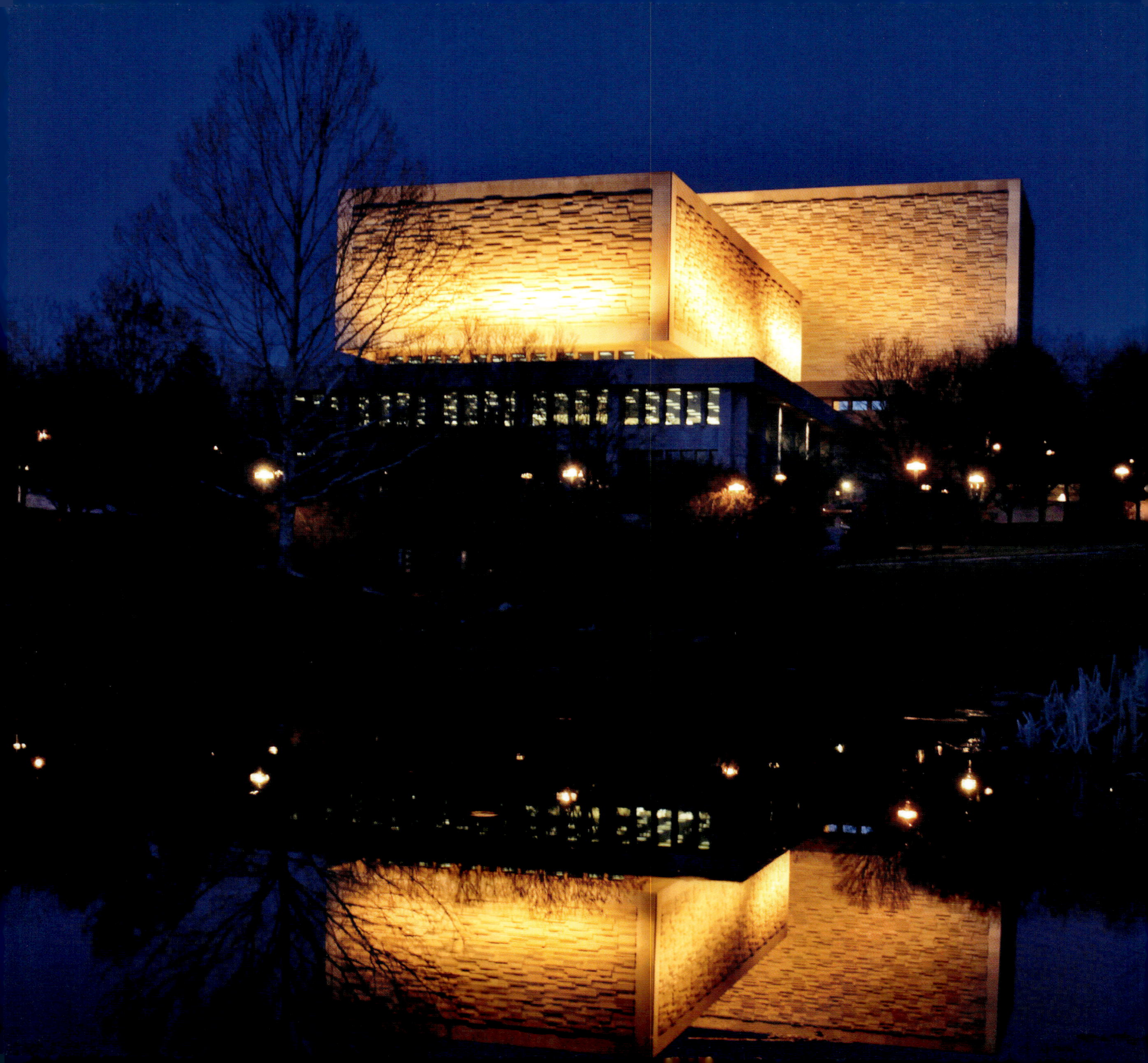

Facing
A reflection of Herman B Wells Library lights up the night.

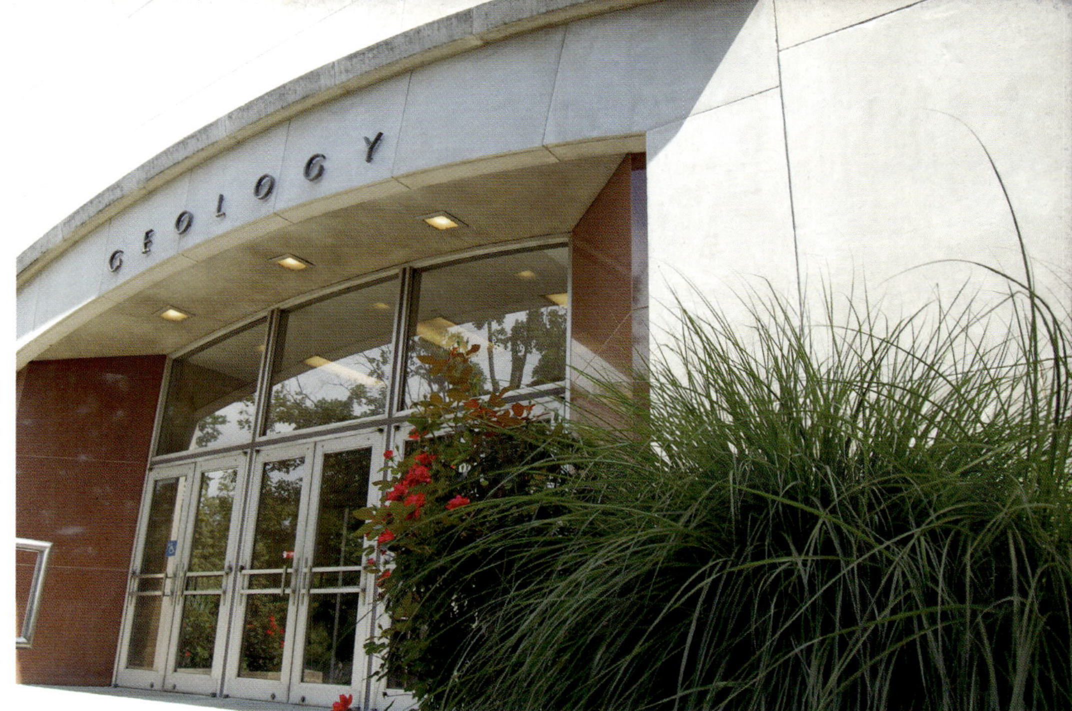

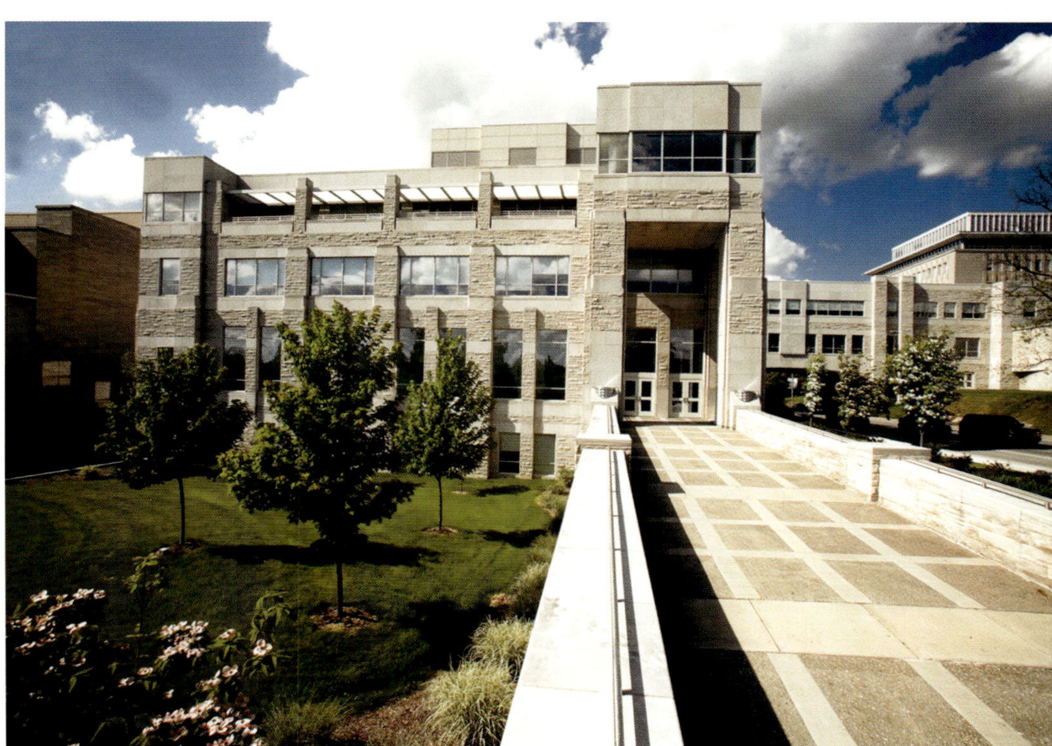

Above
Geology Building.

Kelley School of Business, William J. Godfrey Graduate and Executive Education Center.

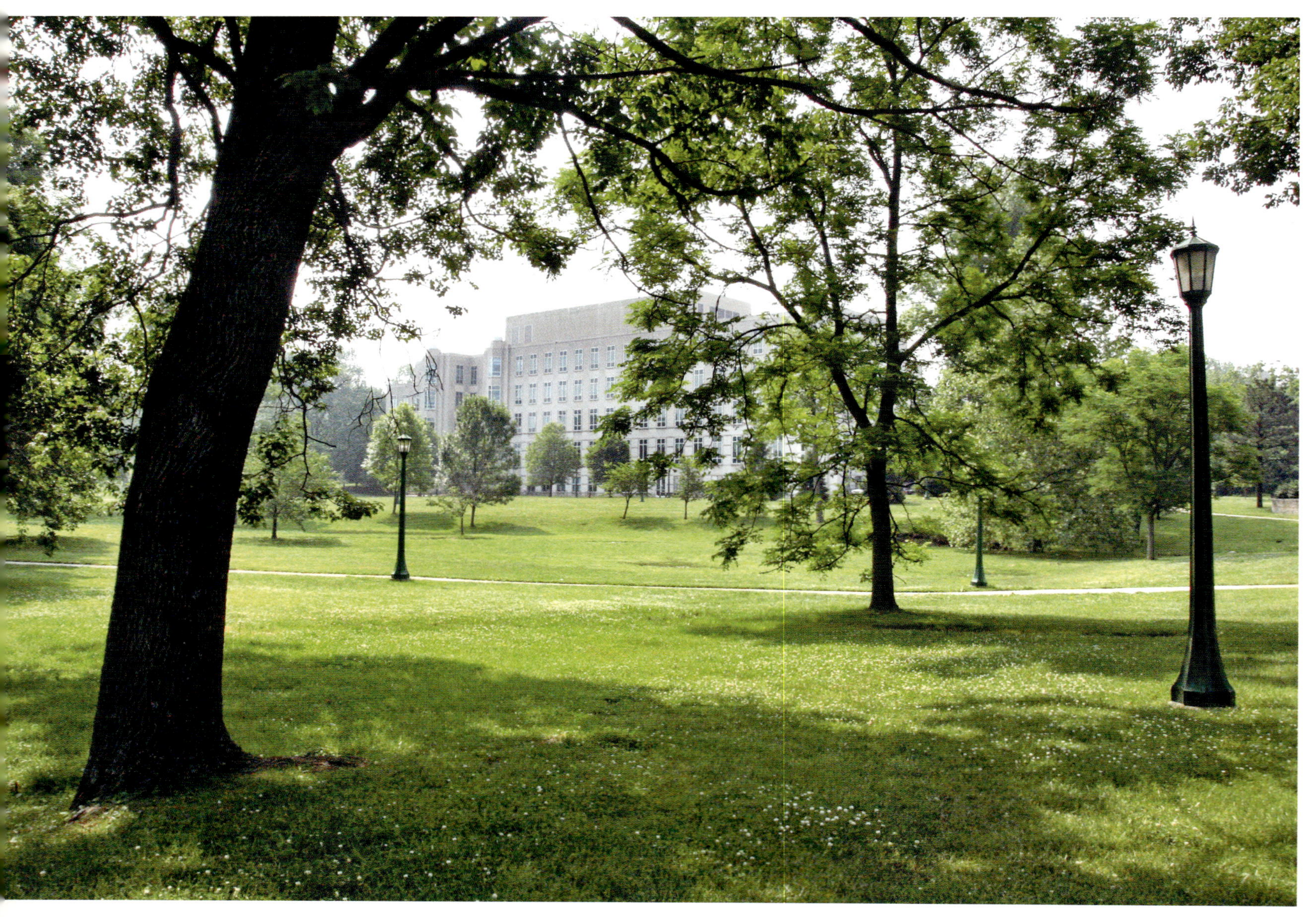

Wendell W. Wright Education Building.

Railroad tracks near Jordan Avenue. *Mandy Hussey*

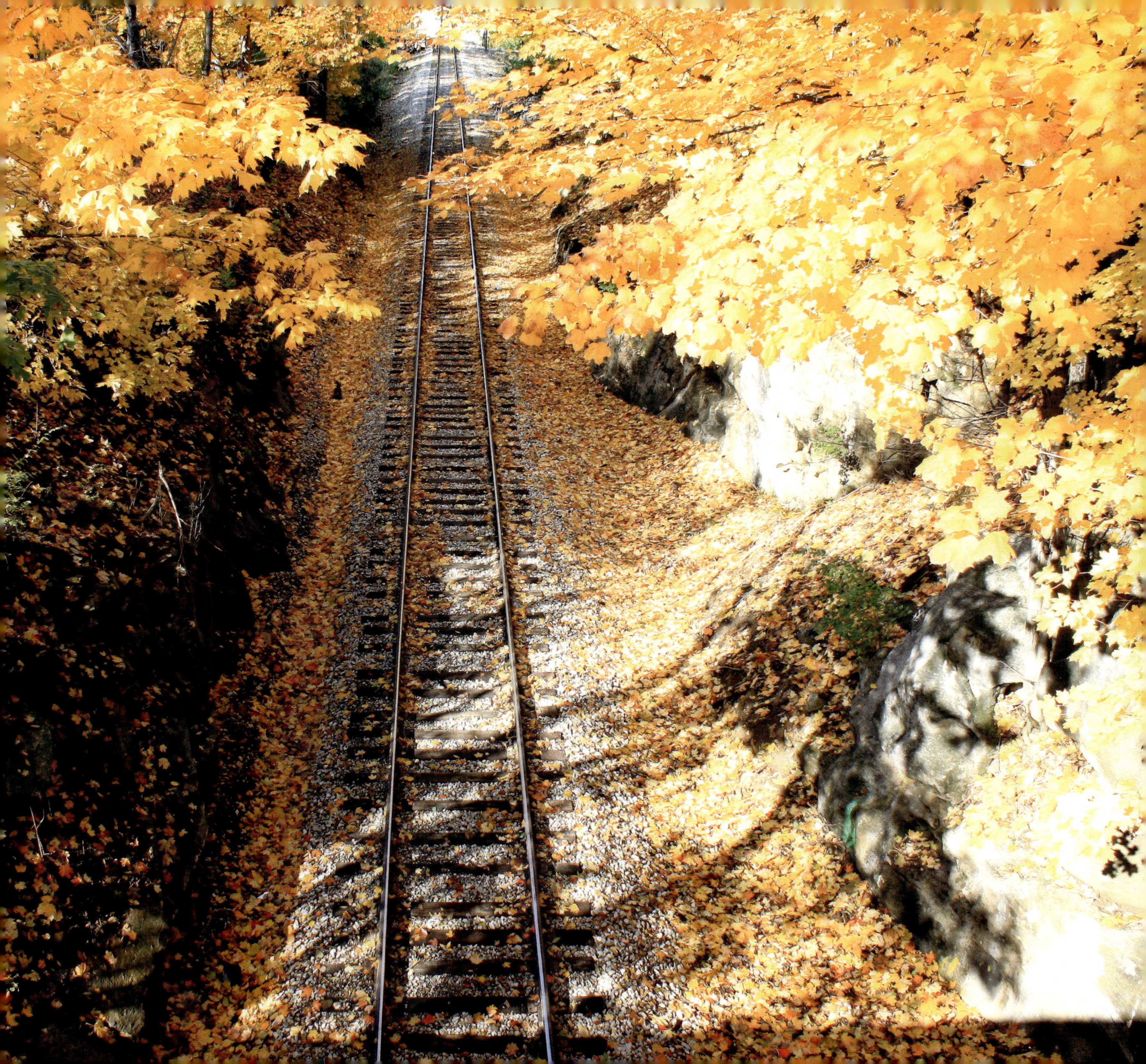

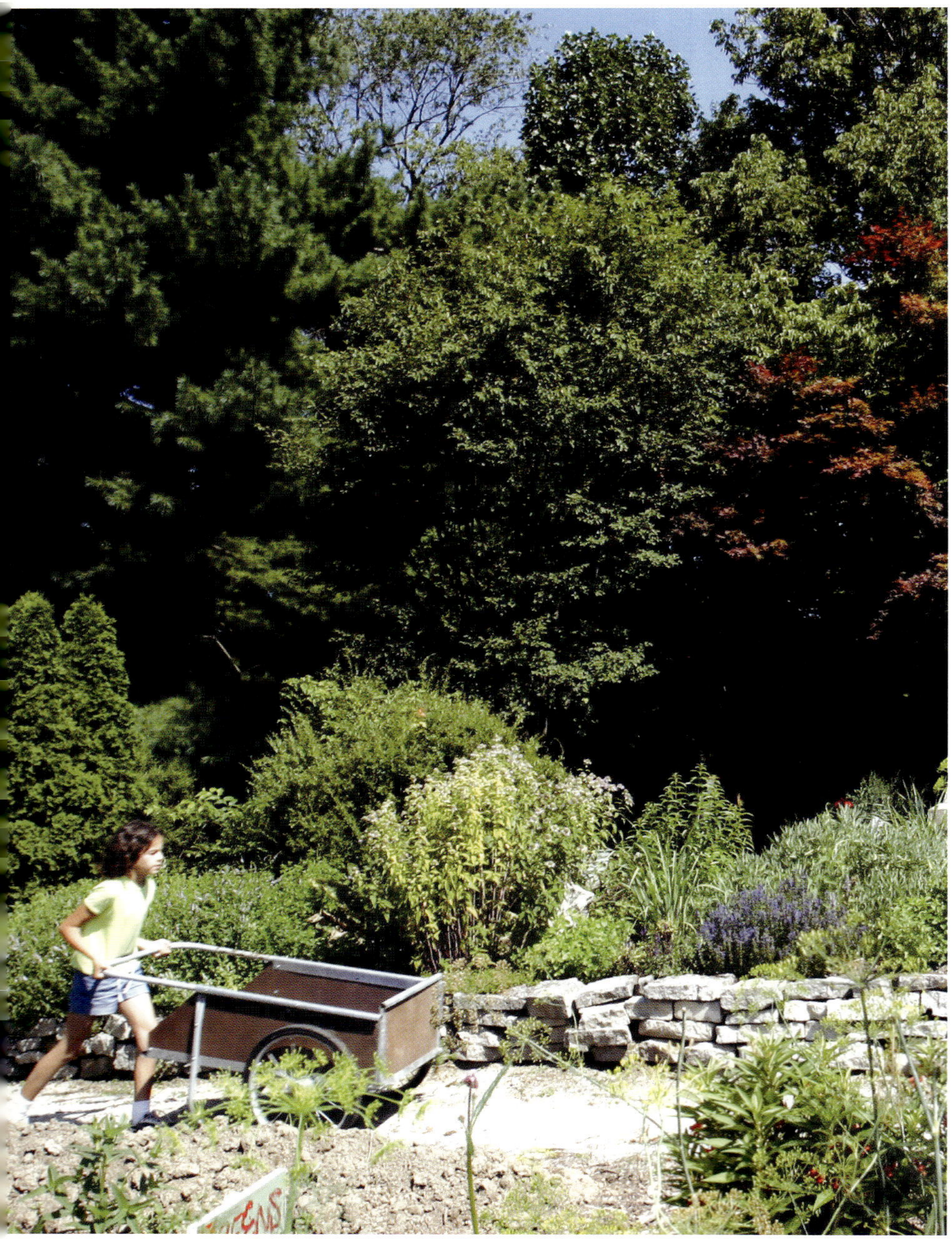

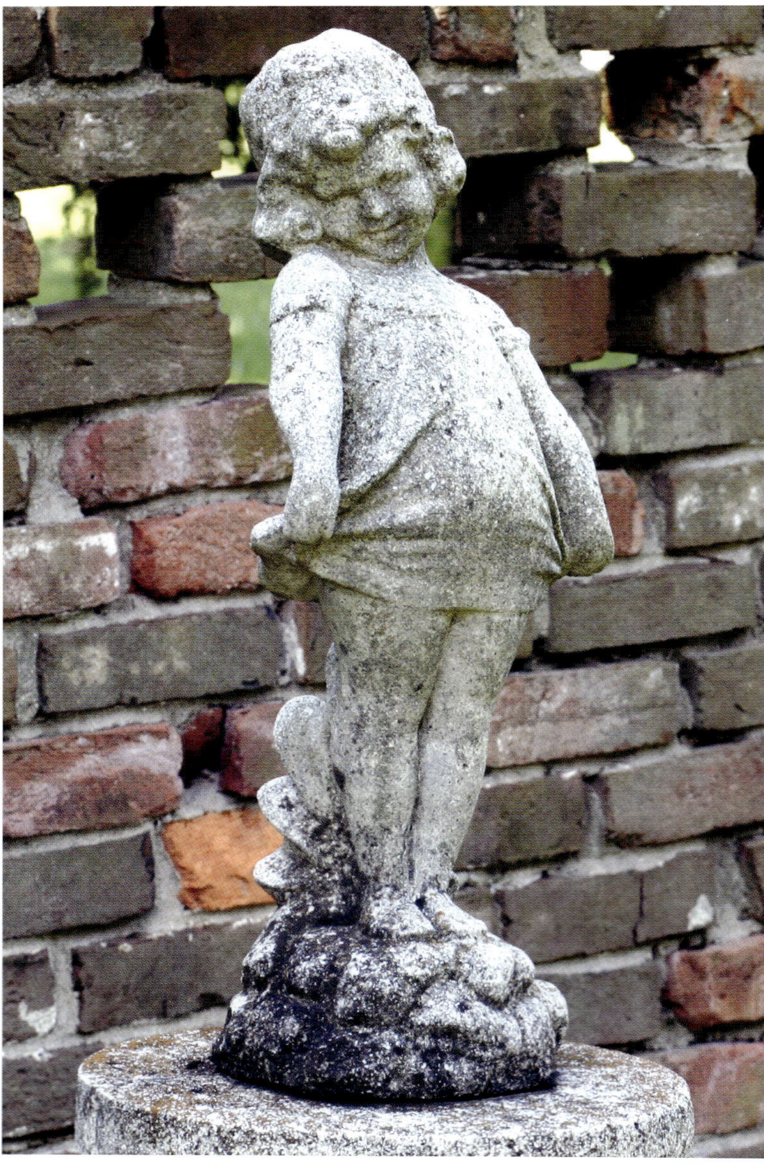

Hilltop Garden and Nature Center.

metz carillon

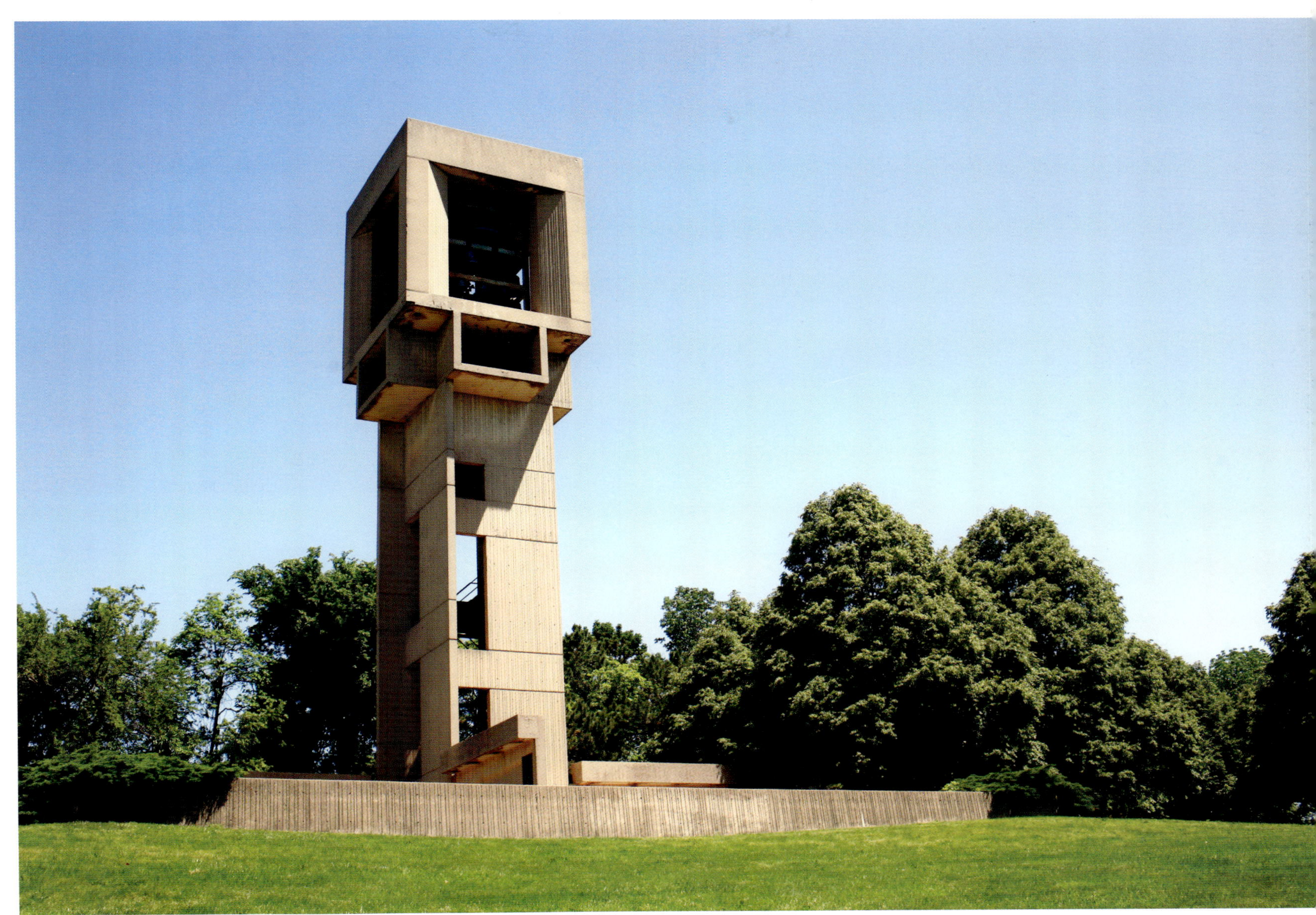

Metz Carillon.

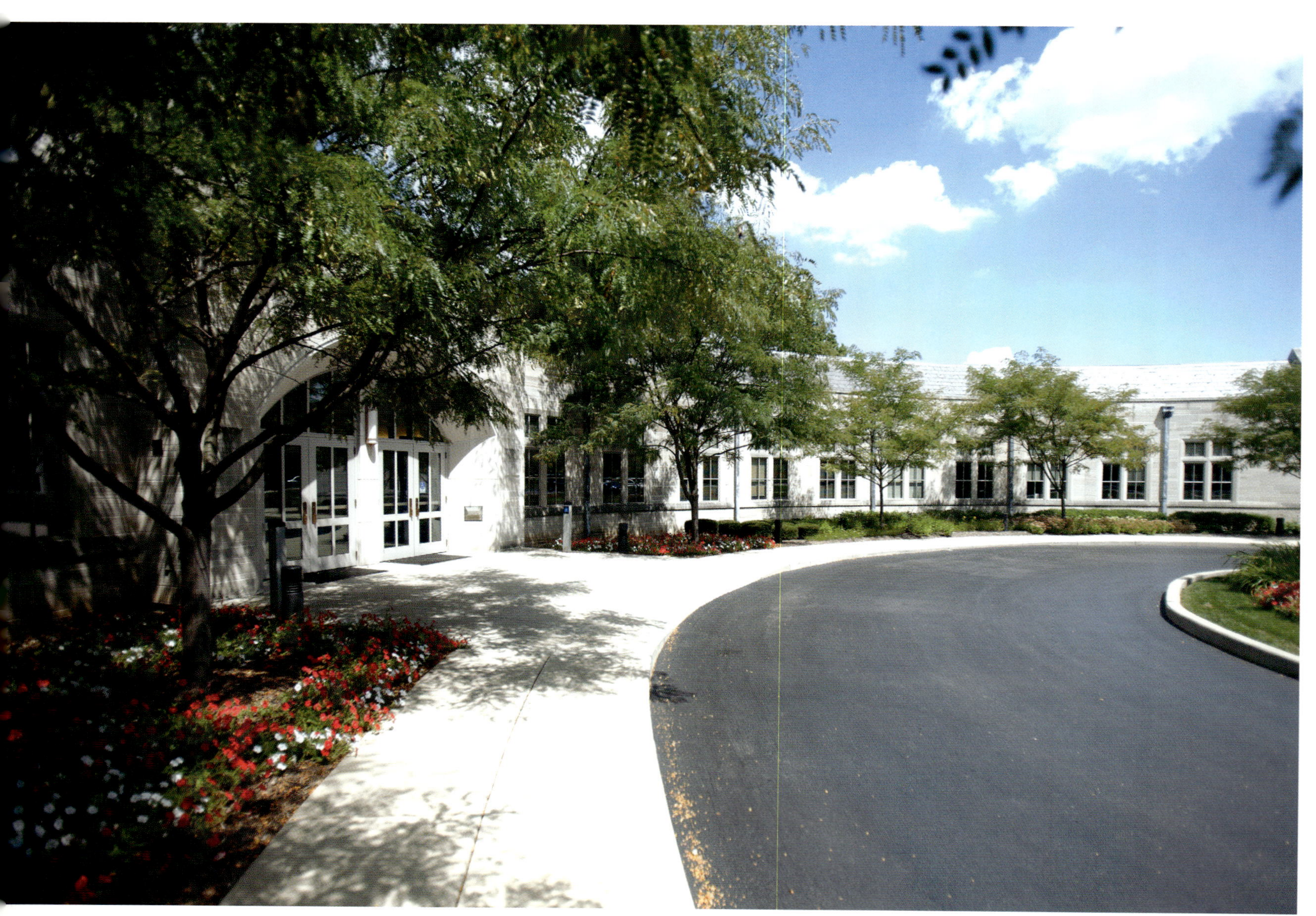

Showalter House, Indiana University Foundation.

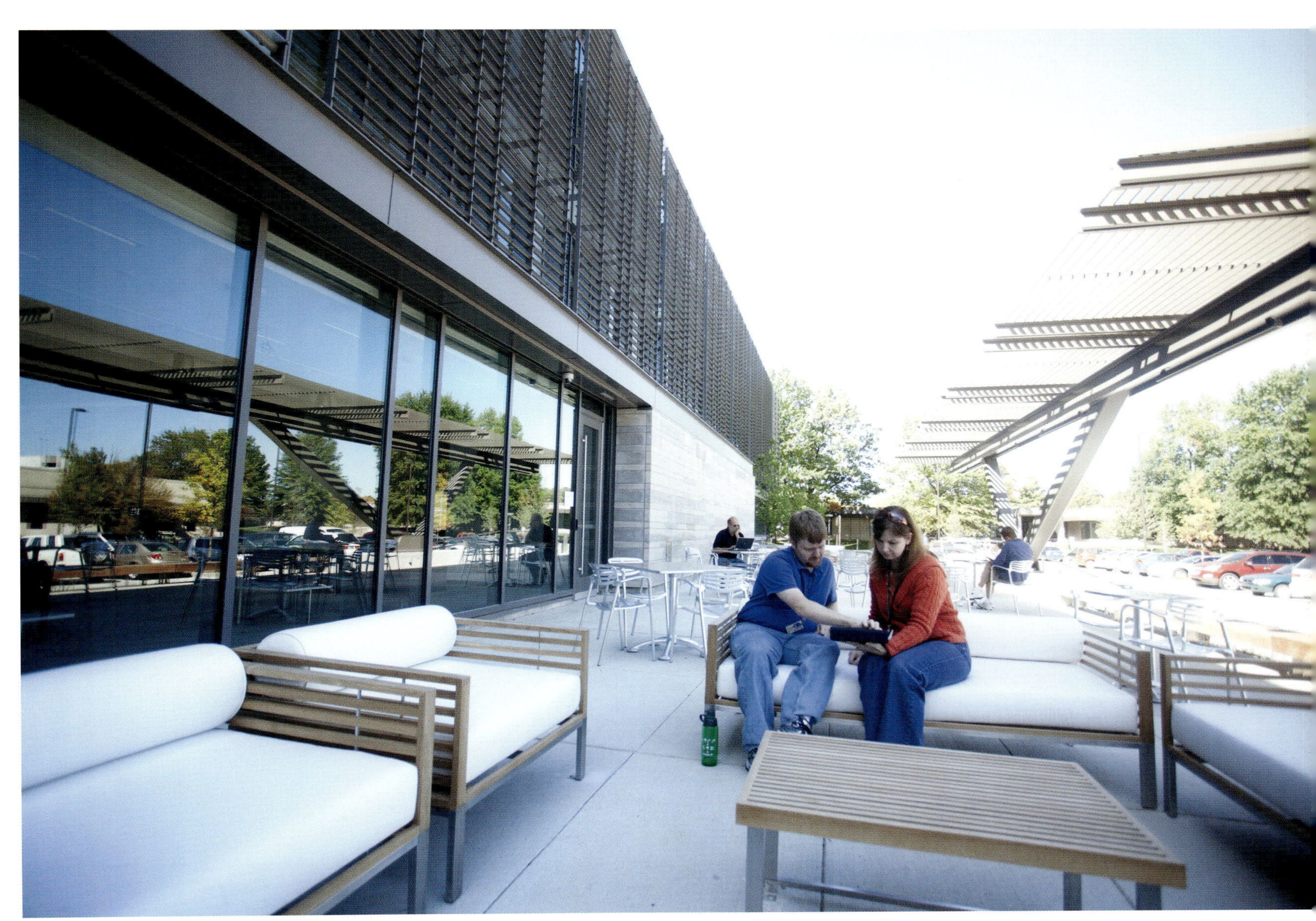

CIB (CyberInfrastructure Building).

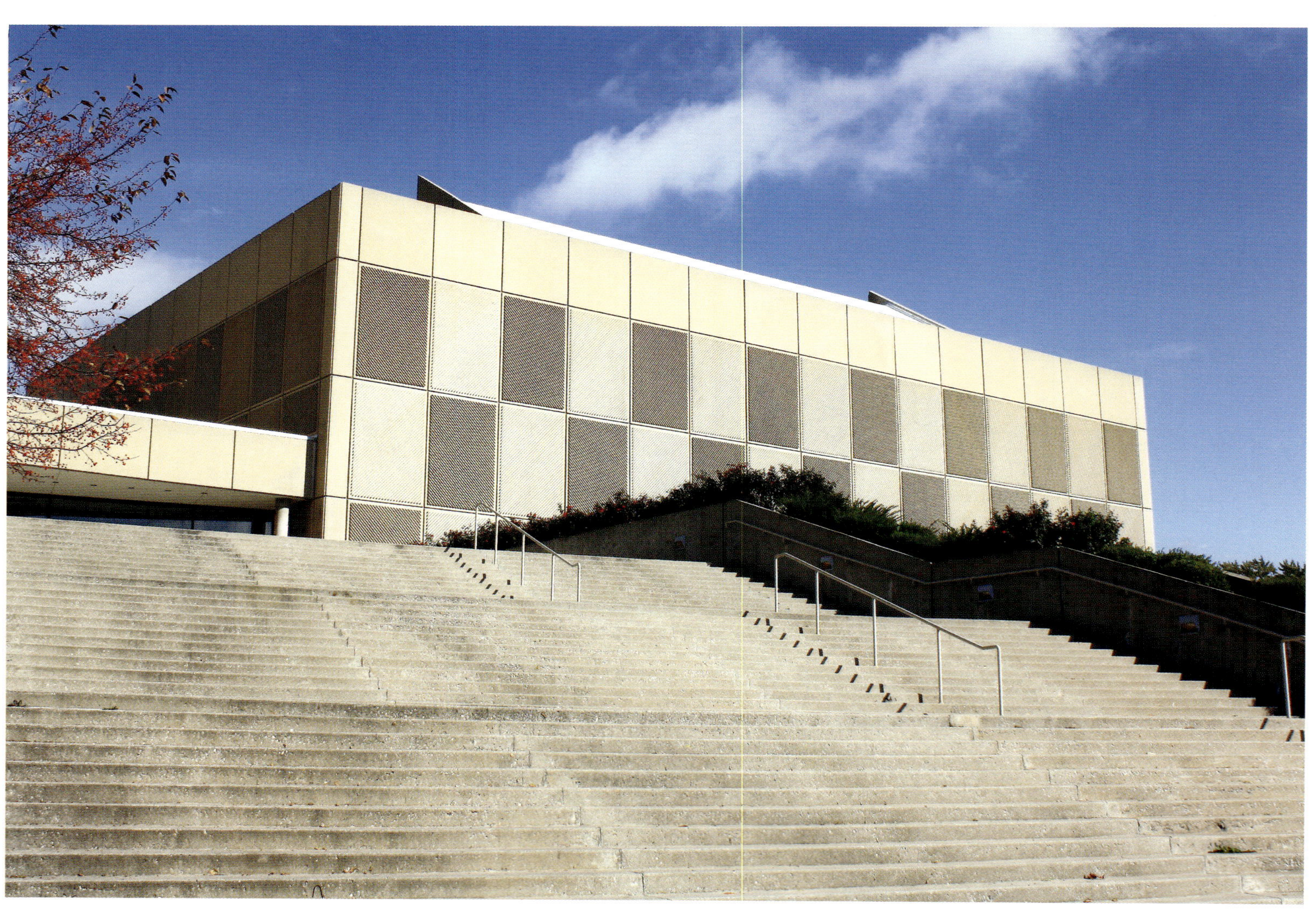

Student Recreational Sports Center, (SRSC). *Mandy Hussey*

Swimmers and divers warm up prior to a swim meet at the Counsilman-Billingsley Aquatic Center in the Student Recreational Sports Center.

athletic venues

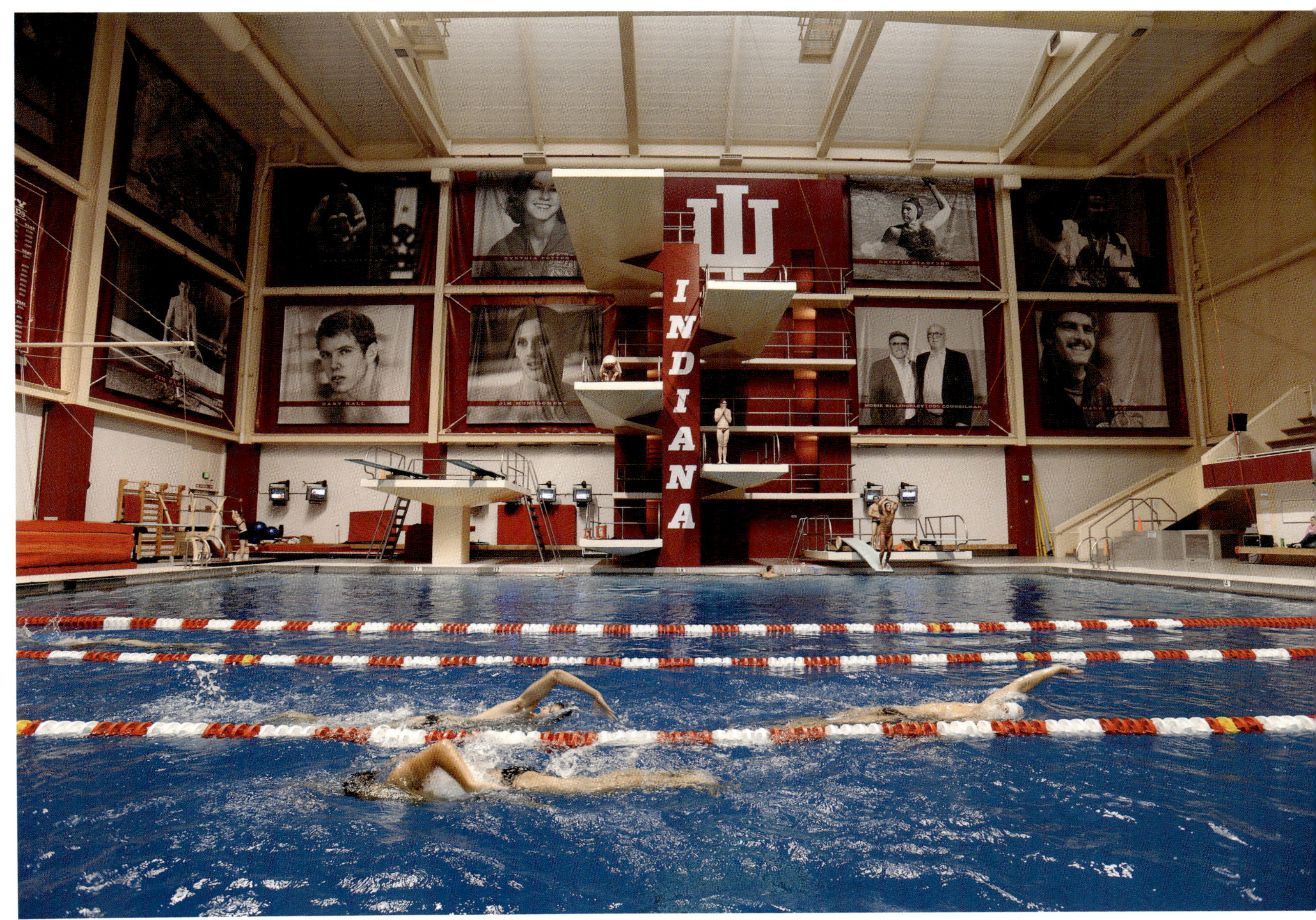

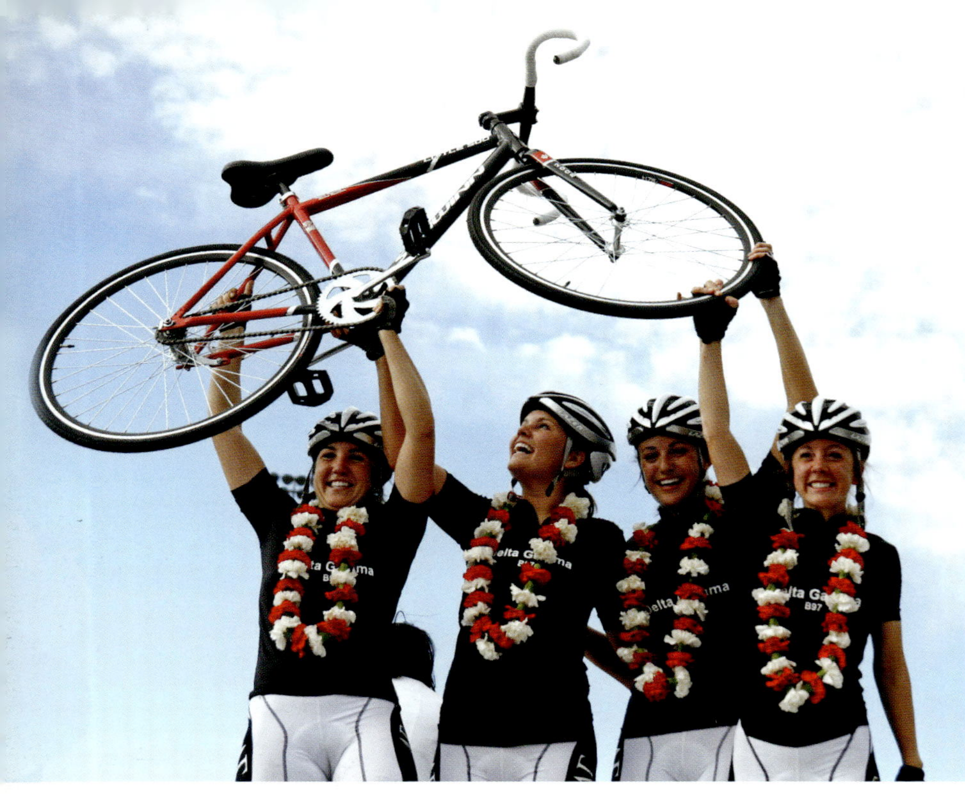

Women's Little 500, left.
Men's Little 500, below and below left.

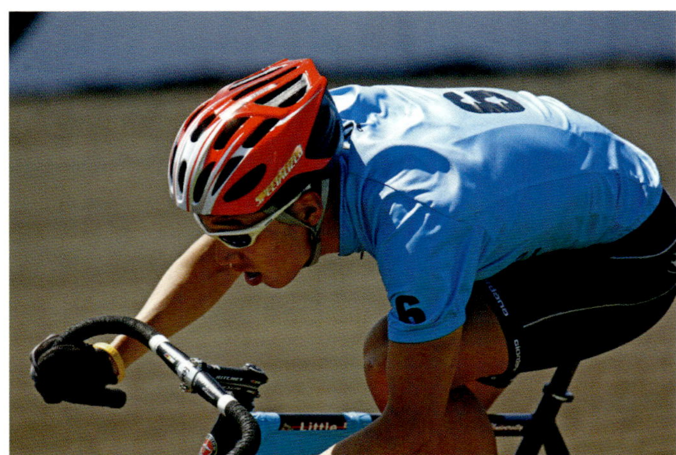

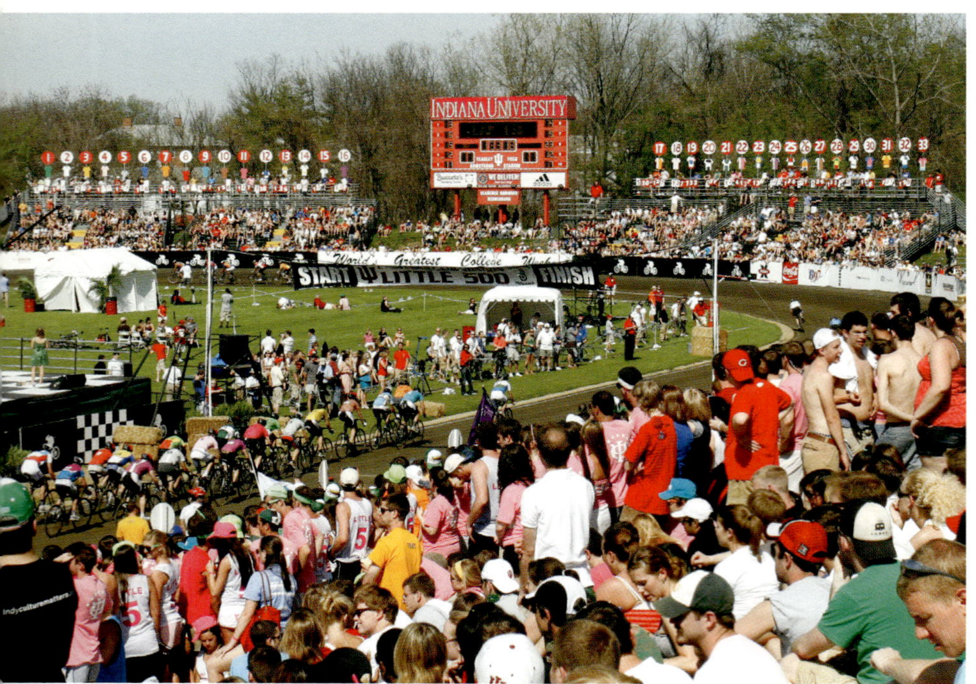

It's really great that the Little 500 has become such an important part of IU. So many people come to our university to see the race, even from out of state.

—*Kristin Ousley,* B.A. STUDIO ART, 2014

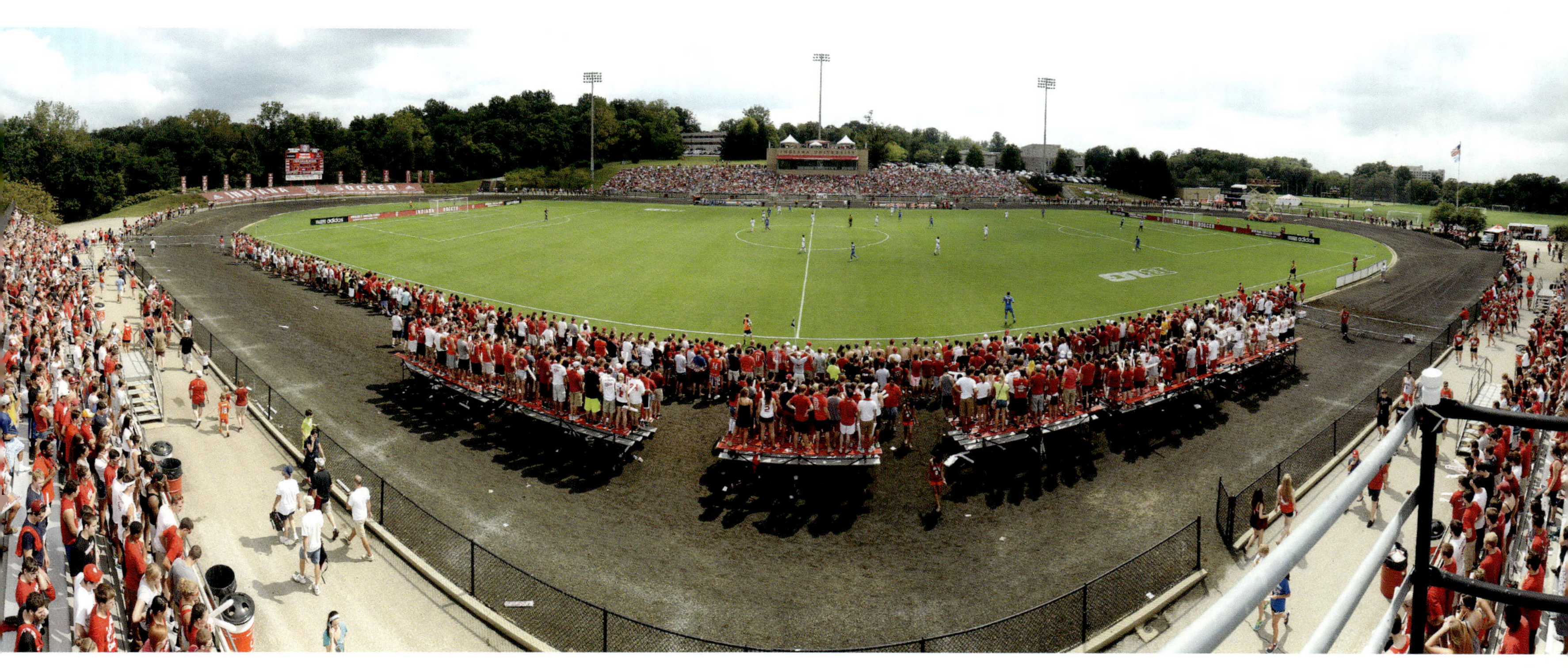

Jerry Yeagley Field at Bill Armstrong Stadium during the IU Men's Soccer game against UCLA, fall 2013. The game set the all-time stadium attendance record at 7,720. The photo is a digitally-stitched composite of multiple images.

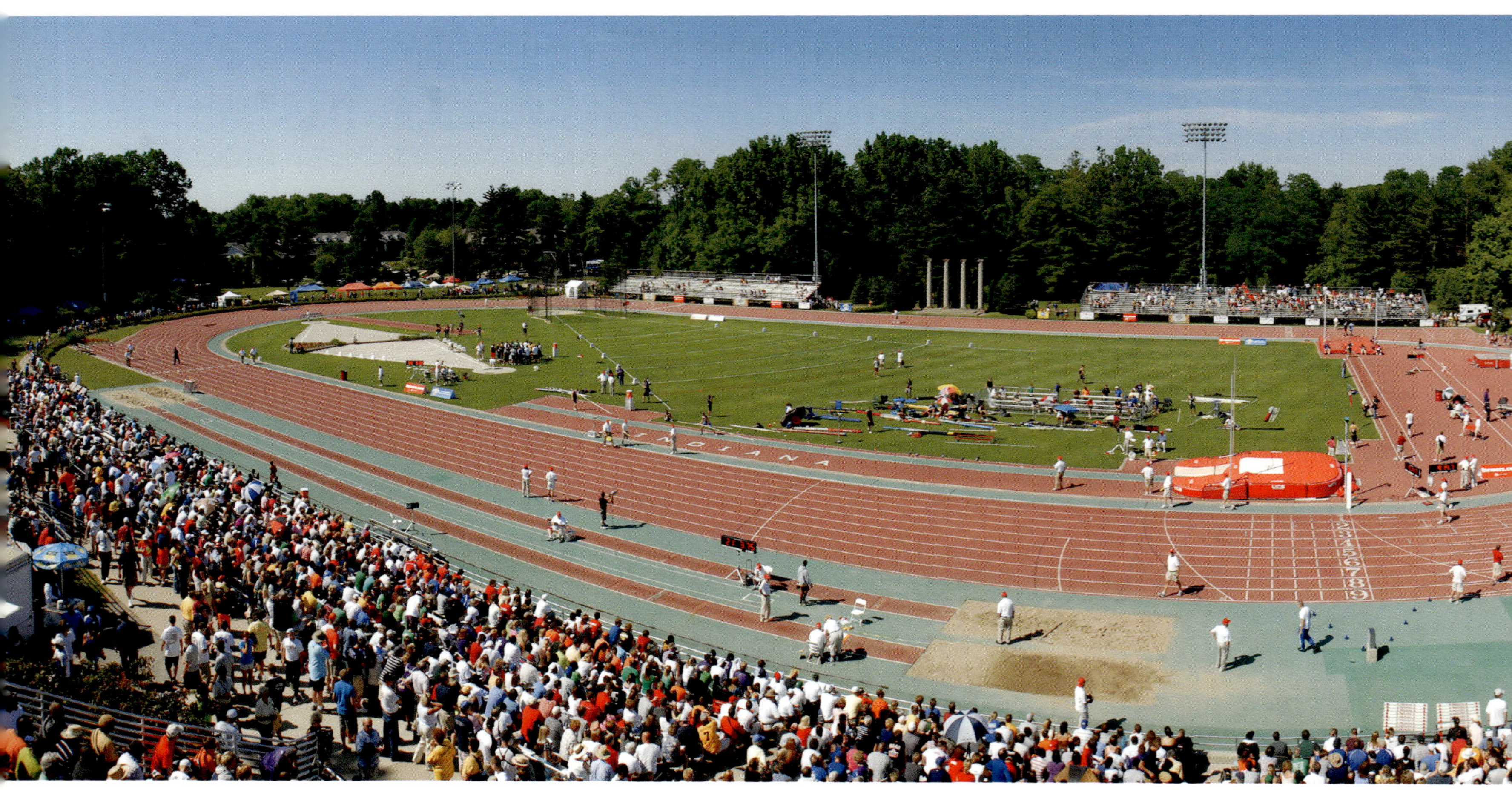

The Robert C. Haugh Track & Field Complex at E. C. "Billy" Hayes Track, during a meet, 2009. The photo is a digital composite of multiple images.

Facing

The IU Men's Cross Country team leaves the starting line during the Indiana Invitational, fall 2007.

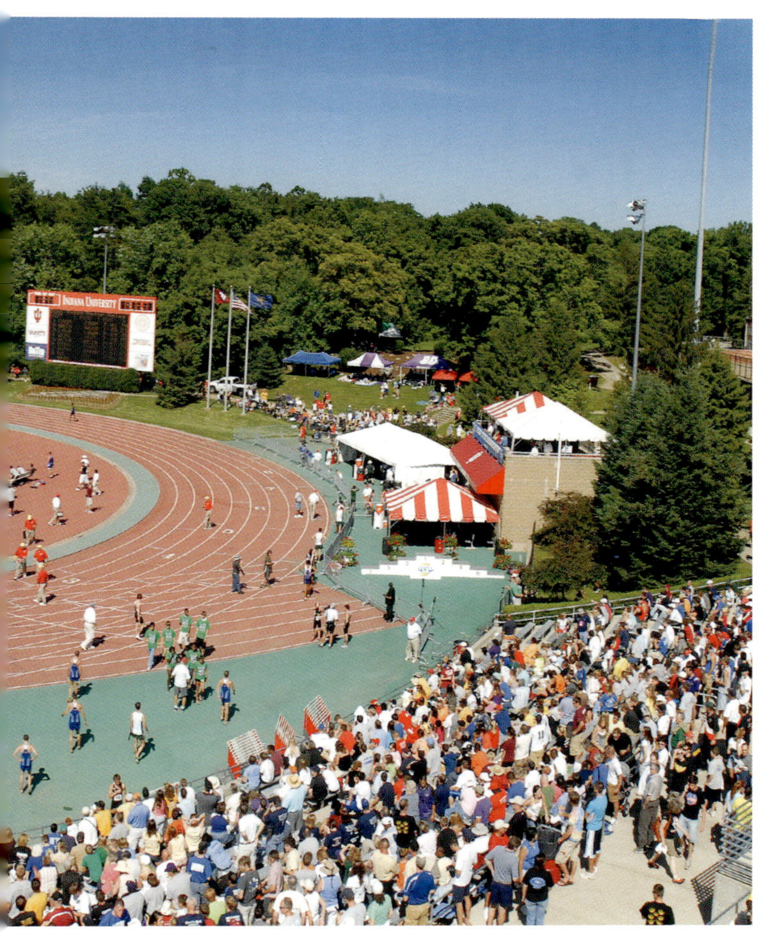

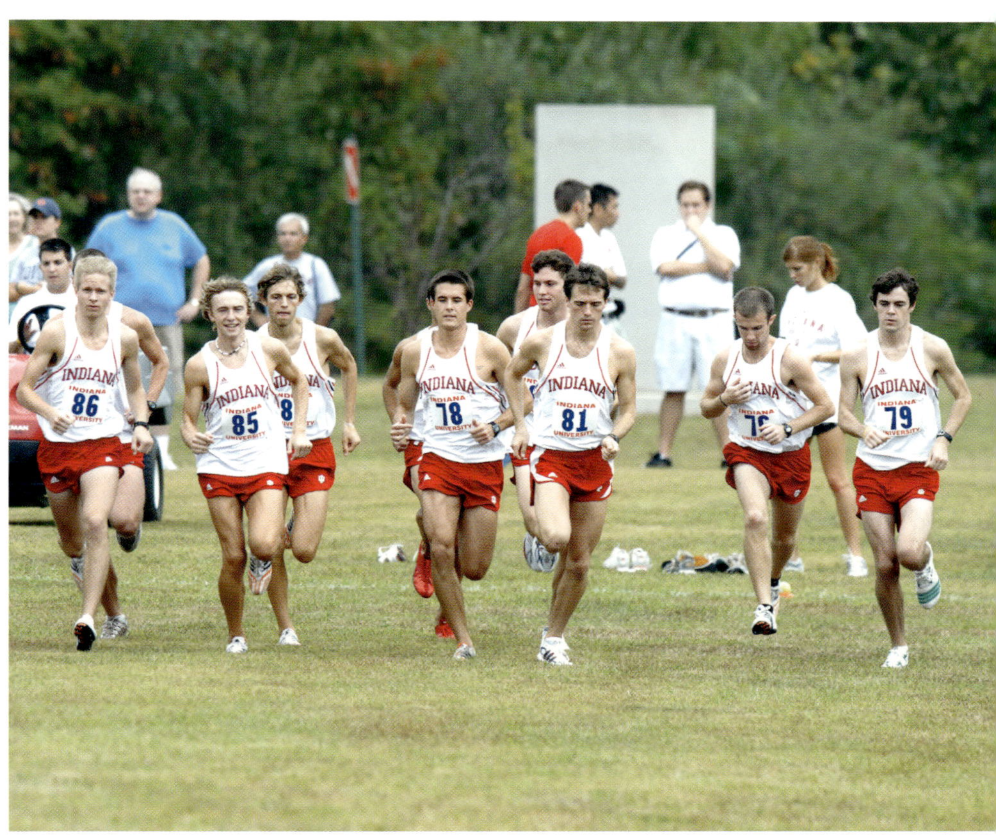
INDIANA
86
85
78
81
79

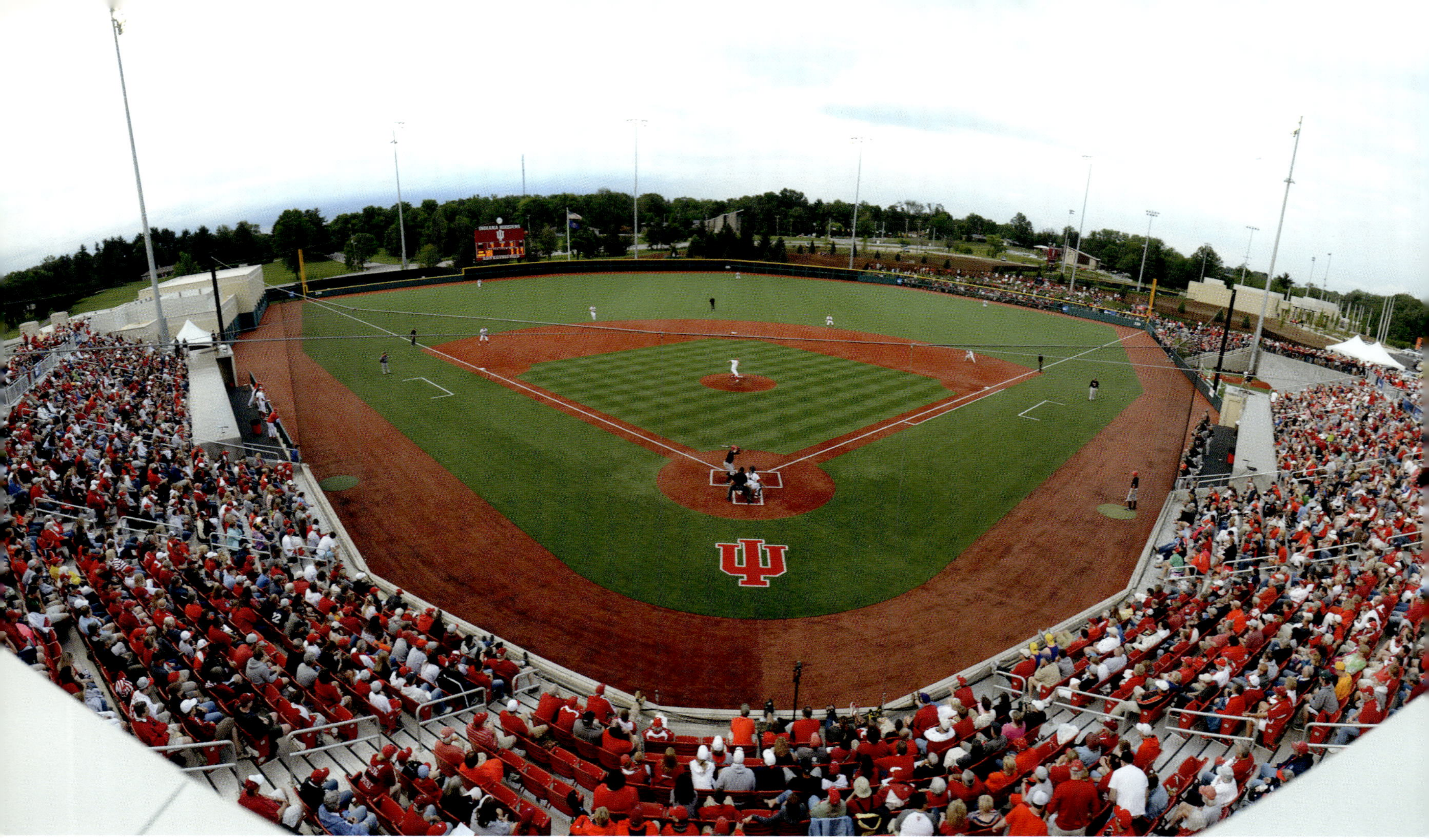

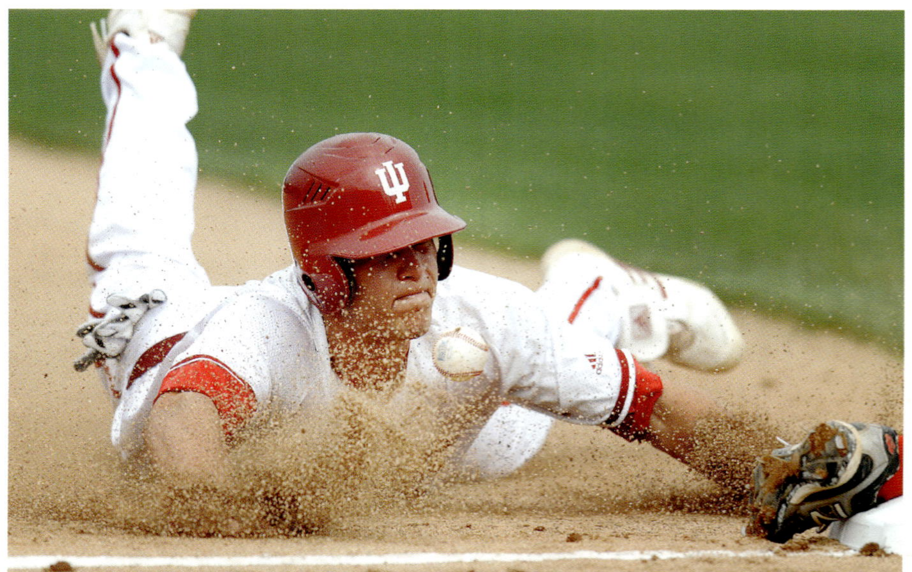

Above

Fans fill the stands at Bart Kaufman Field during the Baseball NCAA Regional Tournament game featuring IU against Austin Peay on June 2, 2013. Photo is a digitally-stitched composite of multiple images.

IU's Michael Basil slides safely into third base against Ball State, spring 2012.

One of my fondest memories at Indiana University was watching IU football on Saturdays with my friends in the student section. The spirit and excitement generated in the stadium is an IU tradition that continues today.

—*Thomas Rude,* B.A. TELECOMMUNICATIONS, 1990; B.S. EDUCATION, 1999

USS *Indiana* prow, Memorial Stadium.

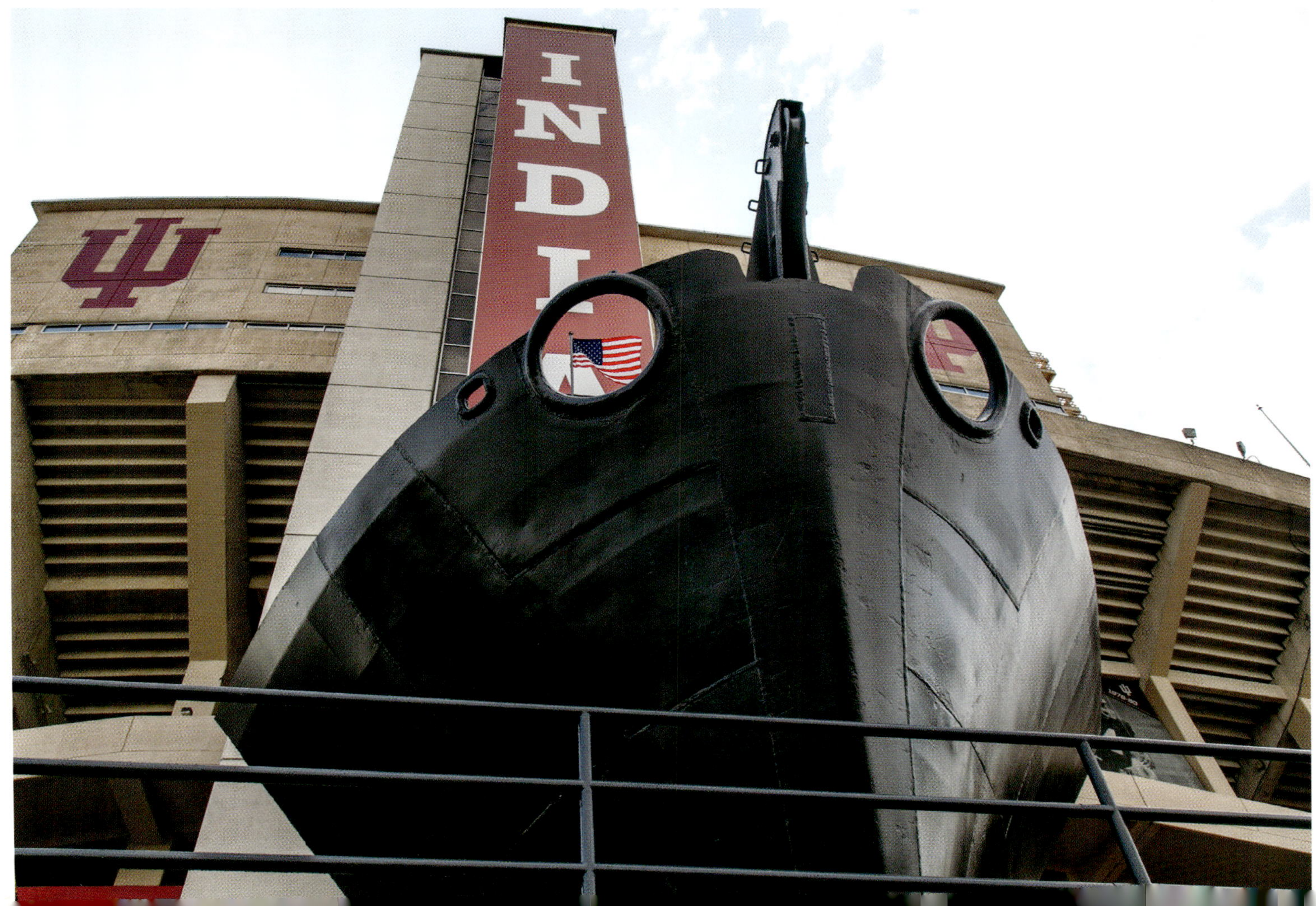

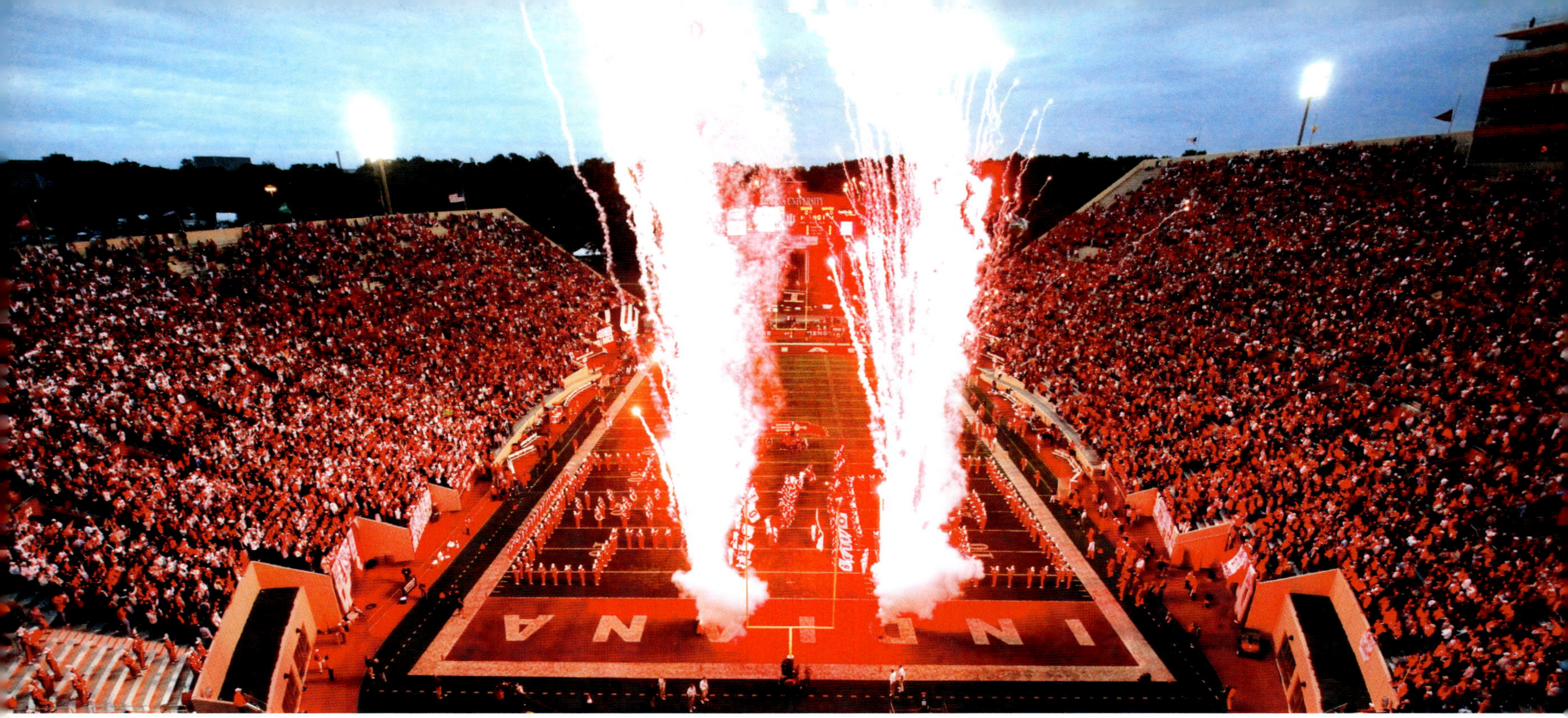

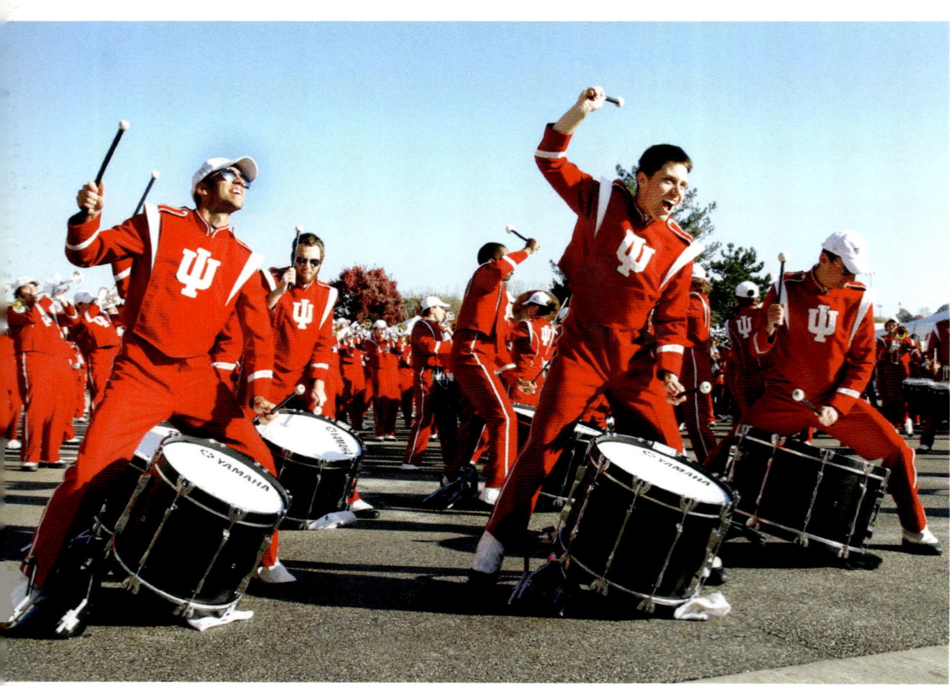

Memorial Stadium and the Marching Hundred.

The North End Zone Student-Athlete Development Center at dusk.

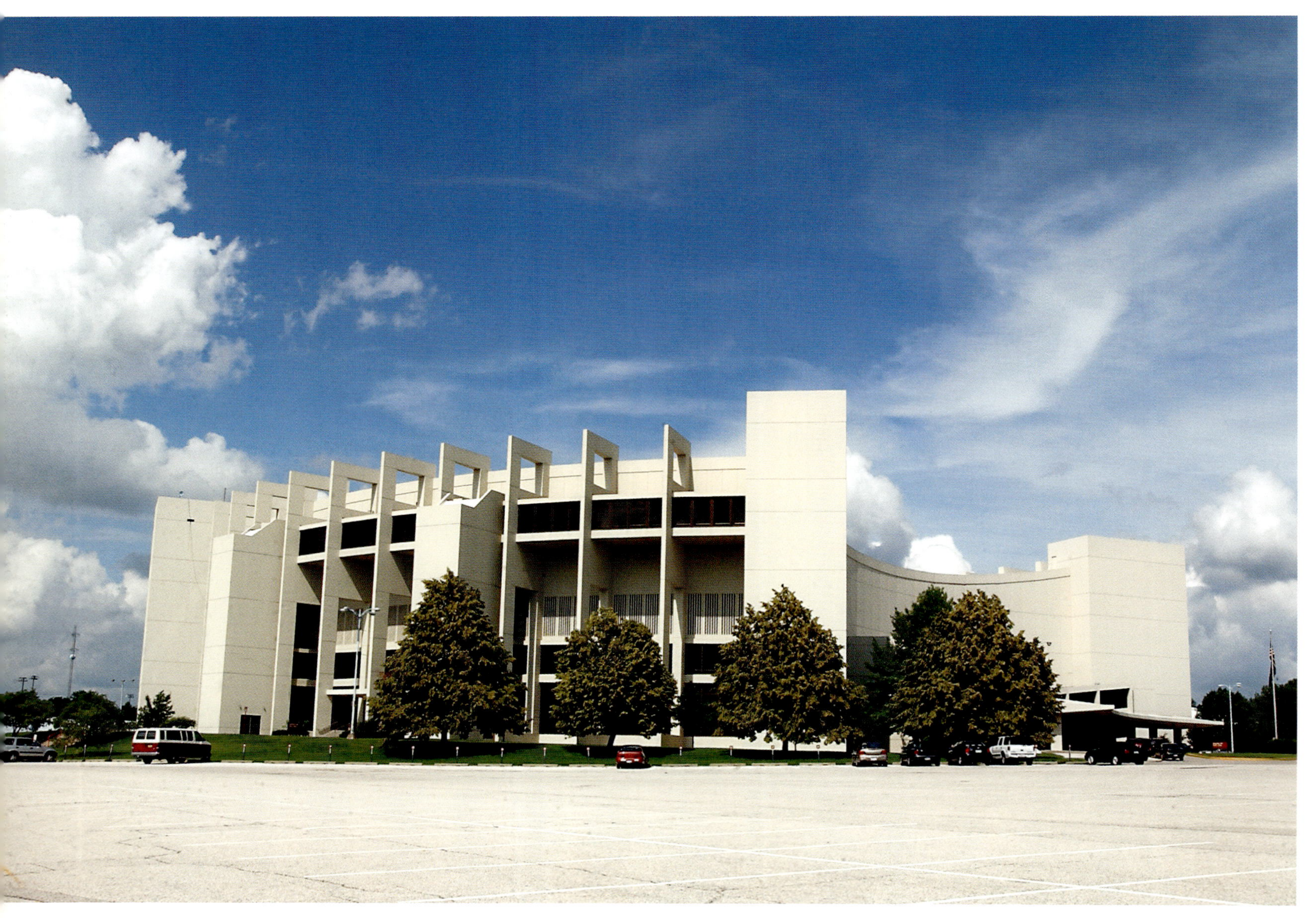

Assembly Hall.

My greatest memories on the basketball court took place at Assembly Hall. That building and our amazing fans have provided a tremendous home court advantage for everyone who has ever played at Indiana.

—*Victor Oladipo,* B.S. KINESIOLOGY, 2013

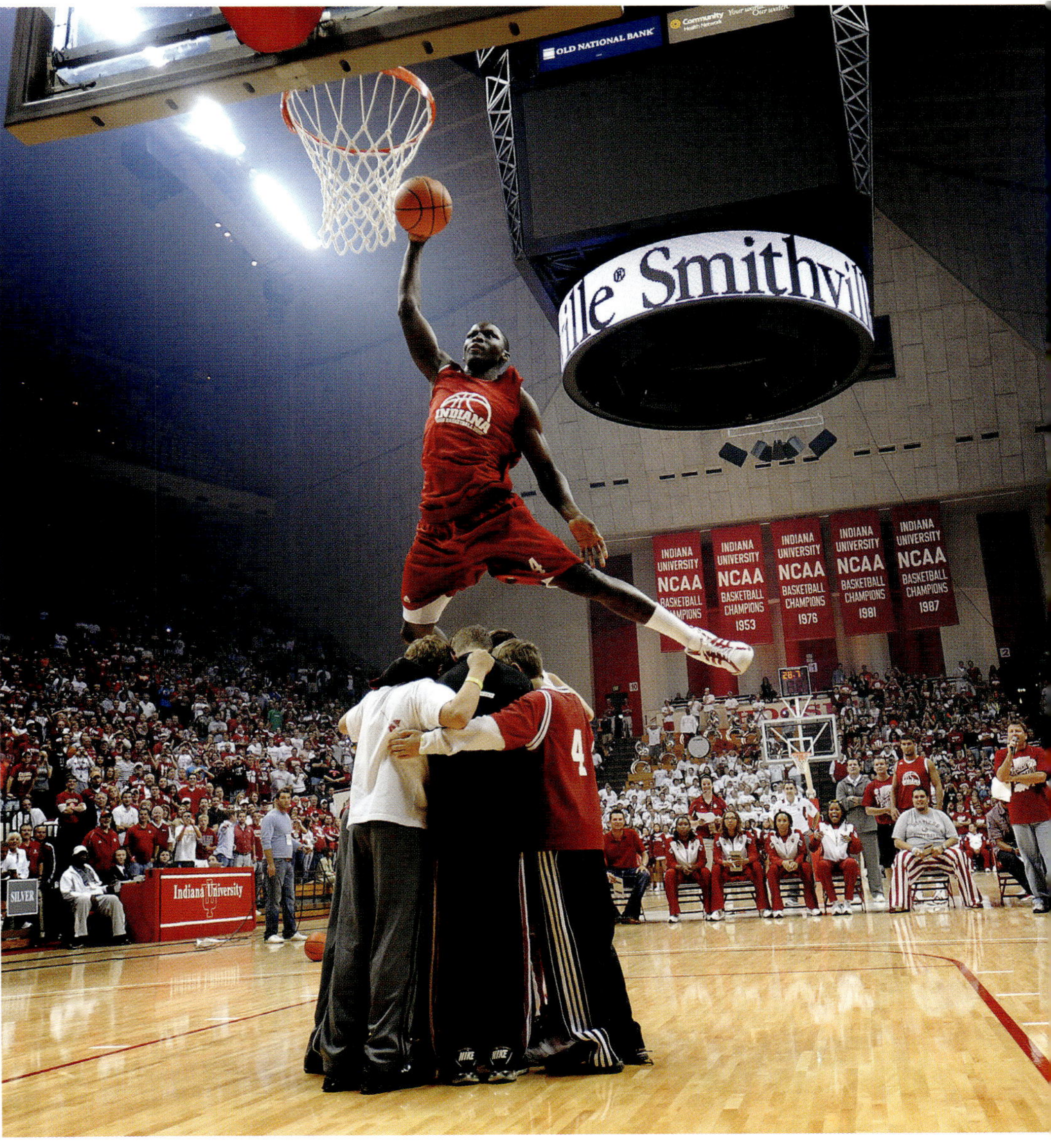

Victor Oladipo soars during the dunk contest at Hoosier Hysteria, 2010.

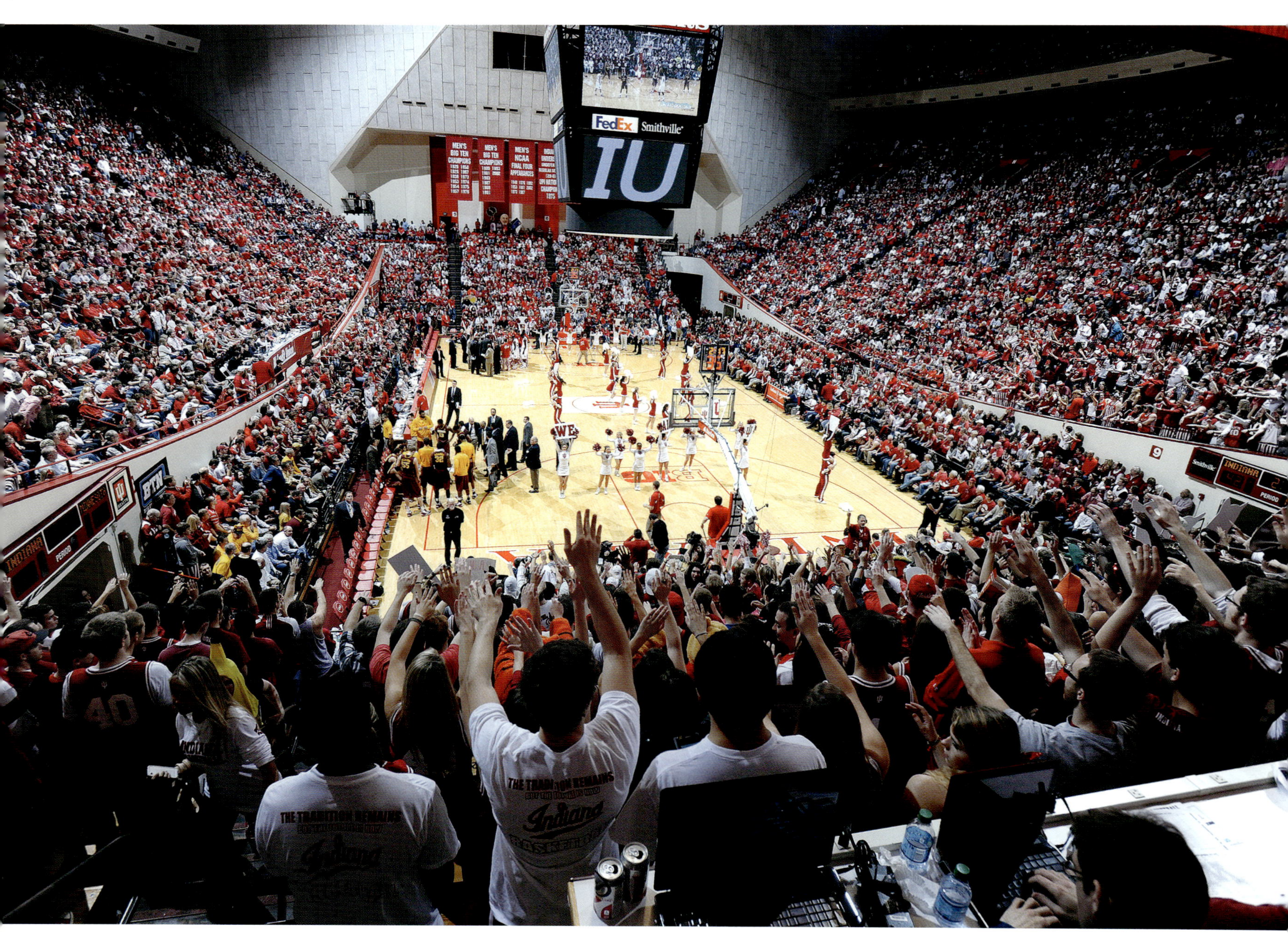

A capacity crowd enjoys the IU Men's Basketball game against Minnesota in 2013.

I grew up going to Indiana University games and have great memories of watching basketball with my father. The atmosphere in Assembly Hall is truly unmatched anywhere in college basketball. Everyone in our family has enjoyed incredible experiences with Indiana University.

—*Cindy Simon Skjodt,* B.A. FORENSIC STUDIES, 1980

I grew up two blocks from the Old Fieldhouse (now Wildermuth Intramural Center). I would frequently walk over to watch the basketball team practice. I became such a familiar presence that I was often invited to rebound for foul-shooting practice. I particularly remember Walt Bellamy and Gary Long. It was where and when I fell in love with Indiana basketball.

—*Angelo Pizzo,* B.A. POLITICAL SCIENCE, 1971

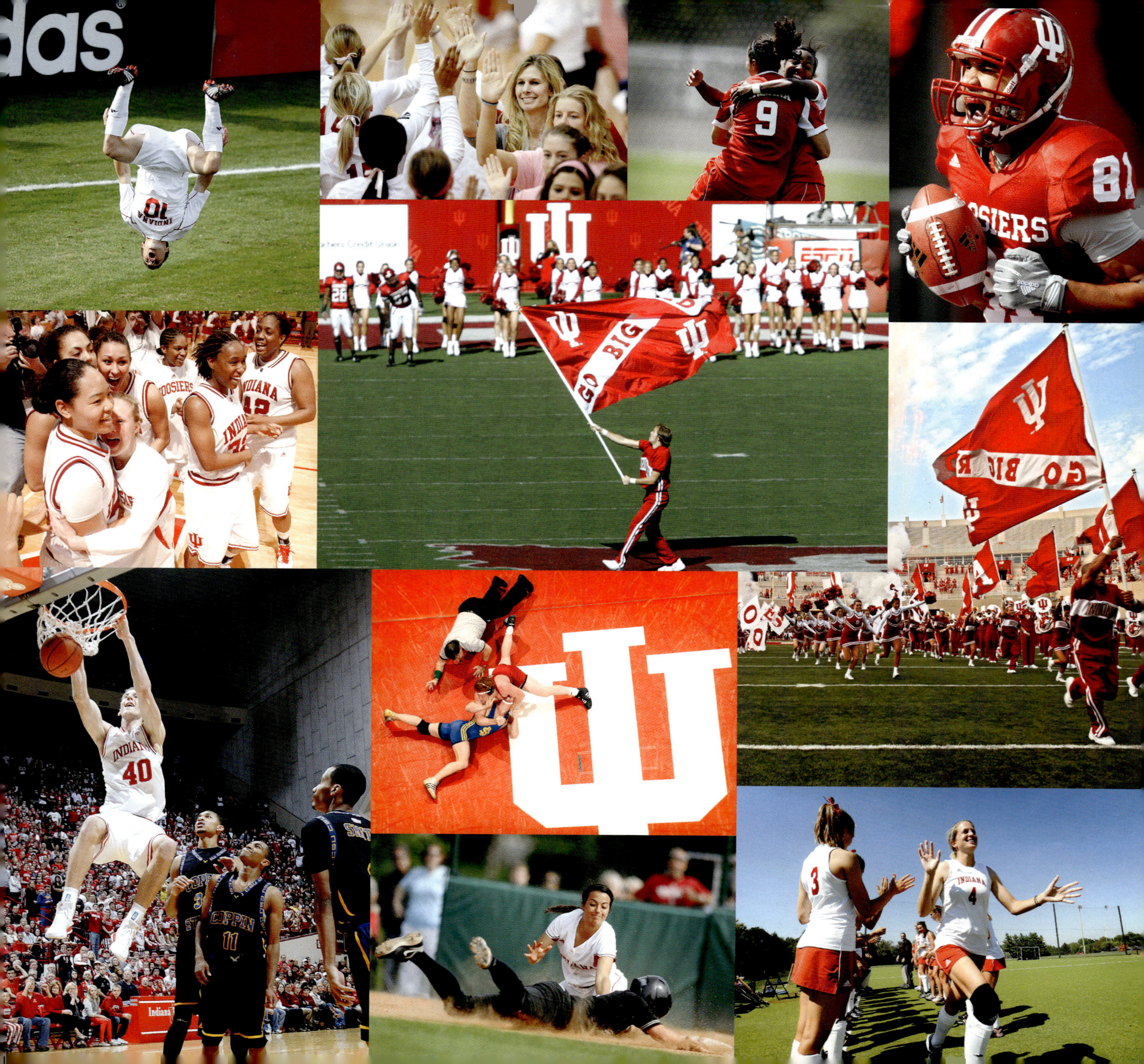

das
9
81
GO BIG
INDIANA
42
INDIANA
40
COPPIN
11
3
INDIANA
4

Indiana, Our Indiana

WORDS BY RUSSELL P. HARKER

Melody taken from "The Viking March," by Karl L. King

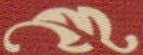

Indiana, Our Indiana
Indiana, we're all for you
We will fight for
the Cream & Crimson,
For the glory of Old IU
Never daunted, we cannot falter
In the battle, we're tried and true
Indiana, Our Indiana
Indiana, we're all for you!

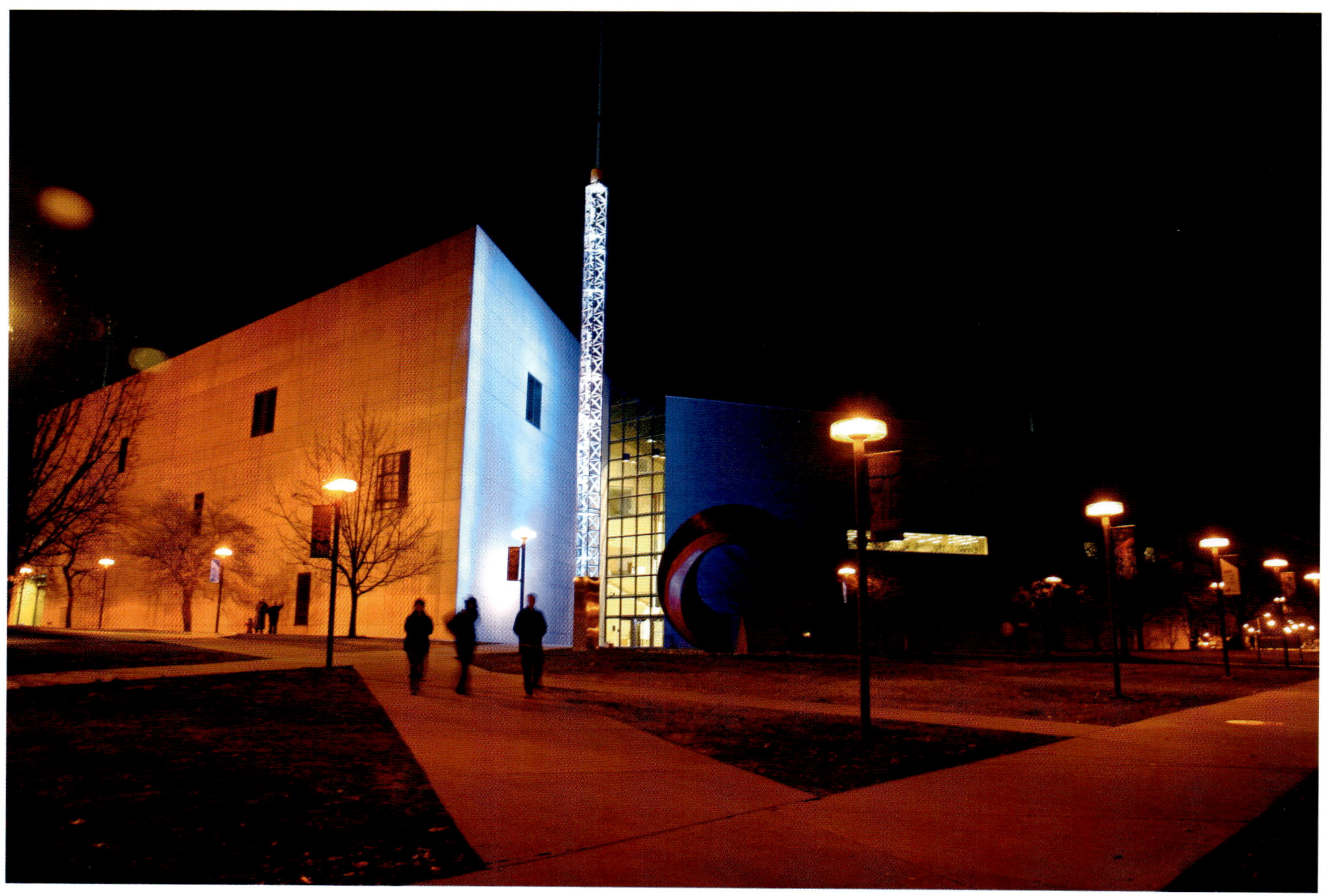

The light totem has become a campus beacon . . .
and the site of wonderful student rituals.
Too, it is the "front porch light" of one of the
great campus art museums in America.

—*Milt Stewart*

B.S. GOVERNMENT; J.D. LAW, 1971

Light totem, IU Art Museum.

About the Photographers

FREELANCE PHOTOGRAPHERS

Rob Guillen is a writer and photographer living in Louisville, Kentucky. He posts photography and prose on his blog.

Milton Hamburger has worked as Art Director for WFIU/WTIU (now retired). He holds a Master of Fine Arts degree from IU.

Mandy Hussey is Marketing and Publicity Manager at Indiana University Press. She is a freelance writer and photographer and graduate of the IU School of Journalism.

Justin Kern is a photographer based in the Chicago area. He runs a photoblog and website.

Chris Robb is Internet2 Director of Operations and Engineering for Indiana University. He has photographed events and weddings.

Sherry Wise is Outdoor Interpreter at Wylie House Museum. She operates the heirloom garden and seed saving project.

INDIANA UNIVERSITY PHOTOGRAPHERS

All photographs courtesy of Indiana University unless otherwise stated.

Mike Dickbernd is the staff photographer for IU Athletics. He is responsible for photographing everything related to the twenty-four Indiana University sports teams. Mike has been at IU since 2008.

Alexandra Lynch has spent most of her life in Bloomington, holds a degree from Indiana University, and worked as a writer and photographer for IU Physical Plant before her retirement in 2013.

Chris Meyer is Director of Visual and Audio Services for IU Communications. He researched and captured many of the photographs that appear in this book.

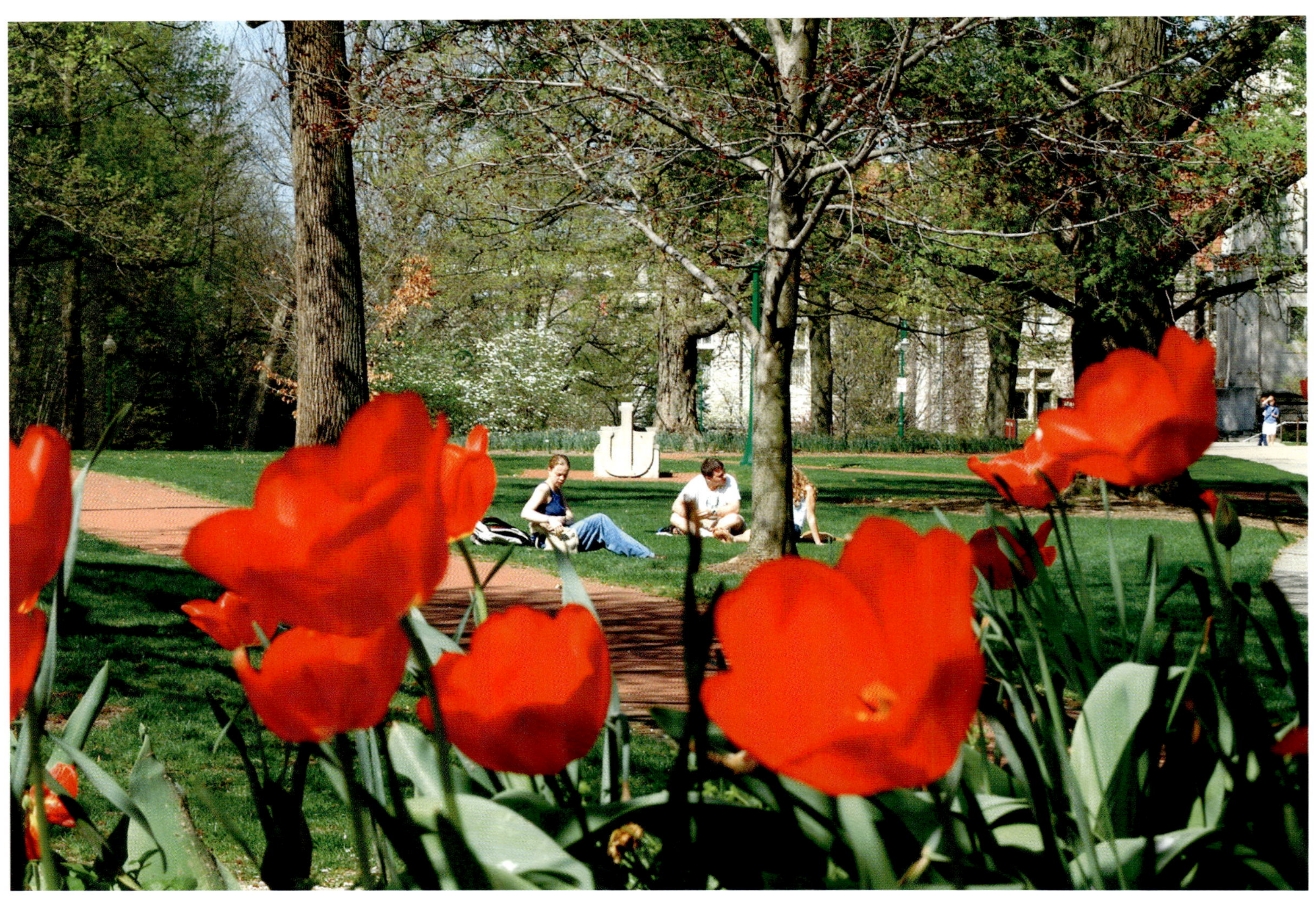

Red tulips, abundant in all corners of the
campus, mark the arrival of spring.

Dave Hulsey: Director of Marketing and Sales
Pamela Rude: Senior Artist, Book Designer
Mandy Hussey: Marketing and Publicity Manager
Linda Oblack: Sponsoring Editor
Sarah Jacobi: Assistant Sponsoring Editor
Bernadette Zoss: Editorial, Design, and Production Director
June Silay: Project Editor
Mary Beth Haas: Sales Manager

Indiana University Press would like to thank Chris Meyer for his meticulous photo research and collection. We thank Mike Dickbernd for research and collection of the athletics photos. For compilation and design, we thank Pamela Rude. For design and research assistance, we also thank Linda Bannister, Dina Kellams, and Abigail Parker.

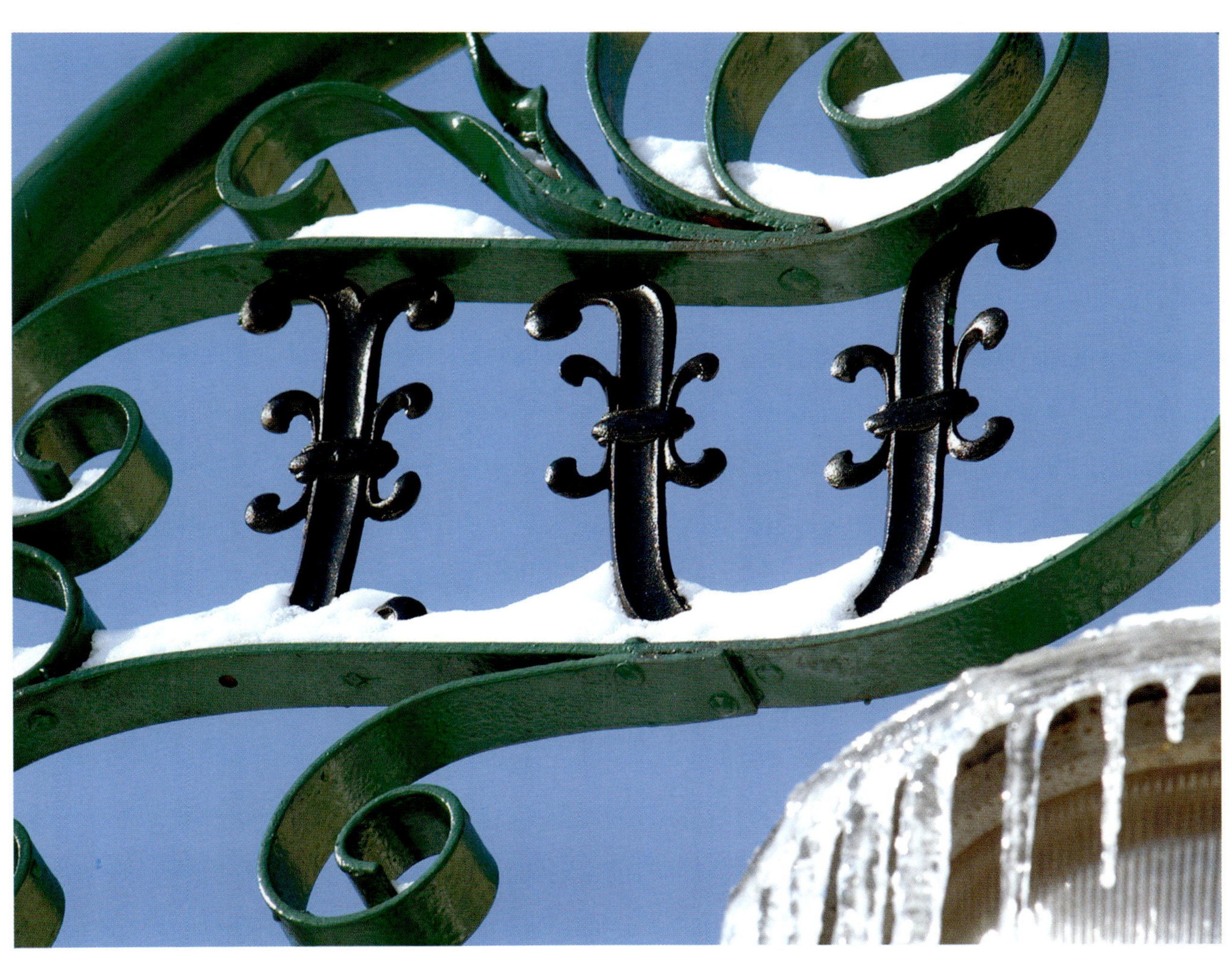